1993

The Suffering Grass

Emerging Global Issues
Thomas G. Weiss, Series Editor

Published in association with the
Thomas J. Watson Jr. Institute for International Studies,
Brown University

The Suffering Grass

Superpowers and
Regional Conflict in
Southern Africa and the Caribbean

■

edited by

Thomas G. Weiss
James G. Blight

Lynne Rienner Publishers ■ Boulder & London

Published in the United States of America in 1992 by
Lynne Rienner Publishers, Inc.
1800 30th Street, Boulder, Colorado 80301

and in the United Kingdom by
Lynne Rienner Publishers, Inc.
3 Henrietta Street, Covent Garden, London WC2E 8LU

Library of Congress Cataloging-in-Publication Data
The Suffering grass : superpowers and regional conflict in southern
 Africa and the Caribbean / edited by Thomas G. Weiss and James G.
 Blight.
    p.   cm.—(Emerging global issues)
 Includes bibliographical references and index.
 ISBN 1-55587-276-X (hc)
    1. Africa, Southern—Politics and government—1975- 2. Caribbean
 Area—Politics and government—1945- 3. World politics—1975–1985.
 4. World politics—1985–1995. 5. United States—Foreign
 relations—1945–1989. 6. United States—Foreign relations—1989-
 7. Soviet Union—Foreign relations—1975–1985. 8. Soviet Union—
 Foreign relations—1985- I. Weiss, Thomas George. II. Blight,
 James G. III. Series.
 DT1165.S84   1992
 327'.09'04—dc20   91-33977
                                                                       CIP

British Cataloguing in Publication Data
A Cataloguing in Publication record for this book
is available from the British Library.

Printed and bound in the United States of America

The paper used in this publication meets the requirements
of the American National Standard for Permanence of
Paper for Printed Library Materials Z39.48-1984.

Whether elephants make war
or love, it is the grass that suffers.

—*Swahili proverb*

Contents

Abbreviations

ANC	African National Congress
ASEAN	Association of Southeast Asian Nations
CARICOM	Caribbean Community
CIA	Central Intelligence Agency
DTA	Democratic Turnhalle Alliance
EEC	European Economic Community
EEZ	Exclusive Economic Zone
EPG	Eminent Persons Group
FMLN	Farabundo Marti Front for National Liberation (Frente Farabundo Marti para la Liberación Nacional)
FNLA	National Front for the Liberation of Angola (Frente Nacional de Libertação de Angola)
FRELIMO	Front for the Liberation of Mozambique
FTZs	Free Trade Zones
G77	Group of Seventy-seven
IBA	International Bauxite Association
ICJ	International Court of Justice
IMF	International Monetary Fund
JLP	Jamaica Labour Party
MFA	Armed Forces Movement (Movimento das Forças Armados)
MNR	Mozambique National Resistance (RENAMO)
MPLA	Popular Liberation Movement of Angola (Movimento Popular de Libertação de Angola)
NAM	Non-Aligned Movement
NATO	North Atlantic Treaty Organization
OAS	Organization of American States
OAU	Organization of African Unity
OECS	Organization of Eastern Caribbean States
PAC	Pan Africanist Congress
SADCC	Southern African Development Coordinating Conference

SADF	South African Defense Forces
SSU	Special Service Units
SWAPO	South West African People's Organization
UN	United Nations
UNAVEM	United Nations Angola Verification Mission
UNITA	National Union for the Total Liberation of Angola (União Nacional para a Independência Total de Angola)
UNTAG	United Nations Transition Assistance Group (Namibia)
USLO	United States Liaison Office
WCG	Western Contact Group
ZANU	Zimbabwe African National Union

Introduction

JAMES G. BLIGHT & THOMAS G. WEISS

In the conclusion to his balanced and thoughtful 1988 essay, "Prospects and Consequences of Soviet Decline," Kurt M. Campbell hints that (as Mark Twain once famously said of himself) reports of the demise of the Soviet Union may have been exaggerated. "It would be premature," writes Campbell, "to suggest that the early signs of Soviet decline may not be irreversible. . . . Having been allowed the opportunity to recover [from World War II] and take a position as a superpower, Soviet leaders do not plan to allow the United States a second chance at superiority."[1] That was the majority view in late 1988, and one supported by the facts.

But, as we know, the USSR proved much less durable than Mark Twain. Almost before the ink was dry on Campbell's and many similar essays, Soviet communism began to disappear in staccato-like stages, as if the old domino theory had been inverted. By November 1989, with the breaching of the Berlin Wall, the external empire gave way. In August 1991, following the failed coup, the Soviet state itself splintered asunder. And in September 1991, Moscow announced that its longest standing ally in the southern Third World, Cuba, was being abandoned and left to fend for itself.[2]

The Soviet Union had all but disappeared. The world seemed to many of us, whose experience of the international political environment has been framed by the depressing, sometimes tense, but centrally stable standoff of the Cold War between the superpowers, to be spinning faster than ever it had before.

Events in the Soviet Union and Eastern Europe, beginning in 1989–1990, turned the world of international political calculations upside down. The trumpet sounding the end of the Cold War tumbled many walls, not just in Berlin, but in chancelleries around the world, where ideology and the accompanying stereotypes of either communist or anticommunist zeal had stratified shibboleths about competition and conflict to the exclusion of the more reasonable approaches of cooperation and negotiation.

1

The chapters in this book lend renewed relevance to the Swahili aphorism that provides its title and captures the growing sentiment in many Third World capitals after the Cold War: "Whether the elephants make war or make love, it is the grass that suffers." There is fear that the great powers will no longer take a significant interest in the Third World as such. With no need to spread the world revolution or to fight communism, the Soviet Union and the United States might simply leave the developing world to rot in the ruins of the conflicts once sustained by Cold War animosities.

Yet the possibilities for collaboration between the United States and the Soviet Union arising from recent global political changes have also increased, especially in the Third World. While détente foundered initially on the shoals of the Third World's regional battlefields, it is all but impossible that the kind of superpower rivalry bolstered by those conflicts in the 1970s and 1980s will be repeated. Perhaps first and foremost, the demise of the Cold War has removed the likelihood of a direct superpower nuclear confrontation. We are unlikely to see again Washington's going to the brink as it did when the Soviet Union hinted it might aid Egypt during the Middle East War of 1973, or when it aided Cuba with nuclear weapons in 1962.

Moscow and Washington have persuaded allies and adversaries in the Third World to negotiate settlements, further contributing to global stability. Even more impressive than the superpowers' use of bilateral negotiation has been their increased reliance on multilateral diplomacy. These tendencies were quite clear before Iraq invaded Kuwait on August 2, 1990, and were subsequently reinforced when an international consensus against that aggression led to a coordination of multilateral military and diplomatic efforts. The growing demand for United Nations peacekeeping and peacemaking under combined superpower leadership is a healthy and startling development, and underscores the novelty of the era into which we have plunged.

At the same time, the Gulf War illustrates the extent to which the new world order heralded by President George Bush will not be characterized by an uninterrupted flight of doves. While the implications of warming East-West relations for conflict management and resolution appear promising, the outlook for reducing violence and suffering throughout the Third World is far from clear.

The Current Research

The long-term effects of changes within the former Soviet Union are impossible to predict. The current asymmetry of the internal cohesiveness and power of the United States and the intense and immense domestic problems of the "Federation of Sovereign Republics" (or whatever the remnants of the central government will be called) will have profound implications for future international relations because Moscow's economic and ethnic difficulties appear increasingly to drive and circumscribe its foreign policy and deny its status as a "superpower." In fact, in the aftermath of the failed coup of August 1991, it remains unclear whether the constituents of the old Soviet Union will have a foreign policy—or several—worthy of the phrase beyond begging for foreign aid from the advanced industrialized countries.

Eighteen months before these events, we had thought it useful in this research to work inductively to examine events over the last several decades in two regions of the developing world—the Caribbean Basin and Southern Africa—to gain some insights into the prospects for and limitations of superpower cooperation in ending long-standing civil strife. History is not an infallible guide and serves as an uncertain base for policy development; but it is the only rational guide we have. The fear of being misled by recent history increases because the end of the Cold War seems clearly to involve a global "revolution," which, by definition, connotes a decisive break with the past.

It has been variously claimed, in fact, that we are now at "the end of history," that the complete Westernization of the world has led to an end to most international conflict; and that we are witnessing "the return of history," the disintegration of stability, the devolution into worldwide ethnic solipsism and endless regional conflict. Extreme versions of these views, however, lead to irresponsibly uninformed improvisation. Revolution or not, we are largely who and what we were, especially regarding the very recent past, such as is under discussion in the following chapters. We do well especially in times like these to keep our eye upon the past even if, as has often been noted, we must thereby proceed backward into the future. The option is worse: to proceed forward into a repetition of past mistakes. With some trepidation, but determined to use the data of the recent past in the two regions that interested us most, we devised a strategy to extract lessons from US and Soviet involvement with the prominent hegemons in those regions, Cuba and South Africa, and on the basis of our examination, to suggest some US policy options.

The logic of our research is as follows: Ever since the United States and the USSR achieved rough nuclear parity in the 1960s and direct confrontations between them became too dangerous, the Caribbean Basin and Southern Africa had been seething with what were called "proxy" wars. We wanted to understand in what ways, and to what extent, the superpowers had contributed to inflaming those conflicts.

Moreover, the regions have historical relationships with the United

States that are quite different: intervention in the Caribbean Basin has taken place virtually since the founding of the Republic, and the putative right to do so is even enshrined in the Monroe Doctrine. Washington's interest in Southern Africa, however, has been almost exclusively derived from a need to counter what has been perceived as Soviet-backed expansion in the region. Thus, we reasoned, a comparison of recent conflicts in the two regions would permit conclusions about both types of Third World fears: being threatened, harassed, or even invaded by the United States, and being ignored by the great powers.

Finally, by early 1990, conflict resolution in Southern Africa seemed surprisingly successful in contrast to similar efforts to end the various conflicts in Central America. Perhaps, we thought, there are reasons for this discrepancy that would shed some light on the fate of these as well as other Third World regions at the Cold War's end.

We pursued a fairly traditional course in commissioning this book's chapters, asking specialists to analyze conflict in the regions, roughly "before" and "after" the end of the Cold War. In addition, in April 1990, we included evaluations of the two anomalous and highly significant actors, Cuba and South Africa, in these unfolding dramas. In April 1991, we gathered the authors together with a distinguished and diverse group of discussants at Brown University. These dates, almost exactly a year apart, are significant because the intervening twelve months were nearly as eventful, and as relevant for this inquiry, as the startling twelve months that had preceded them. They greatly changed the frame of reference of those of us who gathered to discuss the future of the two regions in question. Moreover, subsequent events, especially the failed coup and complete collapse of Soviet communism, have now taken the course of recent history to a kind of preliminary conclusion. Far from being a counterweight to the United States in Third World regions such as the Caribbean Basin and Southern Africa, the former Soviet Union is now the Third World's newest and largest member.

The Suffering Grass

The three sections of this book address three sets of questions: What has been causal and what coincidental about superpower behavior in conflict promotion and resolution? What have been the respective roles of regional hegemons? What was the extent to which war and diplomacy (particularly by third parties) mattered? The concluding section extracts the implications for the foreign policy of the United States, as well as lessons and prescriptions for the Caribbean Basin and Southern Africa, and beyond.

The Superpowers and Third World Conflicts

In the first section of the book, Lloyd Searwar and Gillian Gunn examine why the United States and the Soviet Union have contributed to creating and exacerbating regional conflicts in the Caribbean and Southern Africa. They go on to review how the great powers have carried out their commitments to their allies.

In Chapter 1, "The Caribbean Conundrum," Searwar scrutinizes the geographical notion of the "Caribbean Basin" as fundamentally a geostrategic concept created by the United States that has little or no basis in the scattered, variable reality of the region so described. Central America is Spanish and indigenous in heritage, and, except in Costa Rica, the Spanish-derived political culture has not traditionally been hospitable to US-style democracy. In the Anglophone Caribbean, however, democracy has taken root in the largely black and Indian subcontinental origins of formerly British, French, or Dutch colonies. In Central America, civil strife has been a way of life for as long as anyone can remember, once again with Costa Rica the exception. In the Caribbean islands, intrastate conflict has been rare, with recent significant exceptions in Grenada and Trinidad. The military has been prominent in Central America but "played little part in the retention or access to power in the English-speaking Caribbean since independence."

In spite of the diversity of this mosaic, the so-called Basin is a conceptual reality for decisionmakers and the US public, and consequently for the governments of the Caribbean as well. Searwar argues that US interest in the region has allowed virtually no room for political and economic experimentation by the governments there; he presents a case study of Jamaica under the first administration of Michael Manley.

The United States dominates the Caribbean and largely determines the shape of regimes and their foreign policy. Searwar makes a coherent case that, aside from the significant exception of the Cuban missile crisis in 1962, the Soviets have been very cautious in the region. He argues that each superpower has traditionally justified intervention in comparably proximate "spheres of influence"—Eastern Europe for Moscow and the Caribbean Basin for Washington—with "similar rhetoric or doctrine."

Analytical generalizations are made much more difficult by the presence of Cuba. Searwar contends that Cuba's influence has been complex, and in many ways is actually unrelated to its ideology. In fact, Cuba exports the best aspects of its revolution in the form of doctors, teachers, and engineers.

Searwar summarizes his view: "While superpower tension has not ignited intrastate conflict, it has served to exacerbate such strife and put it beyond the reach of early resolution." Nonetheless, the end of the Cold

War holds out the possibility for change, and Searwar sees a potential new basis for US policy in the region because of the need to ensure safe transit, stop drug trafficking, and halt illegal migration.

In spite of or because of the end of superpower rivalry, Searwar finds the December 1989 invasion of Panama "disturbing." This military action was perceived throughout the region as a reversion to the US gunboat diplomacy of an earlier era. The picture of the region painted by Searwar is bleak indeed: alienation of people too poor to care about the ideology of the left or right, corruption at the highest levels, and shrinking markets for natural resources and crops produced there. In his view, the superpowers have together made a terrible mess of things: the United States by its drive to keep its surrogates in power, and its endless search for socialists, wherever they may be; the Soviet Union by its ceaseless probing for advantage—without much success—and its inability to rein in the Cubans.

Gillian Gunn paints another portrait of Moscow's and Washington's rivalry in Chapter 2, "The Legacy of Angola." She comes to grips with the realities of great-power rivalry through the Angolan case, identifying "characteristics and causal factors that are independent of the warmth or coolness of superpower relations at a given moment, and the ideological idiosyncrasies of Moscow and Washington at a given historical juncture." After presenting a brief chronology of events in the former Portuguese colony's struggle for independence, she describes the gradual involvement of the superpowers, through local agents and Cuban intervention, in the developing conflict.

In her analysis, Gunn derives three lessons from the Angolan conflict. First is the danger of a power vacuum, here complicated by decolonization. "Portugal bitterly resisted African independence . . . [and] no thought was given to transition mechanisms." The strong ethnic and class polarities that framed the regional conflict provide the second lesson. The presence of traditional rivalries and antipathies "made Angola a perfect proxy battlefield for Moscow and Washington, for they could compete without having to expend their own human resources." The final lesson is the unpredictable but often critical role of third parties to such conflicts. Cuba, South Africa, and Zaire contributed to the escalation of hostilities, often manipulating the superpowers and certainly addressing their own agendas.

Gunn extracts three general policy conclusions for the post-Cold War era from her case study. First, avoiding the development of a power vacuum is essential, and an outside third party is required to "patrol the metaphorical playing field to ensure individual competitors play by the rules and outside powers remain outside." She sees the United Nations, enhanced by the demand for its services and with increased support from the superpowers, as the "logical force to fill any empty space," including potential vacuums in South Africa, Iraq, and the former Soviet Union. Second, mechanisms to defuse ethnic and class tensions before they become explosive are critical to prevent the internationalization of regional conflicts. While "perhaps a utopian wish," the reduction of such tensions should be kept in mind as the "top priority for would-be peacemakers." Third, "careful attention must be paid to the interests and mischief potential of local actors, for they are capable of swiftly involving larger countries in conflicts."

In conclusion, Gunn points out that Soviet-US cooperation can promote these goals. While the possibility persists that other actors may become involved, at least the danger that troops of the former Cold War adversaries will be engaged will disappear, as will the tripwire for nuclear confrontation.

Regional Hegemons and Regional Conflicts

The second section of the volume is devoted to understanding the role of regional hegemons that have the strength to project military might beyond their borders. Jorge I. Domínguez addresses the case of Cuba and Newell M. Stultz that of South Africa.

In Chapter 3, "Pipsqueak Power: The Centrality and Anomaly of Cuba," Domínguez explains his title: "Cuba has been anomalous because it has been such an unlikely candidate for a significant international role. A country that had been best known for catchy music, first-rate dancing, and picaresque personal conduct became the Sparta of the late twentieth century as hundreds of thousands of troops served overseas." Cuba's unusual position over the past quarter-century has a number of explanations. First, its actions spring from its psychological state in the aftermath of the missile crisis, when Cuba stood alone. Second, the need to deter the United States from invading the island emerged, producing a military power far greater than Cuba's size and situation warranted. Finally, there was President Castro's inclination and ability to play a role fit usually only for the head of government from a larger country.

The argument of his chapter turns on the organizing concept of Cuban deterrence of US aggression, combining the interpretations of Thomas Schelling with President Fidel Castro's views and actions as leader. This line of argument is clearest in the October–November 1962 period, but Domínguez elaborates other parts of the Schelling argument, beginning with Castro's desire to increase his bargaining leverage through efforts designed "to cultivate a certain image of non-rationality." Castro, notes Domínguez, also juxtaposed talk and action, as well as intention and capability.

Domínguez does not argue that the Cubans thought all this out beforehand. Rather, the Schellingesque framework serves as a useful tool in the search for conceptual clarity in examining "pipsqueak power." One might argue that Castro has used a "strategy of conflict" toward the Third World and a "strategy of conflict avoidance" toward the United States.

The end of the Cold War must, according to Domínguez, create significant psychological pressures on Cubans. Once part of a country that believed itself to be a leader in the vanguard of history, Cubans now resist the new flow of events at every turn. Cuban military intervention overseas has worked. But the "hell of success" is that Cubans must now "live in an island, just in an island." Whether the lives and expense of overseas commitments were worth it will be left to the judgment of historians. However, Domínguez provides his own negative assessment, noting that when the Cubans withdrew from Angola, the "Luanda government was far from consolidated," and its "allies no longer govern Ethiopia, Grenada, or Nicaragua."

In Chapter 4, "South Africa in Angola and Namibia," Newell Stultz addresses many of the same issues as they arise in the Southern African context. He seeks first and foremost to determine how "changes in Soviet attitudes toward the Southern African region as a whole" can explain the "apparent reversal of Pretoria's foreign policy toward the Angola-Namibia subregion." Key to Stultz's analysis of events is his attempt to interpret the thinking of the South African government in terms of abandoning zero-sum for positive-sum thinking. Stultz notes that total onslaught, the idea that South Africa was under siege and the only bulwark against communist aggression in the region, lost credibility as East-West relations warmed and no longer formed the basis for decisionmaking in that country. South Africa's military humiliation at both Cuito Cuanavale and Calueque during the first half of 1988 was a more immediate force in changing Pretoria's approach to regional politics.

Stultz reflects on the difference between today's world and that of 1988, when negotiations that led to launching Namibian independence culminated. International events, like the changes in Eastern Europe, coincided with domestics changes, such as the rise of the relatively reform-minded F. W. de Klerk, the release of Nelson Mandela, and a host of reforms that have begun to lead South Africa back into the community of nations.

Stultz asks somewhat rhetorically, "How different, one might ask, would the results of the 1988 negotiations have been had the Cold War then been intensifying, instead of beginning to wind down?" He does not argue that ending the Cold War will necessarily lead to the millennium in Southern Africa, but he concludes that where superpower competition has sustained conflicts and impeded their resolution, one would hope that ending this competition would have the opposite effect.

Third Parties and Conflict Resolution

In the third section, Wayne S. Smith and Fen O. Hampson elucidate the limits of superpower cooperation in resolving regional conflicts. They review the extent to which other parties have also mitigated war in the two regions under scrutiny.

In Chapter 5, "Conflict Management in the Caribbean Basin," Smith contends that the impact of global political sea-changes may be least felt in the Caribbean, "the oldest and most central US sphere of influence [where] the Monroe Doctrine lives on as a unilateral policy statement." Smith delivers a broadside against two centuries of US policy, arguing that the key justification has always been "strategic denial" of any foreign power's influence in the region. The attempt to deny Moscow any undue influence during the Cold War is only the latest example: "Virtually everything the US did in the area during the forty years between 1945 and 1985 was geared to its rivalry with the Soviet Union." He goes on to note that it is particularly important to begin a process of genuine consultation with the countries of the region and decries the fact that the Monroe Doctrine has not been "multilateralized at all. The United States still decides for itself when to intervene—and how to do so."

Mikhail Gorbachev's ascension to power provides a chance to alter policy toward the region, because the atmosphere now is similar to that in the interwar period and shortly thereafter, the so-called good neighbor period. Like many analysts from the region itself, Smith points out that there is little evidence of a Soviet "blueprint for conquest." Rather, unrest in Central America in particular "stemmed from economic underdevelopment, political instability, and social injustice." Smith believes that in the post–Cold War era, the United States must abandon the illusion of the validity of the Monroe Doctrine. The Soviets are withdrawing everywhere, and nowhere is this clearer than in the Caribbean, where in fact their interests have never gone beyond assisting Cuba, at home and in its overseas adventures. With the Soviet Union departing, and no other foreign power to take its place, Smith asks, what are the issues to be defended by the Monroe Doctrine?

Smith would be more comfortable with multilateral approaches to the region's problems. While Presidents Johnson and Reagan used the facade of regional groups such as the OAS to deploy US troops to the Dominican Republic and Grenada, unilateral decisionmaking has been the norm. While the end of the Cold War provides the opportunity to change policies "by committing itself now fully to respect the UN and OAS

Charters, the United States, under the Bush administration, has become more assertive and has given less rather than more attention to international law." In fact, Smith echoes many of the more skeptical critics from the region in wondering whether the disappearance of the Soviet Union as a superpower will not bring more rather than fewer US troops to the region: "Now that the United States is no longer concerned about retaliatory action by the Soviet Union, will it resort to imposing its will by force in the Caribbean Basin whenever it chooses?"

Chapter 6, Fen Hampson's "Winding Down Strife in Southern Africa," provides a more optimistic case study of conflict management. Hampson carefully dissects the claims of the Reagan administration that the bilateral process of "constructive engagement" with South Africa eventually produced the atmosphere needed for the final negotiated settlement in Angola and Namibia. Several alternative explanations are proposed by Hampson. The first is based on William Zartman's concept of "ripeness" for settlement—"the point at which the parties to a dispute no longer feel that they can win the conflict and both sides perceive the costs and prospects of continued confrontation to be more burdensome than the costs and prospects of a settlement." Another explanation is more systemic, stressing "the importance of great power relationships and the changing dynamics of East-West competition on the possibilities for diplomacy and resolution of Third World conflicts." Hampson gives considerable attention to a question seldom asked so straightforwardly: Were negotiations facilitated by the end of the Cold War and superpower collaboration, or by the fact that the Soviet Union has caved in across the board, including in Southern Africa?

Critical to Hampson's chapter is his contrast of the Reagan administration's constructive engagement with the multilateral approach of the Carter administration's Western Contact Group. He concludes that, far from being a causal factor in the outcome, constructive engagement in reality prompted an eight-year delay, while the WCG, working in tandem with the United Nations, might have brought a solution earlier. In Hampson's view, what ultimately led South Africa to the bargaining table was its "changing perceptions and growing concerns about the costs of the conflict, as well as the emergence of a new leadership within South Africa committed to charting a new course in both domestic and foreign policy."

Hampson's provocative counterfactual history posits that the incoming Reagan administration should have promoted rather than abandoned the work of the WCG. The role of superpower cooperation, then, seems to have been not all that important to the resolution of conflict in the region. In Hampson's words, "US-Soviet cooperation may be a necessary condition for the settlement of regional conflicts . . . [but] it is not a sufficient condition."

*Regional Conflicts and Their
Resolution in the Post–Cold War World*

The final versions of these chapters benefitted from two days of discussion at Brown University in April 1991 among academics as well as government and UN officials from the United States, the Soviet Union, the Caribbean Basin, and Southern Africa. As one might expect, there were disagreements about how to analyze current events in the two regions and globally, for these are vast uncertainties. Few predicted the implosion of the USSR in 1988, yet it has now been accomplished. Many now predict anarchy and civil war in the two regional hegemons under discussion here—Cuba and South Africa—yet the regimes may remain viable for some time, or may adapt to changing circumstances. There are other reasons for feeling both hopeful and despairing of the future of the Caribbean Basin and Southern Africa. Our goal here, therefore, is not prediction, which, in light of the legions of recent, cosmically wrong predictions, is a fool's exercise. Rather, we have sought a comparative understanding of some important causes of war and peace in two regions that have had too much of the former, and which need far more of the latter.

Yet some common themes and lessons arose from our two case studies. In Chapter 7, we attempt to distill them from the essays and discussions. Returning to the metaphor of superpower conflict as enacted in the Third World, we respond, "Not necessarily" to the question "Must the grass still suffer?" There is now only one superpower, or elephant, left in the jungle of world politics. Surely there is a way for the United States to tread lightly upon the grass, and to foster its growth and development. This is the focus of the commentary in the concluding chapter.

The task, we suggest, will be neither simple nor easy. Preaching, or even teaching, democracy will be insufficient, as will US support for regional and international institutions, necessary as both will be. At the heart of the issue for Washington's policy toward the Caribbean Basin and Southern Africa after the Cold War is whether, in light of the rapid evolution of chaos in the former Soviet empire—the new northern Third World—citizens and officials in the US can muster the interest, empathy, and material resources to assist in relieving the suffering in these two devastated regions of the southern Third World.

Notes

1. Kurt M. Campbell, "Prospects and Consequences of Soviet Decline," in Joseph S. Nye, Jr., Graham Allison, and Albert Carnesale (eds.) *Fateful*

Visions: Avoiding Nuclear Catastrophe (Cambridge, Mass.: Ballinger, 1988), 152–169.

2. See David Hoffman, "Soviet Brigade to Leave Cuba, Gorbachev Says," *Washington Post*, 12 Sept. 1991, A34, 1; and Gerald Seib, "Soviets Plan Troop Pullout from Cuba," *Wall Street Journal*, 12 Sept. 1991, A13.

■ Part 1 ■
The Superpowers and Third World Conflicts

■ 1 ■

The Caribbean Conundrum

LLOYD SEARWAR

The Caribbean has always presented the pattern of conflict and competition that we are currently observing there. In the words of Dr. Eric Williams, late prime minister of Trinidad and Tobago: "The Caribbean islands began their association with modern society as the pawn of European power politics, the cockpit of Europe, the arena of Europe's wars hot and cold. . . . Caribbean history, conceived in international rivalry, was reared and nurtured in an environment of power politics."[1]

The actors and contenders, however, have changed over the years. At the height of the Cold War, the revolution in Cuba centered the Cold War agenda on the Caribbean. Long before that, the region had been perceived as the US "backyard," or the "vital American underbelly," which in keeping with the Monroe Doctrine conferred on the United States a right to intervention. Between 1823 and 1945, the US government landed troops in and occupied Cuba (four times) and Honduras (five times); backed the overthrow of the government in Nicaragua and occupied that country (twice); sent troops into Panama (three times); and acquired Puerto Rico.

Intervention in the era of the Cold War, however, was triggered not so much by a threat to US financial interests, but in reaction to the perceived influence or intervention of the other superpower in a region considered of major geostrategic significance to the United States and within its sphere of influence. Governments, fairly elected, or opposition groups espousing ideas or systems associated with the USSR were considered to be "moving East" and were accordingly adjudged hostile and therefore legitimate targets for pressure, subversion, or removal.

Events that have projected the region into the international arena can only be fully understood in the context of the East-West conflict, now drawing to a close. These events have included the US-backed intervention in the Dominican Republic; the fomenting of civil disturbances in Guyana, leading to the imposition of a special electoral system and the

15

ousting at the polls of the Marxist premier Cheddi Jagan; the long tenure in office, despite international pressure, of the Somoza and Duvalierist regimes in Nicaragua and Haiti, respectively; the "regional" intervention in Grenada following the murder of Prime Minister Maurice Bishop; the civil disturbances and the hostile international media campaign leading up to the electoral defeat of the first Michael Manley government in Jamaica; and, finally, the long-supported struggle of the contras against the Sandinistas.

The Caribbean Basin states are all, except Mexico, small, and many of them are islands; most achieved independence only in the past three decades. They have paid a high price. Superpower conflict and the consequent externalization of their problems have not only promoted internal instability and disorder but also constrained their freedom to choose strategies for development appropriate to their smallness and openness.

Now, as the Cold War winds down, regional leaders, policymakers, and scholars are anxious to determine whether a new period, in which the peoples of the region are enabled to take charge of their own history, reasonably free from external pressure or internal faction, is opening. Will the withdrawal of the Soviets from Eastern Europe be accompanied by an analogous disappearance of Soviet influence in the Caribbean Basin? What leverage will be left to small states in the Caribbean if there is a virtual withdrawal of Soviet power? In view of Soviet reduction in its overseas commitments and the reorganization of aid and support, how will Cuba maintain its ascendancy in the Third World given the fact that the Caribbean must remain its diplomatic base? What issues, if any, will replace anticommunism as the dominant principle shaping US policy toward the Basin?

These questions are difficult. The answers, whether based on the implications of the structural adjustment programs now being imposed by the IMF and the World Bank or on the exercise of unipolar power as demonstrated in the Gulf crisis, might not be favorable for the nations of the Caribbean Basin. However, the first steps toward even informed speculation must begin with the analysis of the relationships and conflicts that preceded the end of the Cold War.

One notes, at the outset of such a study, that even the space that is known as the Caribbean Basin has been determined externally. The Caribbean can be defined in a number of ways, but the definition of the geopolitical space mainly derives not from geographical or economic or cultural considerations, but from the strategic concerns and perceptions of the superpowers in the context of the East-West conflict.[2] It is in particular a US geostrategic concept that links two disparate areas, Central America and the islands of the Caribbean, and reflects the belief that conflicts within the Caribbean Basin owed their common origin to Soviet expansionist designs pursued either directly or through its "surrogate or ally," Cuba.

While the definition of the region thus responds to the global concerns of the East-West conflict, intrastate conflicts among the Basin states in fact engage the interest and intervention of the superpowers. Washington is concerned with how such conflict can be instigated or directed toward establishing regimes hostile to the United States and whose existence could have a domino or demonstration effect. The USSR has perceived internal conflicts in the Caribbean Basin as opportunities to support leftist or radical regimes whose emergence could restrict to the Caribbean Basin US strategic resources, which might otherwise be deployed in more distant regions that are of vital interest to the USSR.

A Sphere of Influence

Washington, despite its intermittent genuflections to the sovereign rights of states, has perceived the Caribbean Basin as the core of its sphere of influence and has therefore attempted to ensure that the internal systems of Basin states are similar to those identified with the superpower itself. Deviation has been interpreted as a step toward the other side in the East-West conflict.[3] While recognition of this sphere of influence is seldom explicitly acknowledged as a guiding principle of US foreign policy, scholars have identified its operation. Thus, Robert W. Tucker notes:

> Central America bears geographical proximity to the United States, and historically it has long been regarded as falling within our sphere of influence. As such, we have long exercised the role great powers have traditionally exercised over small states which fall within their respective sphere of influence. We have regularly played a determining role in making and unmaking governments, and we have defined what we have considered to be acceptable behaviour of governments.
>
> In Central America our pride is engaged. . . . If we do not apply policy of our resurgent America to prevent the coming to power of radical regimes in Central America, we have even less reason to do so in other states.[4]

The tacit recognition of the Basin as a US sphere of influence and the rules that flow therefrom have guided the behavior not only of Washington but also of Moscow and Havana. The first rule is that the regional hegemon can exercise supervisory intervention within its sphere without the risk of military challenge by the other superpower, either directly or through a surrogate. Second and consequently, the other superpower will, in the circumstances and on the whole, restrict its

behavior in the sphere to denunciation or discreet probing or prudent
support of radical governments or movements.

In this respect, it is significant that massive Cuban military
interventions (with the support of the USSR) have not been in the
Caribbean but in Africa, an area of acknowledged superpower competition
rather than a region of vital interest to one side or the other. (The
superpowers have used similar rhetoric or doctrine to justify their
respective forceful interventions in the Caribbean and Africa.)[5]

The superpowers' respective levels of interest in the Caribbean Basin
and the forms of intervention they have chosen have been derived from the
Basin's geopolitical characteristics. When considering the possibilities for
superpower cooperation in the management or resolution of conflict in the
Caribbean Basin, it is therefore necessary to recognize that there is a
profound asymmetry in their levels of interest and intervention. At the
same time, one must consider what effects, if any, change in the sphere of
Eastern Europe may have on US relations with the Basin.

The Structure of Other US Interests

In addition to its preoccupation with Soviet designs to instigate or support
radical regimes in the region, the United States is also concerned with the
preservation of certain structural interests, which will persist irrespective
of the diminution or disappearance of superpower competition or conflict.
The US coastline juts into the Caribbean, and Puerto Rico and the US
Virgin Islands are US territories. Moreover, US interests in the Basin have
been reinforced by "regional shifts within the US" itself, "away from the
north-east and towards the southern rim. . . . Defence and space
programmes, agri-business and new manufacturing industries" are
increasingly concentrated in the southern rim, thus enhancing the
importance of ports and industrial areas such as Houston, New Orleans,
and Miami.[6] Major new military installations in Honduras complement
existing military bases and installations in the Panama Canal Zone,
Guantánamo in Cuba, San Juan and Roosevelt Roads in Puerto Rico, as
well as in the CARICOM states—an antisubmarine facility in the
Bahamas and systems involved in underwater communications and
electronic relay in Antigua and Barbuda. Antigua's international airport,
and that of Barbados, provide essential transit points for US military
flights into the South Atlantic.

Indeed, the location of certain territories in the Caribbean is of basic
strategic significance not only for Washington but also for its NATO
allies: for example, the proximity of the Bahamas to the United States;
the location of Dominica between Martinique and Guadeloupe (perceived

by the French as a catalyst for dissent in those territories); and the presence of the Ariane European Space Programme Rocket Base in Korou, Cayenne (French Guyana). There is also evidence corroborating the contention of some analysts that since the US invasion of Grenada in 1983, the Barbados Defence Force and other small SSUs in the OECS are envisaged as elements in US defense arrangements.

The sea lanes of the Caribbean, the major routes of transit for essential raw materials, including oil, are generally recognized as having major strategic significance. More than half of all US oil continues to be refined in the Caribbean. Moreover, sea lanes have increasing long-term importance as Latin American economies become more closely integrated with the North.

It has been suggested that the Caribbean could play an important role in the administration of the provisions of the new Law of the Sea Convention, which updates the international law for oceans arrangement. "The free and co-operative maintenance of harbours and trade facilities [which] is a Western creation,"[7] can be disrupted with far-reaching significance if control of off-shore zones is indiscriminately assigned in the convention.

While the Basin is not a major area of US investment, it is a key zone of circulation for US economic interests, providing a vast trading and financial network with centers in Panama, the Bahamas, and the Cayman Islands. There are off-shore banking facilities in the eastern Caribbean as well as in Free Trade Zones (FTZs), the most developed of which is in Colón, Panama, which reportedly accounts for a greater volume of trade than the rest of Central America combined.[8]

The steadily increasing surge, despite restrictive legislation, of migrants, both legal and illegal, into the United States from the Caribbean already appears to threaten the United States. Caribbean Basin migrants have begun to exercise influence on US politics. While not a significant producer of narcotics, the Caribbean provides transit routes for narcotic trafficking and money laundering into the United States from the Bahamas in the North to Guyana in the South.

A final menace has been the capacity of Caribbean intellectuals to react against the limitations of their small states and fragile economies. In the search for identity that is characteristic of transplanted peoples, they have produced and promoted ideas that have occasionally had catalytic worldwide influence on nonwhite, underdeveloped peoples. These intellectuals have been perceived in the United States as threatening, especially to US capitalist values. Such influences include the initial arousal of black consciousness in the United States by Marcus Garvey and others; the promotion of such concepts as negritude and Pan-Africanism (the work of Aimé Césaire and Padmore respectively, and acknowledged by African leaders as the creation of the black diaspora in the Caribbean); and the expansion of the agenda of nonalignment to include a significant economic content that involves the formulation of fundamental aspects of the demand for a new international economic order.

It seems certain, therefore, that even if the Caribbean Basin is not hereafter seen by the United States as a zone of Cold War competition, instabilities within it may continue to be a source of concern for the United States.

Range of Conflicts

In addition to its strategic concerns, the United States has other continuing interests, in particular the nature of intrastate conflicts. While there are a number of interstate conflicts (the claims to the territory of Guyana and Belize by Venezuela and Guatemala, respectively), these have so far attracted no superpower intervention and are proving amenable to diplomatic amelioration, if not resolution, at multilateral and bilateral levels. Cross-border conflicts have been an important element in Central American conflicts but have not themselves been the occasion for superpower intervention. Refugees and migration have posed nearly unmanageable problems for recipient states, such as Belize in Central America and the Bahamas, but have not erupted beyond bilateral tensions. Claims to the resources of the sea have been reflected in difficult problems of maritime delimitation involving metropolitan powers, especially in the eastern Caribbean. However, it is only in the case of narcotics trafficking that there has so far been interstate conflict involving superpower intervention—invasion in the case of Panama, or punitive action through the assertion of US extraterritorial jurisdiction over the Bahamas.

The dominant pattern is of intrastate conflicts with external involvement. There are significant differences between intrastate conflicts within Central America and those of the English-speaking island and mainland states. With the important exception of Costa Rica, the internal conflicts in Central America turn on the demand by the rural and urban dispossessed for a share in political space and power. It has essentially been a problem of securing entry to the political systems in which the traditional ruling class, closely allied with the military, have sought to protect their present niche through repressive measures and by holding elections that provide no real opportunities for access to power.

In contrast, the military have played little part in the retention or access to power in the English-speaking Caribbean since independence because the transfer of power from the expatriate rulers had begun while the security forces were still under colonial control. In these countries the sources of conflict lie not so much in a demand for opening the political process as in the conviction of some ruling groups that constitutional decolonization or flag independence was only a beginning. To overcome problems such as mass unemployment and maldistribution of income, such groups felt it necessary to use the political power acquired at independence for "the job of reconstructing social and economic society." New ruling groups emerging from the electoral process (Bishop's New Jewel Movement, which had taken power in Grenada in 1974 after a coup, remained an exception) were acutely aware of the limitations on political power and freedom that are imposed by economic structures. Moreover, they saw their states as embedded in an international economic system that ensured that the gains of production accrued mainly to Western industrialized states. They sought to introduce radical measures of transformation that were articulated in terms of socialist or Marxist ideology. There is, however, no hard evidence that in resorting to such programs they were responding to the initiative of any foreign power or agency. Nevertheless, such programs almost invariably attracted US hostility and led to intervention, even when the party committed to those programs had achieved power through elections.

Case Study in Intervention in Intrastate Conflict

In this respect the fate of the first Michael Manley regime is particularly instructive. Manley, an internationally respected statesman committed to parliamentary democracy, had always declared himself as no more than a democratic socialist. After the 1979 electoral victory of his Peoples National Party (PNP) over Edward Seaga's Jamaica Labour Party (JLP), Manley set about implementing a program with the following objectives:

1. To make the process of the production and distribution of goods less dependent on external factors and local oligarchic control;
2. To renounce the Puerto Rican model in which foreign investment is seen as the main engine of development with all policy promoting its entrenchment; and
3. To enlarge the public sector, particularly in strategic areas of the economy.[9]

The program included the nationalization of public utilities and foreign companies that owned most of the sugar industry as well as the negotiation of a new tax structure with the North American–owned bauxite industry to ensure a larger share of accrued wealth for Jamaica.

There were also proposals for underpinning Jamaica's parliamentary system with mechanisms for a politics of participation by the people.

Manley sought a major role in Third World movements dedicated to the negotiation of the so-called New International Economic Order. He also assisted in the foundation of the IBA, a bauxite cartel designed along OPEC lines, which was more directly relevant to the fortunes of his government.

While the Jamaica two-party political system was not deeply divided along class lines, the opposition JLP represented the interests of business and the better-off sections of society and soon presented itself as the advocate and protector of overseas investment. The bitter fight with the bauxite companies inevitably attracted the unfriendly attention of the administration of US president Gerald Ford. However, a new understanding arose with the election of his successor, Jimmy Carter. This honeymoon did not last, as Carter's "liberalism" dissolved under the pressure of regional and international events and change within the US policy formulation process itself with the triumph of Brzezinski's East-West perspective over the North-South concerns of Andrew Young and other advisors.

The campaign against Manley, in which there is abundant evidence of CIA involvement, led to internal strikes, riots and massacres, propaganda smear campaigns in the local and international press, withdrawal of local and overseas investment, flight of the professional middle class, withholding of assistance from multilateral and bilateral agencies, and collapse of the tourist industry, on which the Jamaican economy was heavily dependent.[10] The campaign was organized within and formed part of the internal struggle for power by the leader of the opposition, Edward Seaga. In public addresses, mainly in Washington, he contended that Manley was introducing the Cuban model in Jamaica and that multiparty democracy would soon end. Seaga argued that Marxist systems would soon spread to other countries in the Basin.

After reviewing the Seaga campaign, Vaughan Lewis came to the conclusion that "by the end of 1977, the opposition leader had devised a strategy to influence the American administration away from its basically sympathetic view of the objectives of the Manley administration; . . . and by implication, toward the isolation of a Jamaican Government falling within an allegedly developing Cuba-Jamaica-Guyana axis in the subregion."[11]

Exacerbating intrastate conflict in Jamaica was not simply a matter of US intervention to prevent or obstruct programs of radical change perceived as threats to its security. It was an example of a recurring situation in which regional groups manipulate the US foreign policy process to their advantage because of the known susceptibility of that process to appeals to combat communism.

Manipulation of the US policy process toward the Caribbean created a link between US strategic concerns and the fate of urban/military elites in Central America, the Seaga party in Jamaica, or one side in the ethnic cleavage in Guyana. As Manley's hold on power deteriorated, extreme leftist elements in the party forged deepening linkages with Cuba. Thus, the Jamaican situation became a self-fulfilling prophecy.

The USSR in the Basin

How far were fears of Soviet expansionism really justified? It has been maintained that the opportunities for Soviet action in the Basin have their origin in the profound hostility of the United States toward radical regimes, which in consequence seek security and assistance from "the other side."[12] Except in the case of the Cuban missile crisis, Soviet initiatives have been marked by caution, born mainly of a tacit understanding that there could be no fundamental military challenge without risk of escalation in the other superpower's sphere of influence. Other factors promoted caution, including Moscow's lack of understanding of mixed ethnic/cultural heritage; the failure to develop empathy with regional intellectuals and leaders, including homegrown Marxists; and anxiety to avoid the aid burden of "another Cuba."

Because the Soviet Union has never given high priority to the Basin, its interest in internal developments there has not been steadily engaged. Overwhelming evidence of this lack of interest is its surprise at Fidel Castro's victory and that of the Sandinistas in Nicaragua. The narrative of how mounting US hostility pushed Castro to embrace the USSR is well known. While there was initially a friendly and constructive US response to the Sandinistas, the failure to maintain a consistent policy led not only to strengthening Soviet and Cuban links but to eroding the internal pluralism to which the Sandinista regime had been initially committed. Once its interest was engaged, the USSR established a mission in Managua and initiated a substantial aid program.

While the United States appears to have mismanaged its initial relationship with the Bishop regime in Grenada, it seems that there was a strong internal commitment to the pursuit of Marxist transformation by a small but powerful group of intellectuals in the New Jewel Movement, who long before the takeover had espoused Marxist theories of noncapitalist socioeconomic and political development popular with Soviet scholars. Initially, however, there was so little Soviet interest in Grenada that strong Cuban mediation was necessary to engage Moscow.

What is significant is that the USSR, slow in the development of relations and anxious to limit relationships to party levels and the middle echelon of Soviet officials, went on to conclude a number of major secret military aid agreements with Grenada.

This mixture of caution yielding to growing commitment is demonstrated in the USSR's approach to aid to Nicaragua and Grenada. In both cases, the emphasis in military assistance was mainly on defensive weaponry (considered unlikely to provoke a response from Washington), but the weaponry was suitable for self-defense or coping with counterrevolutionary action. In both instances, Cuba and other Eastern European countries were also involved in supply and training. Nevertheless, the belief that emphasis on defensive weaponry would diffuse US concerns was a serious miscalculation. The scale of supply, although pursued incrementally, was sufficient to arouse fears in neighboring states—fears that would in turn trigger a US reaction.

Anxious to avoid the burden of another aid program along Cuban lines, there was a similar limited approach to economic aid. Nicaragua was provided with oil and foodstuffs on credit, while the USSR imported Nicaraguan products at higher-than-market prices. Economic aid to Grenada consisted of agreements to purchase regularly, at good prices, major exports, such as spices and bananas, together with the supply of foodstuff and construction material. As in the case of arms supply, East European countries and Cuba were prodded to participate.

Although the United States interpreted the scale of aid as destabilizing Grenada's security, the USSR, as the Valentas have pointed out, "was unable or unwilling to provide much help in transforming Grenada into a socialist paradise in the Caribbean."[13] Further pointers to the prudent but rising levels of Soviet engagement were the fundamental changes in their perceptions and policy toward the Basin, especially in Nicaragua. The Soviets, who had hitherto counseled the Cubans against the promotion of violent revolution through the training and arming of guerrilla groups, now saw new possibilities for revolution in the Basin and elsewhere in the Third World in line with the strategies outlined long before by such figures as Che Guevara.

While anxious to avoid confrontation and, more still, humiliation in the US sphere of influence, the USSR thus demonstrated its willingness to support regimes whose existence might lead to the diversion to the Caribbean of US military resources from other areas of the world in which the USSR had vital interests. At the same time, US influence would be weakened as such regimes looked elsewhere than the United States for security assistance, opportunities for trade and aid, and for development models and ideas.

The Role of Cuba

Cubans are frequently portrayed as surrogates for the USSR in their activities in the Caribbean Basin, which oversimplifies the Cuban role. Through the 1960s, the USSR had viewed the Cuban strategy of support for guerrilla groups as counterproductive and provocative in a region recognized as the sphere of US influence, with possible grave consequences for the bilateral superpower relationship. While there had been movement toward a convergence in approaches since the 1970s, fundamental differences persisted. Cubans perceived an urgent need for their own security to promote the establishment in the Basin of friendly, preferably Marxist, governments and to neutralize hostile regimes. The USSR for its part continued to assign an altogether lower priority to the Basin.

The initial Cuban push into the Caribbean Basin had been facilitated by its attraction for radical leaders and intellectuals searching for a program of fundamental change. In addition to ideology, other factors drew leaders—and not only those from the left—to Havana: the success in redistribution especially through the provision of health, housing, and educational services; the creation of a disciplined society, an objective that has so frequently eluded Caribbean and other Third World states; the demonstration of sophisticated organizational skills; and not least, a readiness to stand up to the regional superpower.

Some Basin governments and political parties sought to acquire socialist respectability or to head off the pressure of leftist groups in their states by establishing diplomatic links with Cuba. In 1973, four CARICOM states—Barbados, Guyana, Jamaica, and Trinidad and Tobago—had established diplomatic relations with Cuba, ending its isolation; this step immediately incurred the hostility of the United States.

Cuba's external thrust, to pursue its own security and to advance strongly held ideological objectives, had several phases. Earlier, the emphasis was on support and training of leftist guerrilla groups for similar governments. Later came the mobilization of solidarity through diplomatic links with Basin countries and, further afield, with leading Third World countries. Such solidarity was underpinned by the provision of technical assistance and other forms of economic cooperation.

These two areas of activity were essentially Cuban initiatives owing little to direct support from the USSR. However, the phase of military assistance, including the provision of training, arms, and other support, whether in the Basin or elsewhere, depended heavily on Soviet logistical support and supplies. Such military activities were perceived by Havana not only as a means of advancing Cuba's security and ideological

14 9, 10 1

objectives but as a method of attracting large-scale Soviet economic assistance.

To mobilize the diplomatic solidarity of Third World governments, Castro journeyed to Latin America, Africa, and Asia and hosted the Sixth Summit of the NAM in 1979. Cubans were at pains to build close links with the governments of ethnically Afro-Asian countries of the Caribbean islands, namely the English-speaking states (in particular Grenada, Guyana, and Jamaica), which were at the same time seeking leadership roles in the NAM and the G77. Cuba facilitated this attempt by projecting itself as sharing the common values derived from a similar origin in a plantation economy. While the concerns of the Reagan era have tended to focus attention on Cuban activity in Central America, the major Cuban thrusts for influence have in fact been in the Caribbean islands.

Cuban initiatives, whether in Central America or the Caribbean, were always supported by technical assistance and economic cooperation. For instance, Cuba built schools and hospitals in Jamaica; manned the medical service and built and staffed a university medical school in Guyana; and constructed an international airport in Grenada. Despite the expulsion of Cuban missions from Jamaica, Grenada, and Suriname, and the current reduction in Soviet support, the web of Cuban influence is built on wider foundations than backing revolutionary activity and is thus likely to persist.

The Contribution of the Superpowers to Conflict

While superpower tension has not ignited intrastate conflict, it has served to exacerbate such strife and put it beyond the reach of early resolution. Three types of adverse effects have been particularly significant: internal polarization, corruption of systems, and militarization.

Polarization

As ruling groups or their opponents have sought succor from one superpower or the other, they have frequently projected themselves as pursuing pure strategies, whether it be free enterprise and market economy or Marxist/socialist strategy. In view of the failure of each—socialism in Guyana under Forbes Burnham or in Jamaica under Michael Manley, or private enterprise in Jamaica under Seaga or in Grenada since the invasion—the destruction of a middle ground has hampered the search for consensus for devising economic strategies appropriate to small states.

In Grenada, Soviet disapproval of Bishop's deviation from Marxist/Leninist orthodoxy seemingly disrupted the fragile consensus on which the regime had survived and led to the army coup and murder of Bishop.

Externalization of conflict has led, in Nicaragua, to the premature abandonment of pluralism and unnecessary measures of radicalization; it has also promoted violence that has become endemic in some societies, especially in Central America. Moreover, the true genesis of intrastate conflicts has been obscured, for example, in the ethnic divisions in Guyana and Trinidad and Tobago. As a consequence, the search for agreements through, for example, constitutional arrangements has been postponed. The result, on the one hand, is widespread alienation and the growth of movements outside the civil society (the Black Muslims in Trinidad and Tobago, for example) or, on the other hand, mass migration.

Corruption

Regimes that have felt that their tenure in office was secure because of their commitment, in a US sphere of influence, to free enterprise have corrupted their systems of government. Nothing illustrates better the US protection of corrupt and brutal regimes for security reasons than the way in which the Carter administration, until very nearly the end of the war, sought accommodation with Somoza and his National Guard. Haiti also provides a most dramatic example of US assistance, including military assistance, to a regime that Washington supported as a bulwark against the penetration into that society of Cuban communism. In the small twin-island state of Antigua and Barbuda, a ruling family has been in office for nearly a generation. Their administration has been marked by several well-documented acts of local and international corruption, including the use of the government apparatus for the purchase and transshipment of arms from Israel to drug barons in Colombia. In addition, legislation has been enacted that severely curtailed the rights of free speech and assembly, freedom of the press, and the right of workers to unionize; there has also been widespread use of victimization as an instrument of policy.

Guyana likewise provides an example of the corruption of systems undertaken with impunity because of fears that the alternative would have close ties to Moscow and Havana. Over a period of a quarter-century, elections were rigged; a new constitution was introduced with dictatorial powers for an executive president; and human rights were curtailed. However, the Guyana case has had an unusual denouement. When, under internal pressure, the government resorted to nationalization of major sectors of the economy, thereby incurring the censure of Washington, links were quickly developed with Cuba and the Eastern bloc in a similar search for new sources of security and assistance but also as a ploy to outflank an extreme left opposition.

Militarization

The superpowers have contributed to the militarization of societies in the Caribbean Basin. Soviet military assistance to Nicaragua to counter the contras has been an important factor in militarizing that society, especially through arming civil defense organizations. In Grenada, Soviet large-scale military assistance, leading to a dominant role for the army, facilitated the coup in which Maurice Bishop was murdered.

In the eastern Caribbean, current security trends tend strongly toward militarization. Unlike the case of the Central American states, there is in the CARICOM states no endemic problem of violence or recurring pattern of military intervention (Maurice Bishop's coup remains an exception). In the wake of US intervention in Grenada in 1983, assisted by military personnel from Jamaica, Barbados, and the OECS states, the United States has provided military assistance for training and equipping small SSUs for the OECS states and for the defense forces of Barbados and Jamaica.

The OECS defense arrangements, while providing for joint action to prevent drug trafficking, illegal migration, and the supervision of the EEZ, have as a primary objective coping with uprisings such as had earlier occurred in Dominica and St. Vincent and the Grenadines. It was therefore not surprising that the CARICOM heads of government meeting in Kingston, Jamaica, at the time of the Black Muslimeen uprising in Port of Spain in July 1990, reacted with a call for an extension of the OECS defense arrangements to other territories. The Kingston decision reflects the tendency for governments confronted by rising societal discontents resulting from failed development strategy to resort to military force to quell demands for social change.

While the CARICOM states constitute a grouping committed to parliamentary government, it has been insufficiently noted that the Westminster model is susceptible to authoritarian rule in the absence of traditional safeguards and rules. Moreover, present ruling groups are steadily aware that their colonial predecessors had invariably invoked the military and paramilitary forces to put down internal dissent and uprisings. The risks of militarization that have been detected by a number of scholars are therefore by no means farfetched.[14]

The Ebb and Flow in the Superpower Relationship

While the Caribbean experience demonstrates that intrastate conflict serves as an arena for superpower conflict, the ebb and flow in the superpower relationship itself affects the course of conflict. Superpower relations have been reflected in their relationships with Basin states. For example, before 1969, the Soviets exercised restraint on Cuban activities, which at that time were viewed as a possible source of disturbance in the central balance. However, conflict in the Basin has derived mainly from US foreign policy.

The Carter era provides a clear example of the primacy of US policy for the region. Reacting to the reverses in Vietnam and to the tarnished image of the US government after Watergate, the Carter administration initially pursued a policy of building cooperation with radical regimes that were already in office or had recently emerged in the Basin, including Jamaica, Guyana, Grenada, and subsequently Nicaragua. One of the leading advocates of regional cooperation in the Carter administration, Terrence Todman, then assistant secretary of state for Inter-American Affairs, articulates the new Carter approach to the region as follows: "We no longer see the Caribbean in quite the same stark military security context that we once viewed it. Rather, our security concerns in the Caribbean are increasingly political in nature. The threat is not simply foreign military bases on our doorstep. It is possibly an even more troublesome prospect: proliferation of impoverished Third World states whose economic and political problems blend with our own."[15]

This approach was given policy formulation by Sally Shelton, then US ambassador in the eastern Caribbean, as follows:

- Significant support for economic development;
- Firm commitment to democratic practices and human rights;
- Clear acceptance of ideological pluralism;
- Unequivocal respect for national sovereignty; and
- Strong encouragement of regional cooperation and of an active Caribbean role in world affairs.[16]

Reacting to resurgent domestic conservatism triggered by a recession and international reverses, namely the hostage-taking in Iran and the Soviet invasion in Afghanistan, the Carter administration quickly reverted to the traditional stance of anticommunism. Andrew Young, Carter's first UN ambassador, wrote in the *New York Times* after his dismissal that the Carter administration had begun "to view the Caribbean region through a cold war prism, placing more emphasis on Cuba than on the broad problem of poverty that besets the entire Caribbean."[17]

Ideological Pluralism

In the meantime, the English-speaking Caribbean had taken Carter's representatives who had visited the Caribbean—Andrew Young, Terrence Todman, and Philip Habib—at their word. CARICOM leaders, in the face of their own sharp ideological conflicts within the regional integration movement, adopted the doctrine of ideological pluralism as an organizing principle. The CARICOM foreign ministers' meeting in Saint Lucia in February 1980 declared that "ideological pluralism is an irreversible fact of international relations and should not, therefore, be permitted to constitute a barrier to the strengthening of the mechanism of CARICOM,"[18] a position which was reinforced in a similar declaration by CARICOM heads of government two years later.

Maurice Bishop, prime minister of Grenada, invoked the doctrine as an international norm that might provide security by deterring intervention:

> Our third principle is that the principle of ideological pluralism must be respected in practice. Every single country in the world, including racist apartheid South Africa, will speak in theory of accepting the principle of ideological pluralism. But theory is not enough; we want to see in practice that the people of this region are in fact allowed to build their own processes in their own way, free from outside interference and free from all forms of threats or attempts to force them to build a process that somebody else likes. This principle today must be recognized and practised. It is a fundamental principle that reflects the reality of today's Caribbean.[19]

In the wake of the Grenada invasion, the doctrine may appear to be irrelevant. However, the episode remains significant as an example of how a US foreign policy response to change in the region can ameliorate or exacerbate conflict.

Changes in US Perceptions and Policy in the Post–Cold War World

At the very moment the US government seems willing, because of the radical decline of Soviet expansionism, to accept radical Caribbean Basin governments, socialism collapsed in the Basin, and the IMF and the World Bank imposed market regimes on the deeply indebted Basin states, including formerly socialist states such as Jamaica and Guyana, that have sought their assistance. In the region, there is an increasingly widespread acceptance of private enterprise as the principal engine of growth. Dwindling US concerns about Marxism may greatly reduce the need in the immediate future to send in the gunboats. The IMF will ensure that colonies in the Caribbean Basin adopt the free enterprise system.

One sign of relaxation is that the US concern with anticommunism seems to be giving way to a commitment to democratization and free elections, even though they might bring to office regimes not completely supportive of US policies. The thrust toward democratization is apparently based on the twin beliefs that democracy will lead to a more stable and peaceful international environment and that the free enterprise system is an essential concomitant of democracy.

While these trends were being celebrated, however, the disturbing Christmas 1989 invasion of Panama took place. The demonization of Noriega (an admittedly corrupt and brutal dictator) in order to rationalize the invasion appeared to many observers in the region as an all-too-familiar scenario, with the substitution of drug barons for communists. It had the traditional ending—the establishment of a compliant government served by US-trained security forces, which administers the Panama Canal in a way acceptable to the United States.

In Nicaragua a fragile consensus prevails. The unexpected victory of Violeta Chamorro might seem to justify the use of force in resisting and turning back undesirable change. However, it has left a situation in which violence is endemic to the Nicaraguan society and in which, despite commitments of the winning coalition—the UNO—to massive privatization, it will prove difficult to dismantle socialist state structures that respond to the deep needs of that society. Moreover, the Sandinistas remain the majority party and are thus a considerable force in society.

In Jamaica, Michael Manley has regained power after an election that was, by Jamaican standards, nearly free of violence. It has been contended that the violence that accompanied the run-up to the previous election, in which he was defeated by Seaga, had been organized by the CIA. Diplomatic relations with Cuba, broken off as one of the first acts of the Seaga government, have been restored. The relationship with Washington is cordial. However, since Manley's victory, there has not been indication of a greater willingness by the United States to accept democratic socialism in the Basin. Manley, in providing assurances to Washington, has sharply modified his program, which exalts the major role of private enterprise and foreign investment.

Modestly hopeful was the holding of free and fair elections in Haiti, despite the ephemeral victory by the radical-oriented presidential candidate, Father Bertrand Aristide. Previous feeble attempts to hold fair elections, ending in the massacre of voters by the army, attest to the strength of US concerns about a possible communist takeover in this state, which is strategically located close to Cuba. The speed with which the army, always responsive to US admonitions, moved to put down a Duvalierist coup in the wake of the election of Aristide seemed momentarily to be significant, though his subsequent ouster was discouraging.

Perhaps of equal significance has been the pressure exerted recently by

Washington to hold fair elections in Guyana. The US role in the removal of the government of Marxist Cheddi Jagan in the mid-1960s has been well documented.[20] Therefore, recent US insistence on the establishment of an acceptable and transparent electoral system, despite the possibility of electoral victory by socialist elements, may likewise point to a new flexibility. However, it remains to be seen whether, in the absence of an East-West Cold War, the US government will be prepared to accept strategies other than total free enterprise that may be adopted as a result of the outcome of elections, whether in Haiti, Guyana, or elsewhere in the Basin.

Changes in the USSR's Perceptions and Policy

Soviet post–Cold War behavior in the Basin must for its part respond to such new and important factors as disintegration of its influence and control in Eastern Europe, widespread renunciation of the communist system as one capable of providing acceptable standards of living, and threats to the structure of the Soviet Union itself. But it must also take account of developments within the Basin that may have an impact on its policies.

Grenada and Nicaragua are of particular relevance. The events leading up to the US invasion of Grenada marked not only the end of the Bishop regime but also the failure of the orthodox and doctrinaire strategy that the USSR had pursued within the country. Moscow found unacceptable the links that Maurice Bishop had built with a number of relatively capitalist regimes in the other English-speaking states, especially Trinidad and Tobago, and viewed with even greater suspicion and hostility his efforts to build bridges to Washington. The Soviets tacitly encouraged an internal faction led by Bernard Coard, a rival for power who was impatient with the slow pace of socialist transformation and the failure of Bishop's New Jewel Movement to provide a Marxist vanguard. While the nature and extent of Moscow's support for this strongly ideological faction has not been established with certainty, the Soviets had frequently manipulated factions in pursuit of their own objectives in similar crises in Eastern Europe and Afghanistan. Not only was Soviet behavior dominated by rigid ideological considerations, but it also failed completely to understand US security concerns, especially the overarching need to preserve the unity of the ruling group and national consensus.

The details of the bloody denouement need not be retold, but the remarkably different subsequent Soviet approach to events in Nicaragua probably owed something to their failure in Grenada.[21] The Soviet approach in Nicaragua was characterized by flexibility and pragmatism and acceptance of a mixed economic system. While a mixed system had always been perceived by the Soviets as a stage in socialist transformation, they now recognized it as an end in itself.[22] Moreover, at an early stage Moscow appeared to have grasped the security value of national reconciliation for Nicaragua.

The new pragmatic Soviet approach might have been responsive to perestroika within the USSR itself. But it also recognized that the national leadership must devise strategies appropriate to local circumstances rather than accept models adopted to secure USSR approval and assistance. Soviet perception of the need for national unity may be a spin-off from insights derived from the Afghanistan situation.[23] However, it is not farfetched to see in it lessons learned from the failure in Grenada.

The USSR will likely maintain its interest in the Basin because this collection of small states will continue to link the regions of developing countries. The USSR has prolonged its aid program to Nicaragua and has recently concluded a trade and information agreement with post-Noriega Panama.

Superpower Cooperation in the Resolution of Conflict

Can superpower cooperation by itself serve to wind down and resolve such conflicts that in the Caribbean Basin are primarily intrastate in origin? There are positive signs, most notably in the recent reduction of conflict in Nicaragua. The withdrawal of US assistance to the contras was matched by Mikhail Gorbachev's assurance to George Bush that the Soviets had terminated military assistance late in 1988. There is also evidence that there was strong pressure from Moscow on Daniel Ortega to hold acceptable elections.

More significant was the existence of a regional initiative that, by eliminating the need for negotiations between the superpowers, provided a ready-made basis for cooperation. The Arias Plan, signed by all Central American governments in August 1987, required measures to democratize Nicaragua, including ensuring freedom of expression and assembly and holding elections under foreign supervision. Washington, in response to congressional pressure, curtailed assistance to the contras, and Moscow's openness to new ideas promoted disengagement in the Third World. Yet, the essential condition for the resolution of the conflict had been the agreements reached by regional states that had enlisted international support.

If superpower cooperation in the resolution of conflicts is to succeed, however, there are several lessons from the Caribbean experience that are relevant for other conflicts in the region and elsewhere in the Third World.

1. Superpower interventions have served to obscure and conceal the true sources of conflicts, exacerbate divisions, and make such conflicts altogether more difficult to resolve in the following ways:
   - Development models imposed from outside the region have proven inadequate instruments for development, their failure leading to widespread alienation and the growth of movements that challenge civil society.
   - Superpower insistence on pure strategies, whether of the left or right, makes it impossible for the state to promote internal consensus and to begin on that basis to search for appropriate strategies.
   - "Protected" regimes have felt free to indulge to their own advantage in corrupting systems and thwarting democratic processes.
   - Violence has become endemic in some states, especially in Central America, against the background of persistent militarization, and there is a growing trend toward militarization in the English-speaking insular Caribbean.
2. Superpowers have from time to time been maneuvered unwittingly into situations of competition or conflict by their clients who have sought through the externalization of the internal conflict to strengthen their own positions within the state.
3. While events in the Basin reflect to some extent the ebb and flow in superpower relations, changes in such relations are purveyed in the Basin mainly through the US policy process.
4. The resolution of intrastate conflicts will require not only restraint and support from the superpowers, but also, as a necessary condition, agreements negotiated within the region in which middle powers might play decisive roles.
5. While the processes of cooperation at global levels might have a mutual restraining effect on superpower action, parallelism will persist with US action in the Basin matched by similar action by Moscow to maintain the integrity of its union.
6. It is too soon to predict with confidence whether Soviet acceptance of pluralism in Eastern Europe will facilitate US acquiescence to experimentation in the Basin by freely elected governments or whether, in the absence of competition from the other power, the United States will pursue punitive or supervisory action.

Conclusion

Contrary to the wishful thinking of some analysts, there can be no total withdrawal of Soviet power from the Third World, including the Caribbean Basin (the Basin was never an area of priority interest, however). It is most unlikely that Moscow will throw away several decades of foreign policy gains. Too hasty a withdrawal from the Third World could further fuel a resurgence of hard-liners within the USSR itself, which would threaten perestroika. The USSR has never been a major aid donor in the region, assistance being limited (except for Cuba) to the provision of arms and training, as in the case of Grenada and Nicaragua. It can, therefore, more easily pursue diplomacy to secure the support of regional countries in recognition of the catalytic role it plays in the Third World.

It now seems likely, however, that the USSR will abandon Cuba, though this will jeopardize Moscow's influence in the Third World. The Soviet Union is unlikely to maintain security assistance to Cuba at existing levels even if the United States and Cuba fail to achieve accommodation. Trade will be restructured toward greater emphasis on mutual gain, at a pace that will likely threaten the Cuban economy. In response, Cuba, already pursuing a diplomacy of solidarity with the region, is likely to intensify these initiatives in the conviction that such relationships enhance its own security. It has already begun to expand diplomatic representation in the eastern Caribbean.

Far more important for the immediate future will be developments within the countries of the Basin themselves and the evolution of US foreign policy in a context in which anticommunism will no longer be the dominant preoccupation. The Caribbean Basin has entered the post–Cold War era in varying degrees of disorder and internal conflict and with heavy dependence on traditional export industries that are weak and deteriorating. They are bedeviled by institutional decay or irrelevance, lack of a clear strategy, and the alienation of large sections of the population. Most of them are engulfed in debt crises; some are among the most indebted countries in the world.

The IMF and the World Bank have assumed responsibility for monitoring internal systems and have insisted on maintenance of or transformation into market economies. The magic of the marketplace has so far failed to rescue beleaguered economies in the region, but this failure has not revived radical leadership. Instead, there is a profound turning away from, and disbelief in, all existing institutions, including political parties and trade unions.

This situation will almost certainly lead to political instabilities that could threaten safe transit as well as lead to an increase in drug trafficking and a further surge in mass migration into North America. It remains to be seen whether Washington will see these threats to US security as deriving mainly from poverty and deprivation and whether such perceptions will lead to a more relaxed attitude toward letting regimes choose mixed strategies that might yield acceptable standards of living.

However, it seems equally possible that any thrust toward social and economic transformation that is not considered sufficiently enthusiastic about free enterprise may be seen as challenging fundamental US assumptions and thus require corrective intervention. It may be that despite structural interests, the United States may lose interest altogether in the region, especially at a time when the developed world turns increasingly toward major trading blocs. Indeed it seems possible that current US trade proposals, namely the Enterprise for the Americas Initiative aimed at creating a free trade area from Alaska to Argentina, will subsume the region in an amorphous trade bloc in which the small states of the Caribbean Basin will become little more than tourist paradises or export production zones.

It cannot be confidently argued that such disinterest will exclude intervention. It may be that the lower profile of Soviet power will encourage disinterest. After all, nothing can go far wrong. And if it does, as Grenada, Panama, and, more recently, the Gulf crisis have demonstrated, there can be quick intervention that, with proper management of the press, can be portrayed as "surgical" and successful.

There may also be a chance for a more optimistic scenario. In view of the remarkable international leadership roles taken by a number of CARICOM states, Washington might in the future perceive its relationship with the small states of the Caribbean Basin not only in terms of possible security risks but also as providing important diplomatic opportunities for the projection and interpretation of its views and interests into the developing world.

Notes

1. Eric Williams, *From Columbus to Castro, the History of the Caribbean—1492–1969* (London: Adre Deutsch, 1970), 69 and 71.

2. William Demas has identified three definitions of the Caribbean: (1) the English-speaking Caribbean or Commonwealth Caribbean including the mainland states of Guyana and Belize; (2) the Caribbean archipelago plus the mainland extensions of Guyana, Suriname, Cayenne and Belize; and (3) the Caribbean Basin consisting of the countries of the Caribbean archipelago plus the littoral states of Central and South America. See Demas's "Foreword" to *The Restless Caribbean*, edited by Richard Millett and W. Marvin Will (New York: Praeger, 1979), vii–xix. It should be noted that the US Trade Act,

known as the Caribbean Basin Initiative, omits the littoral states of South America.

3. Modesto Seara Vasquez, "Zones of Influence," *Year Book of World Affairs, 1973* (London: Stevens and Sons, 1974): 301–315.

4. R. W. Tucker, "The Purposes of American Power," *Foreign Affairs*, 59, no. 2 (Winter 1980–1981): 241–274.

5. For discussion of parallelism, see Thomas M. Franck and Edward Weisband, *Word Politics: Verbal Strategy Among the Superpowers* (New York: Oxford University Press, 1971), 3–32.

6. Fitzroy Ambursley and Robin Cohen, *Crisis in the Caribbean: Internal Transformations and External Constraints in Crisis in the Caribbean* (Jamaica: Heinemann, 1983), 17.

7. Richard Sim and James Anderson, *The Caribbean Strategic Vacuum* (London: Institute for the Study of Conflict, Publication No. 121, 1980), 2. The Caribbean states have had a dominant role in the negotiation of Law of the Sea Convention. Jamaica has been chosen as the location for the UN Sea Bed Authority.

8. Xavier Gorostiaga, "Towards Alternative Policies for the Region," in *Towards an Alternative for Central American and the Caribbean*, George Irvin and Xavier Gorostiaga, eds. (London: G. Allen & Irwin, 1985), 15.

9. Michael Manley, *Jamaica, Struggle in the Periphery* (London: Third World Media Ltd., 1983), 3-14.

10. Michael Kaufman, *Jamaica Under Manley, Dilemmas of Socialism and Democracy* (London: Lawrence and Hill, 1985).

11. Vaughan Lewis, "The Small State Alone, Jamaica Foreign Policy, 1977–1980," *Journal of Interamerican Studies* 25, no. 2 (May 1983).

12. S. N. MacFarlane, *Superpower Rivalry and Soviet Policy in the Caribbean Basin*, Occasional Paper No. 2 (Ottawa: Canadian Institute for International Peace and Security).

13. Jiri and Virginia Valenta, "Leninism in Grenada," *Problems of Communism* 33, July–August, 1984 (Washington, D.C.: Documentary Studies Section, International Information Administration): 1–23.

14. See articles in special issue of *Bulletin of Eastern Caribbean Affairs* 2, no. 6 (January–February 1986), and in particular "US Military Expansionism in the Eastern Caribbean," by Alma Young, 19–22.

15. Hearings, House Sub-Committee on Inter-American Affairs, June 28, 1977, 30, as quoted by Anthony Maingot in "The Difficult Path to Socialism in the English-Speaking Caribbean" in *Capitalism and the State in US–Latin American Relations*, Richard R. Fagen ed. (Palo Alto, Calif.: Stanford University Press, 1979), 293.

16. As summarized in George Belle's *USA, Imperialism and the English-Speaking Caribbean* (Mt. St. Benedict, Trinidad: Caribbean Conference of Intellectual Workers, January 1984).

17. As quoted by Kaufman, *Jamaica Under Manley*, 189.

18. "Communiqué issued by Fifth Meeting of Standing Committee of CARICOM Foreign Ministers," Saint Lucia, February 1980.

19. Maurice Bishop at mass rally in Grenada to mark first anniversary of the revolution, March 1980, in *Maurice Bishop Speaks* (New York: Pathfinder, 1983), 80–95.

20. Richard J. Barnet, *Intervention and Revolution* (Mentor, NY: World Publishing, 1971), 278–284.

21. Valenta, "Leninism in Grenada."

22. Voytek Zubek, "Soviet New Thinking and the Central American Crisis," *Journal of Interamerican Studies* 29, no. 3 (Fall 1987): 87–106.

23. Olga Alexandrova and Uwe Halbach, "The Change of Government in Nicaragua: The Regional and Global Significance," in *Aussen Politik* (October 1990), quotes a statement by Eduard A. Shevardnadze at a Foreign Ministry conference in July 1988 as follows: "The policy of national reconciliation has been born, that significance of which extends far beyond the borders of Afghanistan. A glimmer of hope has appeared in the complicated world of national conflicts, a certain model, a unique type of settlement has come about."

■ 2 ■

The Legacy of Angola

GILLIAN GUNN

Scholars currently studying the role of the superpowers in regional conflicts face a daunting task. Is the Cold War truly over? If it is, how should we interpret the lessons gleaned from studying US and Soviet involvement in Third World hot spots over the past 40 years? Are those lessons irrelevant in light of the new, more accommodating relationship between the superpowers? If the Cold War is not over, but has merely entered a temporarily less frigid stage with potential for returning to the deep freeze, will the rules of the old Cold War apply in a new one? How should we interpret these lessons if, as history suggests is inevitable, today's superpowers become tomorrow's empires in decline, and new economic and military powers lock horns in the Third World?

The questions have a nightmarish quality. Scholars find themselves in the position of scientists who know the results of past experiments but are not certain what the specimen jar actually contains today and therefore are unsure if the rules gleaned from past research are still conclusive.

This cloud of confusion could have a silver lining, however. Past regional conflicts can be reexamined with an eye to identifying characteristics and causal factors that are independent of the warmth or coolness of superpower relations at a given moment and of the ideological idiosyncrasies of Moscow and Washington at a particular historical juncture. Analytical tools could perhaps be identified that might remain useful whether we are presented with a continuing thaw or a new cooling. On the assumption that no country has ever permanently retained superpower status, consideration should be given to whether these conclusions might remain relevant if we find ourselves speaking, 40 years hence, of a Japanese/German or an ASEAN/EEC superpower rivalry.

In this chapter, only one regional conflict, that in Angola, will be examined. One is by no means a statistically valid sample; therefore the conclusions must be classified as highly tentative and compared with results of the reexaminations of other regional conflicts.

The Setting in Angola

Before proceeding with an analysis of the factors that contributed to superpower intervention in Angola, memories can be refreshed about the political scene in that territory before the move to independence began. Only a thumbnail sketch is provided here, as considerable literature exists on the subject.[1]

The main actors involved in Angolan politics on the eve of the independence process were Portugal's MFA and three Angolan nationalist groups. The MFA comprised a group of Portuguese military officers who opposed the continuation of military campaigns against nationalist movements in Portugal's overseas territories. The MFA's membership had a variety of political views, ranging from center right to far left. They disagreed on whether the African wars could best be stopped by adopting a federal system with decentralized decisionmaking or by granting independence to the rebellious colonies. MFA members were united, however, in their determination to overthrow the government of Marcello Caetano, prime minister of Portugal, and after several false starts, they mounted a successful coup on April 25, 1974. Within two months the radical wing of the MFA emerged as the dominant political force and promised to rapidly grant independence to the country's colonies.

At the time the MFA took power, three rival nationalist movements were fighting for the cause of Angolan independence and, with increasing frequency, squabbling among themselves. The MPLA, founded in 1956, was strongest in the Angolan capital, Luanda, and among the Mbundu people of the surrounding area. Its leadership was dominated by members of the small community of educated Africans and mixed-race nationalists. A few leftist whites also played important roles in the organization. The MPLA had cordial relations with Cuba, an on-and-off relationship with the Soviet Union, and expounded in pro-socialist rhetoric.

A rival nationalist group emerged in 1962. It went by a variety of names initially but became known eventually as the FNLA. With a political base among the Bakongo people of northeastern Angola, it had a reputation for antiwhite action; its public statements revealed no socialist ambitions. In 1962 the CIA provided the FNLA with arms and money, but when Portugal protested, support was reduced in 1969 to a $10,000 intelligence retainer. The FNLA sought to expand its foreign backing in 1973 by courting Beijing. Within Africa the FNLA had close relations with the government of Zaire.

In 1966 a portion of the FNLA split to form UNITA. UNITA's core support was found among the southern Ovimbundu people. Though it initially vacillated between black nationalist and socialist ideas, by 1974 it had settled into consistently anticommunist rhetoric. Modest Chinese aid to UNITA began in 1970.

Chronology of Intervention—1974 to 1976

The MFA coup and the prospect of rapid Portuguese decolonization triggered intense activity in Portugal's African colonies. In Mozambique, where nationalists were unified, preparations began for a direct transfer of power to a single movement, FRELIMO.[2] In Angola, however, the multiplicity of nationalist groups complicated the transition to independence. (The transition processes in Portugal's West African colonies, Guinea-Bissau and Cape Verde, are not discussed here because they lie outside the Southern African region.) From June 1974 to January 1976 the MPLA, FNLA, and UNITA jockeyed for position. As tensions rose, they called on their existing allies and appealed to new ones for assistance. Maintenance of law and order was complicated by Portugal's unwillingness and inability to administer forcefully the agreed-upon rules for transition that were laid out in the Alvor Accords.

The events, briefly stated, unfolded as follows:

June 1974—Chinese instructors arrive in Zaire, Angola's neighbor to the east, to help the FNLA.

July 1974—The United States is preoccupied with the Watergate scandal and the implications for Portugal of the overthrow of Caetano's government. It devotes little attention to pending Angolan independence, though the CIA does disburse a small amount of funds for the FNLA. At this time the MPLA is still on poor terms with its chief benefactor, the Soviet Union, which had suspended aid some months earlier because of unhappiness with the movement's internal factionalism.

August 1974—US intelligence reports that the Soviets are delivering $6 million in military supplies to African liberation movements through the Tanzanian port of Dar es Salaam, though it is not certain how much of this material is destined for the MPLA. During the same month, 450 tons of Chinese arms are delivered to the FNLA.

November–December 1974—Western observers suspect, but cannot confirm, that the Soviet Union is sending supplies to the MPLA through Congo Brazzaville, Angola's northern neighbor. US secretary of state Henry Kissinger becomes alarmed at the expanding role of the pro-Soviet Communist Party in Portugal and begins to pay greater attention to Angola.

January 1975—Portugal, the MPLA, the FNLA, and UNITA sign the Alvor Agreement, which declares all three nationalist movements legitimate, outlines procedures for pre-independence elections, and sets November 11, 1975, as the date for decolonization. The CIA finds evidence that the Soviet Union is shipping weapons to the MPLA through Congo Brazzaville and suggests token support for the FNLA and UNITA to give Washington leverage with the "likely future rulers of Angola." Washington authorizes a covert grant of $300,000 to the FNLA.

February 1975—The FNLA begins to spend money ostentatiously in Luanda, alerting observers that it is obtaining funds from somewhere. US diplomats in Luanda receive unconfirmed reports that Soviet arms have been sighted in the hands of MPLA members. The FNLA begins small-scale attacks on the MPLA in Luanda.

March 1975—The FNLA increases attacks on MPLA installations. Soviet arms supplies to the MPLA increase. Portuguese administrators are unable or unwilling to control the growing civil disturbances.

April 1975—FNLA/MPLA fighting escalates. At the end of the month, the North Vietnamese army captures Saigon, negating US claims that its withdrawal a year earlier had brought "peace with honor." Washington decisionmakers become increasingly anxious that the Soviet Union will interpret US failure to prevent Saigon's fall as a sign of weakness, and that Moscow will begin to test US resolve elsewhere.

May 1975—The MPLA counterattacks, forcing the FNLA from Luanda. The MPLA asks the Cubans for light arms. UNITA and FNLA leaders go to Namibia for discussions with the South Africans.

June 1975—American diplomats suspect that 230 Cuban military advisors are arriving at MPLA training camps. South African troops occupy positions just inside Angola, allegedly to protect South African–funded water projects. Fearful that the Soviet Union believes Washington's resolve has been weakened by the Vietnam War and the Watergate scandal, the United States perceives the situation in Angola as a key test. If the United States does not take a stand in Angola, Kissinger argues, the Soviet Union will feel free to intervene throughout the world. Realizing that the US Congress will not authorize full-scale intervention, the secretary of state and the CIA push for a program designed not necessarily to install the FNLA in power but to prevent an easy victory by the MPLA.

July 1975—On July 16 Castro requests that the MFA arrange Portuguese consent for the Cuban military to enter Angola. The very next day, the United States, unaware of the Castro-Lisbon communication, authorizes $32 million for arms to the FNLA and UNITA. On July

20, FNLA forces based in Zaire, with US and Chinese personnel assisting in the background, begin an offensive designed to take Luanda before November 11.

August 1975—The MPLA asks Moscow for assistance. Moscow promises to provide arms but not troops. The MPLA then asks Cuba for additional training officers, and by the end of the month, 200 more arrive. South Africa does not know of the Cuban actions but moves northward to occupy additional Angolan territory, and it agrees to set up training camps in southern Angola for UNITA and FNLA forces.

September 1975—South African instructors arrive at UNITA and FNLA training camps, and South African troops move further into Angola. Later in the month, Cuban ships arrive in Angolan and Congolese ports bearing small amounts of Cuban heavy arms and a few hundred soldiers.

October 1975—On October 14 South Africa begins a drive for Luanda from the south with FNLA, UNITA, right-wing Portuguese, and South African forces. Chinese and US-backed FNLA forces, moving in from Zaire, get within 12 miles of Luanda.

November 1975—On November 4 the MPLA asks Cuba for manpower to help defend Luanda. The Cubans agree on November 5 and inform the Soviets after the fact. On November 8 a battalion of Cuban soldiers is airlifted in Cuban planes to Luanda. The MPLA, with Cuban help, hold Luanda against the FNLA and on November 11 declare Angola independent. The South Africans, with their Angolan allies, continue to advance northward and by November 14 are 500 miles into Angola. Additional Cuban troops are dispatched in Cuban ships. Cuba asks the Soviet Union to send heavy arms and airlift Cuban troops to Angola. The USSR agrees to both requests but suspends the latter operation twice in response to US protests, suggesting Soviet ambivalence. The Soviets do not want to appear to be abandoning allies for fear other friends might see them as unreliable, but they are reluctant to confront the United States.

December 1975—Cuban troops continue to arrive. South Africans encounter MPLA/Cuban units with Soviet arms 120 miles south of Luanda, which stall their advance. The extent of US involvement in Angola is made public, and the US Senate passes legislation halting aid to Angolan guerrilla groups.

January 1976—The Soviets become less reticent about airlifting troops, and the number of Cubans in Angola rises to 12,000. The FNLA is eliminated as a fighting force, the South African/UNITA/FNLA unit withdraws to Namibia,[3] and the MPLA begins to consolidate its hold on power.

Lessons from Angola

Four lessons emerge from the superpower actions in Angola.

1. A power vacuum creates great temptation for superpower intervention.
2. Ethnic and class polarization provides a fertile environment for superpower intervention, because opposing groups are already predisposed to assume that their enemy's enemy is their friend.
3. Third parties, allied tacitly or overtly with rival superpowers, can undertake independent actions designed to protect their own rather than their superpower ally's interests. These actions can pull or push one or both of the great powers into a regional conflict quickly and deeply, regardless of superpower intentions.
4. The context of a regional conflict can greatly influence superpower reaction. If a conflict evolves when a superpower believes it is perceived as weak or distracted, it is likely to react more vigorously than it might otherwise.

The Power Vacuum

The power vacuum that existed in Angola from 1974 until 1976, a combination of weak Portuguese authority and intense competition among Angolan nationalist factions, was perhaps the most critical factor in facilitating superpower intervention. Angola resembled a championship soccer match without referees to discipline players who violate rules and without policemen to prevent fans from racing to assist their favorite club. The superpowers, metaphorically speaking, were free to rush from the grandstands to the playing field, where each sought to assist its team and trip up the other superpower.

For a variety of reasons, Portugal had long resisted independence pressures, claiming that African colonies would remain integral parts of Portugal indefinitely. Lisbon, therefore, had done virtually nothing to prepare its own people or the colonized Angolans for independence.

Among the many motives for Lisbon's intransigence, the most decisive consideration seems to have been economic. At the time Lisbon began to consolidate its colonial relations with Africa in the nineteenth and early twentieth centuries, Portugal was poorly developed and in fact was itself a semi-colony of the more industrialized countries of Europe. Portuguese raw materials and agricultural products—cork and wine, for example—were traded for finished goods produced by more developed economies on the continent.

Because of its economic underdevelopment, Portugal's relations with its colonial holdings differed markedly from those that France and Britain enjoyed with their possessions. London and Paris oversaw a trade flow in which the metropole imported raw materials from the colony, processed them, and exported finished goods to the colonial holdings as well as to other countries. Lisbon, in contrast, obtained raw materials from Africa and sold them to more developed countries in return for finished goods, largely for consumption in Portugal. The colonies acted as an extension of the Portuguese extractive-agrarian economy.

Even the manner in which Portugal acquired raw materials from Africa reflected its underdevelopment. Because it did not have the capital or industrial capacity to develop its colonies, Portugal leased huge tracts of the colonized lands to other nationals in concession agreements. In return for payments to Lisbon, the concessionaire held essentially sovereign power in a given area, developing agriculture or mining activities, and frequently maintaining independent tax collection and police forces.[4]

As the winds of change swept Africa after World War II, Portugal faced a situation quite different from that confronting France and Britain, which could contemplate decolonization without complete loss of the economic profits generated by the African territories. These countries had developed trade ties not based on the formal colonial relationship, while Portugal remained dependent on legal title to the land for the profits generated by concession agreements.

Because it could not lease what it did not own, Portugal bitterly resisted African independence movements and mounted protracted wars against nationalist guerrillas. It made no effort to train African administrators and gave no thought to transition mechanisms. The conflicts between the metropole and nationalists strained Portugal's own social fabric to the breaking point, provoking a coup that threw the African territories into a rush for independence. The Portuguese military, anxious above all to get home, had little interest in risking still more soldiers' lives to ensure that African participants adhered to agreed-upon independence procedures. The Portuguese collected their transportable belongings and fled home virtually en masse, leaving many administrative and military posts unmanned.

The power vacuum in Angola from 1974 to 1976 was maintained by the rivalry among three nationalist organizations: UNITA, the FNLA, and the MPLA. During the liberation struggle, the groups at times spent more energy fighting each other than fighting the Portuguese, and therefore they harbored long-term mutual resentments as they fought to control the transition to independence. Because of the three-way competition, Lisbon did not choose to directly hand over power, as it had done in Mozambique, but opted for a more difficult, albeit democratic, electoral procedure outlined in the Alvor Accords. This complex transition, supervised by a demoralized and distracted Portuguese administrative and military machine, was supposed to resolve the competition between bitter rivals. This situation created a highly tempting environment for superpower intervention.

Two elements could have ensured more positive transition. First, if Portugal had exerted a strong military and administrative authority, confining rival nationalist groups to separate areas and preventing arms inflows, as the British did during the Rhodesia/Zimbabwe transition,[5] foreign intervention might have been significantly curtailed. Second, consensus among the three nationalist groups would have promoted a peaceful transition. In Mozambique, the Portuguese administrative and military presence was at least as weak as it was in Angola; however, no power vacuum developed because only one "liberation movement," FRELIMO, emerged, to which power was handed without elections.

Ethnic and Class Polarization

Ethnic and class tensions that existed in Angola at the time of independence developed during the colonial period. Scant attention was paid to existing social patterns when the borders delineating the Angolan state were decided by the colonial powers. In Angola, as in much of the rest of Africa, borders divided some people from their kin and united them with others whom they either did not know or actively resented. Class divisions created by Portuguese colonial policies overlaid and further inflamed ethnic problems. Angola's population settled in three large groups, which were eventually represented in each of the nationalist factions.

MPLA. The Mbundu people in the area around Luanda formed the constituency of the MPLA. This group had a distinctly different culture from the Bakongo, associated with the FNLA, and the Ovimbundu, associated with UNITA. The leadership of the MPLA was mixed race (*mestiço*) and white; indeed its first leader, Agostinho Neto, was married to a white Portuguese woman. Many considered the inclusion of *mestiços* and whites in a nationalist movement tantamount to treason because some members of those races had mistreated Angolan blacks during the colonial period.

Equally important were the class characteristics of the MPLA, which included a high proportion of *assimilados*, literally "assimilated ones." These Africans could read and write Portuguese, earned wages from a trade, and acquired Portuguese cultural habits. *Assimilados* had special rights and privileges in Angolan society, including the treasured exemption from forced labor. Portuguese colonial policies placed many obstacles in the way of Africans seeking education, so few native Angolans acquired *assimilado* status.[6] Other blacks, termed *indigenas*, bore the full brunt of Portugal's harsh labor policies and resented the life-style of their "assimilated" countrymen.[7]

FNLA. Based among the Bakongo tribe of northeastern Angola, the precursor to the FNLA had desired only the restoration of their ancient Kongo kingdom as a secessionist, independent state and made no claim on the rest of Angola. FNLA supporters were rural people, with little or no education, and naturally resented the urban educated leadership of the MPLA.

FNLA history strongly suggested that it would find coexistence with the MPLA difficult. In a 1961 uprising in northeastern Angola, *assimilados*, *mestiços*, and whites had been targeted for execution—the whites because of their colonial position, and the *mestiços* and *assimilados* because they were considered allies of the whites.

The connection of the FNLA leadership with Zaire estranged the movement from its two rivals. The head of the FNLA, Holden Roberto, was the brother-in-law of the president of Zaire, Mobutu Sese Seko. Much of the FNLA leadership had grown up in Zaire and spoke French rather than Portuguese. The Zaire connection was not illogical, for the Bakongo people straddled the Angola-Zaire border.[8]

UNITA. Members of UNITA, like those of the FNLA, were mostly rural *indigenas* of the Ovimbundu in central and southern Angola. They, too, were suspicious of the *mestiços*, whites, and *assimilados* in the leadership of the MPLA. Once allied with the FNLA, UNITA, led by Jonas Savimbi, split from that group in 1966 because the FNLA refused to promote Ovimbundu members to positions of prominence and was reluctant to risk its guerrillas' lives conducting warfare within Angolan territory.[9]

Ethnic conflicts in Mozambique, Portugal's other large African colony, had a different impact on nationalist politics. Mozambicans divided into many small units rather than three large groups. Though antipathies among them were sometimes intense, no one group was large enough to intimidate its neighbors. Mozambique also had far fewer *assimilados* than Angola, in part because it was a poorer colony and acquiring funds for education was more difficult. Class and ethnic resentments were clearly present but were less acute than in Angola. As a result, Mozambique developed a single nationalist movement that itself contained ethnic and class divisions rather than a multiplicity of movements.[10]

Class and ethnic tensions in Angola contributed to superpower intervention in two ways. First, they created groups with natural antipathies who tended to view their enemy's enemy as their friend, predisposing the nationalist movements to seek out opposing external allies. Second, viewed externally, the three-way competition made Angola a perfect proxy battlefield for Moscow and Washington, where they could compete without expending their own human resources.

Actions of Third Parties

On several occasions between June 1974 and January 1976, third parties undertook independent maneuvers that pushed or pulled the great powers into the Angolan conflict more quickly and deeply than the superpowers had perhaps intended. Cuban, Chinese, Zairean, and South African actions all influenced decisionmaking in Moscow and Washington.

Cuba. Cuba came to the aid of the MPLA for a variety of reasons. Cuban officials had long-standing personal ties with the MPLA leadership. The Cuban government, aware that many of its citizens trace their roots to Africa, could through intervention demonstrate its commitment to an African cause. Castro was aware that fighting apartheid would vastly enhance his country's prestige in the Third World, a goal he cherished. Finally, aiding a prosocialist movement was in line with Cuba's strategy of fomenting "many Vietnams," thereby dissipating the energy of the "imperialists."

There is now consensus among analysts of the Angolan war that the Cubans decided to intervene in that country without first consulting their allies in Moscow. Fidel Castro was largely disbelieved when he told Barbara Walters in a 1977 interview, "You should not think that the Soviets were capable of asking Cuba to send a single man to Angola. . . . That is totally alien to Soviet relations with Cuba and to Soviet behavior. A decision of that nature could exclusively be taken by our party and our government on our own initiative at the request of the Angolan government. . . . The Soviets absolutely did not ask us."[11]

Recent revelations by Soviet decisionmakers, now able to speak more freely about such matters, eliminate lingering doubts. Castro's claim has been supported by Soviet defector Arkady Shevchenko, who wrote in his memoirs that Deputy Foreign Minister Vasily Kuznetsov laughed when Shevchenko asked in 1976, "How did we persuade the Cubans to provide their contingent?" Shevchenko explained that "after acknowledging that Castro might be playing his own game in sending about 20,000 troops to Angola, Kuznetsov told me that the idea for the large-scale military operation originated in Havana, not Moscow. It was startling information. As I later discovered, it was also a virtual secret in the Soviet capital."[12] This version of events has now been further confirmed by Soviet academics.

By sending forces without first consulting Moscow, Cuba placed the

Soviet leadership in a difficult position. Moscow could either refuse to provide arms and logistical support, and thereby appear weak and ineffectual, or agree, and strain relations with the United States. Left to their own initiative, the Soviets would probably have been far more circumspect in Angola; when the issue was forced by the Cubans, they chose intervention over concession.[13]

China. During the early stages of the conflict, China moved faster than either Washington or Moscow to aid its friends. China's motives were straightforward: it was competing with the USSR for influence throughout the Third World, and it perceived Angola as an ideal opportunity to flex its muscles.

Chinese maneuvers irritated the Soviet Union, and indeed, some observers have argued that Moscow's decision to endorse and assist the Cuban involvement was motivated more by the desire to compete with Beijing than by Cold War competition with the United States.

Zaire. Angola's neighbor to the east, Zaire, influenced superpower behavior in two ways. It pressured Washington, its long-time ally, to aid the FNLA and then provided critical logistical support without which the US intervention could not have occurred.

President Mobutu was motivated to intrude in Angola both by family concerns—the FNLA leader was his brother-in-law—and by strategic considerations. With only a sliver of territory linking it to the sea, Zaire traditionally sent its mineral wealth to foreign markets through Angola's Benguela rail line. In addition, the mineral-rich Zairean province of Shaba bordered Angola, and Mobutu constantly feared Angolan actors would assist secessionist Shaba rebels. Helping a friendly leader take power in Luanda was therefore clearly advantageous to Mobutu.

South Africa. Support by South Africa for UNITA/FNLA was a means of assuring that "the most friendly power possible" would be installed in Angola. South Africa feared that a hostile government would aid both the ANC's anti-apartheid efforts and the struggle of Namibian guerrillas to force South African troops out of their homeland.

South Africa became involved in Angola in a haphazard manner. In the words of a South African military official present when the decision was made,

> We had a request from these movements [the MPLA's rivals] for aid, and we decided to expend a relatively small sum initially. . . . Our intuitive feeling was that we should have the most friendly power possible on that border. . . . We [subsequently] found that our new allies were totally disorganized. They could not utilize cash, so we provided arms. They could not use the arms, so we sent in officers to train them to use the arms.

> The training process was too slow, so we handled the weapons ourselves. We got pulled in gradually, needing to commit ourselves more if the past commitment was not to be wasted.[14]

While South African moves may not have been officially coordinated with Washington, Pretoria made the prospect of a UNITA/FNLA victory appear more plausible and thus US aid to those movements a better gamble. If neither Pretoria nor Kinshasa had stepped into Angola, the scale of Washington's involvement probably would have been far lower. There would have been no troops ready to fight beside Washington's Angolan allies, absorbing the inevitable casualties. Channeling US aid to the combatants would have been far more difficult, if not impossible.

South Africa's actions strengthened Cuban resolve, for the Cuban leadership was delighted to be able to portray itself as defending black Africans against white racists. As detailed previously, Cuban involvement helped pull in the Soviet Union, which further provoked Washington, and a self-reinforcing cycle of intervention was established.

The Mozambican Case. Comparison with Mozambique is instructive. FRELIMO had cordial relations with both the Soviet Union and China. Thus Sino-Soviet tensions produced no motivation to intervene. FRELIMO was on friendly terms with the Cubans, but the leadership had not developed the close personal ties that emerged between MPLA and Cuban leaders. Perhaps most important, South Africa decided not to intervene in Mozambique, even though FRELIMO's socialist and antiapartheid rhetoric made it an unpalatable neighbor. Mozambique's economy was tightly integrated with that of South Africa, so Pretoria was confident it could ensure FRELIMO compliance with its concerns through economic rather than military pressures. Unlike the MPLA, FRELIMO made some effort to reassure South Africa that it would not threaten Pretoria's interests once it took power, thus making the prospect of that government less threatening.[15]

The only government that did seek to intervene in Mozambique was its neighbor Rhodesia. Rhodesia neither endangered the independence process enough to encourage FRELIMO's socialist allies to intervene nor was it on sufficiently good terms with the West to entice assistance.

The Context of the Superpower Challenge

If a primary reason the Soviet Union became involved in Angola was agitation by its Cuban ally, a main reason the United States became involved in Angola was the belief by key US officials, specifically

Secretary of State Henry Kissinger and like-minded analysts in the CIA, that the Soviet Union was probing for US weaknesses in the aftermath of the Vietnam War and Watergate. Kissinger remarked in his memoirs: "Whether it was Watergate that caused Moscow to put East-West negotiations into low gear in the spring of 1974, whether it was the general trend of our domestic debate; or whether both of those were used as a cover for decisions Moscow made for its own reasons cannot be established. . . . The fact is that during April 1974 Soviet conduct changed. . . . Negotiations stalemated."[16]

When Nixon resigned in August 1974, Kissinger became even more concerned that the Soviets might seek to take advantage of US domestic problems to expand their international influence. The fall of Saigon in April 1975 heightened Washington's suspicion that Moscow would see it as weak and vacillating. Kissinger concluded, therefore, that the United States had to "resist marginal accretions of Soviet power even when the issues seem ambiguous."[17] Angola just happened to be the next perceived "marginal accretion."

Of course, with historical hindsight we can now see that the Soviet Union had not carefully decided to test Washington's will in Angola. Rather, the Cubans intervened for their own reasons and put Moscow in the position of losing face or supporting the intervention. The Soviets could not alert the United States to this reality, keeping the fact that the tail had wagged the dog a closely held secret in Moscow for fear of losing credibility itself.

If history were a computer program and one could adjust certain variables and replay the time period, it would be interesting to see what Washington's reaction would have been if events in Angola had not been immediately preceded by developments that the United States feared suggested a lack of will. If the United States were not stung by the defeat of its ally in Vietnam and internally wracked by the Watergate controversy, would it have been so quick to conclude that the Soviets were seeking to test its resolve in Angola? Would it have assumed that a failure to stand up to the challenge would only provoke greater Soviet adventures in the future? Perhaps not.

Conclusion

What, if anything, does the story of the superpowers' 1974–1976 intervention in Angola tell us about possible developments in the post–Cold War era? Can any causal factors be identified that might be independent of the warmth or coolness of superpower relations at a given moment or the ideological idiosyncrasies of Moscow and Washington at a specific historical juncture? And can any lessons be derived that might be relevant should we find ourselves dealing with an entirely different set of superpowers in the future?

The preceding discussion suggests that four lessons can be tentatively articulated and then compared with lessons arising from an examination of other case studies.

First, those individuals, governments, and multilateral institutions wishing to avoid intervention in regional conflicts by today's or tomorrow's superpowers would be well advised to ensure that political and economic transitions do not entail a power vacuum. It is essential that some central authority patrol the metaphorical playing field to ensure that individual competitors play by the rules and that outside powers remain outside. Given the increased activities and visibility of the United Nations, it should perhaps be considered the logical force to fill any empty space. Future transition processes in such areas as South Africa, Iraq, the Soviet Union, and Eastern Europe all provide the potential for power vacuums, so thought should perhaps be given to how they might be responsibly occupied.

Second, ethnic and class polarization creates an environment highly conducive to superpower intervention. Political actors hoping to prevent such internationalization of regional conflicts should therefore seek to establish mechanisms by which ethnic and class tensions can be defused in their early stages, before they become explosive. While perhaps a utopian wish, diminution of ethnic and class tensions should, nonetheless, remain a priority for all would-be peacemakers.

Third, the importance of third-party actions can hardly be overstated. Whether in the future we witness a reemergence of the Cold War, or competition between two or more new superpowers, careful attention must be paid to the interests and potential for mischief of local actors, for they are capable of swiftly pulling larger countries into conflicts.

Fourth, the prevailing global context as well as superpowers' domestic climate greatly influences how actions in a distant regional conflict are perceived. If a superpower believes recent events elsewhere make it appear weak, it is likely to react vigorously to any perceived threat, no matter how small or irrelevant to its own immediate security interests. Governments and analysts should therefore bear in mind how vulnerable a potential adversary believes it appears, and how the actions of a rival power might be interpreted in that context if they are not to be surprised by the reaction.

Might these recommendations remain valid should relations between Washington and Moscow continue to improve? Most likely, yes. If Moscow and Washington are willing to cooperate, they can achieve some of these four goals, reducing the chance that either their own or other countries' military forces will be tempted to intervene in future regional strife.

And what if we eventually witness the emergence of a multipolar world, in which a host of powers compete for influence? Intervention by major and middle powers would presumably be less threatening to world peace, because the potential for nuclear confrontation would be reduced. But conflict can still be highly destructive, as the actions of Iraq recently demonstrated.

In sum, the four prescriptions—avoid power vacuums and ethnic/class tensions, monitor self-interested maneuvering by smaller powers, and be cognizant of how recent events may heighten a rival's sensitivity to perceived challenge—would all appear to have some validity regardless of what the future holds. The remaining task is to examine other instances of superpower intervention in regional conflicts and see if they confirm, expand, or contradict the Angola findings.

Notes

1. For more information see John A. Marcum, *The Angolan Revolution: Exile Politics and Guerilla Warfare (1962–1976)* (Cambridge, Mass.: MIT Press, 1978); Lawrence Henderson, *Angola: Five Centuries of Conflict* (Ithaca and London: Cornell University Press, 1979); Keith Somerville, *Angola: Politics, Economics and Society* (Boulder, Colo.: Lynne Rienner, 1986).

2. Barry Munslow, *Mozambique: The Revolution and Its Origins* (London: Longman Group, 1983), 79–149.

3. Adapted from Gillian Gunn, "Cuba and Angola," in George Fauriol and Eva Loser, *Cuba: The International Dimension* (New Brunswick, N. J.: Transaction, 1990), 193–195.

4. David and Marina Ottaway, *Afrocommunism* (New York: Holmes and Meier, 1981), 99–127; and Somerville, *Angola: Politics, Economics and Society*, 1–71 and 152–154.

5. Ken Flower, *Serving Secretly* (London: John Murray, 1987), 251–271.

6. Marcum, *The Angolan Revolution*, 48.

7. Somerville, *Angola: Politics, Economics and Society*, 71–73; and Marcum, *The Angolan Revolution*, 46–57.

8. Ibid.

9. Fred Bridgeland, *Jonas Savimbi: A Key to Africa* (New York: Paragon House Publishers, 1987), 64–77.

10. Munslow, *Mozambique*, 53–114; Allen and Barbara Isaacman, *Mozambique: From Colonialism to Revolution* (Harare, Zimbabwe: Zimbabwe Publishing House, 1983), 4.

11. Tad Szulc, *Fidel: A Critical Portrait* (New York: William Morrow and Company, 1986), 639.

12. Ibid.

13. Gunn, "Cuba and Angola," 158–163.

14. Author's interview in Pretoria, in 1985, with a retired South African Defense Force officer, who wishes to remain anonymous.

15. Gillian Gunn, "Learning from Adversity: The Mozambican Experience," in Richard Bloomfield, *Regional Conflict and U.S. Policy* (Algonac, Mich.: Reference Publications, 1988), 148–149.

16. Henry Kissinger, *Years of Upheavel* (Boston: Little, Brown, and Company, 1982), 1163.

17. Ibid., 301.

■ Part 2 ■
Regional Hegemons and Regional Conflicts

■ 3 ■

Pipsqueak Power: The Centrality and Anomaly of Cuba

JORGE I. DOMINGUEZ

The future of US-USSR relations, the US government indicated as the Cold War in central Europe came to an end in 1989–1990, rests in part on the future conduct of the Soviet Union toward Cuba. As President Fidel Castro stated after the Malta Summit between Presidents George Bush and Mikhail Gorbachev, the United States "tries to blackmail the USSR into ending its economic and military assistance to Nicaragua [then still governed by the Sandinistas] and Cuba."[1] A version of that sentence could have been written in the summer of 1960, in the spring of 1961, in the fall of 1962, in the second half of 1970, or in the second half of 1979.

Though the reasons vary and have changed over time, Cuba has mattered a great deal for both the United States and the Soviet Union. From 1959 to 1961, the United States and Cuba focused on the breakdown of centuries of close entanglement—a relationship that many in the United States and some in Cuba had considered benign and that many in Cuba and some in the United States had considered exploitative. In those years, the Soviet Union welcomed a new and unexpected faraway friend—that rarest of cases, not "surly" Poles or "ungrateful" Chinese, but Cubans who had apparently *chosen* to throw their lot with the Soviet Union. In 1962, of course, the triangular entanglement brought the world to the edge of nuclear war; the stakes had changed much from the romance, tragedy, and farce of the preceding three years.

In the years that followed, however, Cuba ordinarily entered the direct, bilateral US-USSR relationship mainly by exception (especially in 1978–1979): the need to manage the debris of the November 1962 crisis as well as the need to manage the politics of major Cuban military deployments to Angola and to Ethiopia in the mid- and late 1970s. At these times Cuba was perhaps only in principal explicitly on the agenda of US-USSR relations. However, Cuba figured at least as "background noise" in a great many exchanges between the US and Soviet governments in other circumstances, including those bearing on Central America.

The effective "founding moment" of these triangular relations occurred

57

during the fall of 1962. To be specific, the October 1962 crisis settlement proved to be reasonably straightforward: Soviet missiles and nuclear warheads were removed from Cuba. The November 1962 crisis, however, focused on the aspects of the US-USSR-Cuban relationship that could not skip this triad's third member in order to reach a successful settlement: what would or would not happen to military aircraft in the hands of the Cuban armed forces, the presence of Soviet military personnel in Cuba, the inspection of military activities in and around Cuba, and, by US declaration but *not* by negotiation, the Cuban government's own international activities in regional conflicts.[2]

In 1990 the Soviet Union turned over to Cuba MiG-29 aircraft (the Cuban Air Force's first modernization since 1978). Thousands of Soviet military personnel remain in Cuba as do Soviet electronic intelligence facilities, while Soviet BEAR aircraft continue to fly along the Atlantic coast of the United States to gather intelligence, using Cuba as a base for these operations.[3] Cuba is just as defiant about its assertions of sovereignty. Only in relation to Cuba's participation in regional conflicts elsewhere has there been an appreciable decline in US concern over Cuba.

By the beginning of 1990, Cuban troops had left Ethiopia, where they had arrived in large numbers in 1977, leaving behind several hundred Soviet military specialists.[4] By spring 1990, all Cuban military and most civilian personnel had left Nicaragua, although Cuban medical personnel continued to work there.[5] By mid-1990 Cuba's troop withdrawal from Angola was only a month behind schedule; about 15,000 Cuban troops remained in Angola along with civilian and military advisors.[6] The repatriation of these troops was completed in May 1991. Throughout 1990 thousands of Cuban civilians returned home from Eastern Europe. Namibia became independent, in large measure because Cuba bloodied the South African armed forces, eliminating the need for Cuban support for the SWAPO guerrillas who had fought for Namibia's independence. The ANC came to negotiate with South Africa's government so that Cuban military support for the ANC may end as well.

Cuba, alas, has become an island again. From the mid-1970s to the end of the 1980s its people lived all over the world. In the early 1990s Cubans returned to Cuba, and, for the first time since the early 1960s, the number of high Cuban government officials who defect has been rising as well. The Cuban leadership's insularity is especially noteworthy: Fidel Castro and his associates, long accustomed to thinking of themselves as part of the vanguard of history, have come to witness world-historical trends elsewhere that they vow to oppose and resist at home.

Thus, for example, in December 1989 on Armed Forces Day, the chief of Cuba's navy, Rear Admiral Pedro Pérez Betancourt, felt compelled to speak about the importance of the concept of loyalty of Cuba's military to the political regime, in opposition to those Cubans who are "chicken-hearted and mediocre people . . . [who] have no faith in their land and its accomplishments." And in an early 1991 discussion about preparations for the forthcoming fourth Communist Party Congress, party secretary José Ramón Machado chided party officials who, in effect, were insufficiently intolerant because they responded with "passivity in the face of certain inaccurate and hypercritical views incompatible with our principles."[7]

Thus in the early 1990s the "Cuban question" in international affairs was no longer Cuba's role in regional conflicts elsewhere, with the important exception of Cuba's continuing support for the insurrection in El Salvador and, to a lesser degree, in Guatemala. The question returned to its origins in 1959–1962: What ought to be the nature of Cuba's domestic political regime, and what ought to be the nature of the Cuban-Soviet relationship? These are not, of course, trivial issues; they consumed time, energy, and resources in 1959–1962 and could do so again.

A consideration of Cuba's role in regional conflicts elsewhere, therefore, focuses principally on a period of history that seems to be over for the most part—a period marked by the deployment of Cuban armies overseas and the commitment of Cuban support to various kinds of armed challenges to established governments the world over. (Cuban leaders have not formally renounced their "right" to assist governments and revolutionary movements elsewhere, and it should be assumed that they will do so if circumstances are appropriate.) To examine the history of Cuba's role in those conflicts, we will focus on Cuba's own approach to international affairs in response to the central issue of its foreign policy: how to deal with, and how to deter, the United States.

The US Approach to Cuba's Role in World Affairs

The US approach to Cuba's role in world affairs has been generally clear and consistent: Cuba does not exist as an autonomous actor. This approach has had substantive and procedural implications.

Since at least late 1959 the US government has looked at Cuba and "seen red." It has seen the regime evolve into a hard-line bureaucratic socialist state allied with Moscow and engaged, as a "Soviet surrogate," in mischief-making in much of the Third World. Of course, the US government has also "seen red" in the sense of anger, fury, and obsession that this "tin horn dictator," this country that may compete for the title of the world's least efficient economy, this source of illegal migration to the United States, this "cesspool" in the "US Mediterranean" could play the role that it has in international affairs.

By "seeing red," most US governments have ordinarily preferred not to deal with the various versions of the Cuban question. When forced to because of heightened US-Soviet military confrontation over Cuba, they have done so by addressing Moscow, not Havana. This pattern was most clearly evident during the 1962 missile crisis.[8] It was a part of

Washington's response to the dispatch of Cuban troops to Angola and to Ethiopia in the mid- and late 1970s and in the Reagan administration's reaction to the revolution in El Salvador. The pattern has rested on the profound disbelief of the US government that Cuba could have had a sufficient margin of foreign policy autonomy to act so boldly: the Soviets somehow were the real culprits.[9]

This pattern became evident again at the US-Soviet summit at Malta in late 1989. At the meeting, the United States invited the Soviet Union, in effect, to join in burying the Monroe Doctrine—that long-standing US policy posture that seeks to keep extracontinental powers from involvement in the Americas and that had led the US government in the 1980s to avoid negotiating with the USSR over Central America. (Soviets were told about US wishes, not engaged in negotiations over them.[10]) By late 1989 Washington wanted Moscow very much involved in the international and internal affairs of Central America and the Caribbean in order to put pressure on the Sandinistas in Nicaragua, on the various guerrilla movements in El Salvador and Guatemala, and especially on Cuba, all in part as a means not to engage the Cuban government in negotiations.[11] To be sure, the United States did not necessarily recognize that the USSR had legitimate interests in the Americas; the Soviets were invited only to join the United States in accomplishing US interests.[12]

As a corollary, Washington was predisposed to ignore Cuba's particularities. At various times, the United States has looked at Cuba and "seen Khrushchev" and "seen Brezhnev." The United States has rarely focused on prospects for domestic change in Cuba by means of depriving the Cuban leadership of the threat of a real enemy. Fortress Cuba has endured thanks in part to the existence of US policy.

Cuba's Approach to Its International Role

Fidel Castro's foreign policy strategy has addressed the "Cuban anomaly" by insisting on "Cuba's centrality." Cuba is an anomaly because it has been such an unlikely candidate for a significant international role. A country that was best known for catchy music, first-rate dancing, and picaresque personal conduct became the Sparta of the late twentieth century as hundreds of thousands of troops served overseas. From 1975 to 1991 it sustained that deployment, as a percentage of its population, at a higher rate than the United States did in Vietnam in the peak year of that war.

Cuba is also an anomaly because it is a small country of not quite 11 million people whose main export, sugar, is unhealthy if consumed in excess and by the early 1980s was in nearly perpetual worldwide over-supply. Cuba's economy has performed so badly that it has depended on massive Soviet assistance, especially since 1975, to remain afloat. Indeed, whenever Soviet assistance faltered, as in the late 1960s or the late 1980s and early 1990s, economic conditions in Cuba became grim. The reality of Cuba's economic dependence on the USSR had made it much more difficult for anyone to envisage that Cuba could act on its own in any way.

In 1989 some Soviet government spokesmen invoked "the Sinatra doctrine" as a way to explain Soviet policy toward the dramatic changes in Eastern Europe: everyone could say, "I did it my way." Fidel Castro, of course, is Frank Sinatra's true temperamental heir, for he has sought to do things his way for most of his life. To address Cuba's objective dependence, Castro took bold action to convince the Soviets that he had been a closet communist and that they had no better ally, and that the USSR must be ready to fight for the defense of Cuba and fund his development projects.[13]

It was, in part, to strengthen his alliance with the Soviet Union that Castro sent his troops across the Atlantic to fight in African wars.[14] Cuban leaders took the initiative—now a point commonly agreed upon by most scholars and many policymakers[15]—to send troops to Angola in 1975 to demonstrate to the Soviet government, and to the world, that bold action and military prowess could change the structure of international relations in Southern Africa. Cuban troops went to Ethiopia in 1977 in part for the best of strategic reasons: to shed their blood next to Soviet officers to establish the depth of Cuban commitment to the Soviet-Cuban alliance. In 1990–1991 those actions helped explain why Soviet military officers had become the best defenders of Cuban interests inside the Soviet Union. The triumphalism of Soviet foreign policy in the late 1970s—premature, at best—was made possible partly by the success of Cuban arms on African battlefields.

By the early 1980s, Cuban troops had accomplished their objective in Angola and in Ethiopia, swiftly and decisively, while the United States had been defeated in Vietnam and Soviet troops were bogged down in Afghanistan. In 1979, as the Afghan regime faltered, Cuban-aligned revolutionaries rose confidently to power in Grenada and Nicaragua. In the 1970s and 1980s the essence of Cuba's "pipsqueak power" had been to demonstrate its political-military value to the Soviet Union.

In retrospect it is also clear that President Fidel Castro addressed as well the first part of the Cuban anomaly: How could Gomorrah be turned into Sparta? He believed that Cubans made better heroes than workers, that Cubans could improvise better (at dancing, love, or war) than they could ploddingly plan, and that Cubans were such fun people that they could get along anywhere. Let the Soviets give the guns or the equipment and then step aside so the Cubans could manage the interpersonal relations with Africans, Grenadans, or Nicaraguans. That Castro's instincts proved right explains much about Cuban success in the world in the 1970s. That his instincts proved right also explains much about the crises that afflict Cubans at home in the 1990s. It is much harder to be a hero on Monday morning and every day at the workplace.

The strategy of Cuban leaders has had several more specific dimensions that add to pipsqueak power. It is unclear, perhaps doubtful, whether Cuban leaders had thought of this strategy in advance. It is much clearer, however, that they discovered three general elements in the course of responding to specific foreign policy problems in the conduct of their relations with the United States and the Soviet Union.

1. *Learn from NATO*. An early concept in the formulation of the strategy of the NATO was the importance and utility of the "trip wire." Were the Soviets to invade Europe, they would fight against and kill US soldiers, making it necessary for the United States to declare war on the USSR to defend Western European allies.

The Cuban government has welcomed Soviet personnel in Cuba since the early 1960s. In the fall of 1990, for example, Cuban leaders claimed that, at the time of the 1962 missile crisis, they understood that a US "invasion of Cuba, on whose soil there were 43,000 Soviet soldiers, all of whom were at risk, would have meant war against the Soviet Union."[16] In 1962 one important dimension of Cuba's security against a US attack was the Cuban leaders' view that Soviet troops in Cuba were ready to die defending Cuba against the United States. As Division General Sergio del Valle, Chief of the General Staff of Cuba's armed forces in 1962, has stated, "at that time the Soviets were ready to fulfill their missions alongside with us . . . to die there with us." The identification of many of those Soviet soldiers with the Cuba they were sent to defend was such, according to General del Valle, that eventually "many cried . . . because they did not understand the dismantling of the missiles."[17] Certainly that seems to have been the view of Soviet Lieutenant General G. A. Voronkov: "I felt the situation could not be allowed to continue. The Americans felt unchallenged. On the twenty-seventh [October 1962] I was told a U-2 spy plane was crossing the island and flying nearby . . . I gave the order to fire."[18] The US U-2 was shot down and its pilot died, the only combat death from the crisis.

Consistent with the "trip wire" concept was the "Soviet brigade," a legacy of the Soviet ground troop deployment from 1962 that Washington rediscovered in 1979. But the most recent version has been Cuba's welcoming in 1990–1991 of thousands of the "Chernobyl children" for recreation and treatment.[19] Cuba demonstrates thereby the skill of its public health system, the charm of its tourist facilities, and its friendship for the peoples of the Soviet Union, also signaled by sending blood donations to the victims of the earthquake in Armenia. In these ways, Castro adds to the number of Soviet citizens on Cuban soil whom the United States would encounter in a confrontation.

More generally, Cuba worked hard to involve the Soviet Union, and specifically Soviet personnel, in its most sensitive international operations. Though in late 1975 Cuban troops went to Angola unescorted by the Soviets, Cuba quickly endeavored to engage the Soviet Union in support for the MPLA government in Luanda. In Ethiopia, Cuban troop deployment was closely coordinated with the Soviet Union.[20] Especially noteworthy are the cases of Nicaragua and Grenada, where Cuba worked very hard to engage a Soviet government that had been initially reluctant to provide support. The documents captured by US armed forces in Grenada show that the Cubans even coached the Grenadans confidentially on how to deal with the Soviets.[21]

The stronger the alliance with the Soviets, the greater Cuba's clout and the less likely a US attack. Therefore, one partial explanation for Soviet involvement in regional conflicts in Africa, the Caribbean, and Central America was Cuba's sustained effort to involve Moscow as an ally in these regional issues.

2. *Learn the lessons of the missile crisis.* The Soviets could make a deal with the US government behind Cuba's back. Therefore, the Cuban government had to prepare for the worst by building its own military capacity to withstand a direct US attack as well as to fight on its own overseas in the event that the Soviets would not come to Cuba's defense.

This situation explains the Cuban government's continuing development of an impressive military apparatus committed to self-reliance. Cuba's doctrine was first put succinctly, in public, in 1967, in a comprehensive statement by Armed Forces Minister Raúl Castro: "Should the national security, which is our very existence in this case, depend exclusively on foreign support? We think not. Why not? Because that would ill accustom our people to depend on others for the resolution of our problems. Do we have that support? Yes, we do. Is it good? It is. Should we depend on it exclusively? No."[22]

Cuba's self-reliant military doctrine was formalized in late 1984 when the Tenth Plenum of the Cuban Communist Party's Central Committee explicitly proclaimed Cuba's decision to adopt a "strategy of resisting by means of our own forces," noting that the principal purpose of Soviet military assistance was to empower the Cuban military itself to defend Cuba.[23] It was put more poignantly by President Fidel Castro on July 26, 1988, a year prior to the collapse of communist regimes in Eastern Europe: "Were imperialism to attack us, who is there to defend the island? No one will come from abroad to defend our island; we defend the island ourselves."[24]

This self-reliant military posture explains as well Cuba's decisions in 1975 and again in 1987 to deploy its forces to Angola on Cuba's own airplanes and ships without requesting Soviet transportation, at least during the crucial early moments.[25] This posture explains the development of Cuban logistical and military capability to act alone and swiftly anywhere in the Caribbean Basin. From Cuba's perspective even in the best of times, the Soviets were not always reliable.

Thus over the years Cuba has also advised its closest allies in the Third World to plan for self-sufficiency. Though perhaps the Angolans, the Grenadans, and the Nicaraguans would have discovered the importance of this concept on their own, the Cubans reinforced the view that it was good to have Soviet support but that one had to be prepared for the eventuality that it might not be forthcoming. For these same reasons, Cuba's economy has emphasized a strategy of import substitution to achieve the self-sufficiency needed for a war economy.

3. *Learn from US foreign policy.* US influence in the world, the Cuban leaders had learned from their own experiences, stemmed from the overflow of domestic life in the United States at least as much as it did from specific government policies. The innovations of technology, the vibrancy of the consumer economy, and the images of Hollywood seemed fundamental. Moreover, the United States did not rely on its actions alone, or even on its actions in coordination with a small number of allies. After 1945 the United States founded a new international economic order, including several key institutions, that engaged its government, its firms, and its citizens in a web of influential relationships.

Cuba was among the first Latin American countries to join the Non-Aligned Movement. Havana contributed to the transformation of what the Soviets in the early 1950s had called the US "automatic majority" in the United Nations General Assembly into what the United States in the early 1970s came to call the Soviet and radical Third World's "automatic majority" in that same body. If Cuba could not come close to matching the impact of the United States in the economic organization of the world, it could at least become a leader in challenging the structure of a world economy organized along market principles. This dimension of Cuban policy seemed effective in the 1970s; in the 1980s Cuba invoked it, with less success, on the issue of the debt of Third World countries and especially Latin American countries.

As has been the case with the United States, much of Cuba's influence abroad—and an explanation of what was, for a long time, its relatively good image—has rested on the spread overseas of aspects of Cuban society that have worked well at home and abroad: education, public health, and sports. Cuba's activities in international cooperation in these civilian sectors have flourished. Cuban teachers, coaches, doctors, and nurses, supplemented by construction workers, have constituted the bulk of Cuban civilian personnel in African and Latin American countries that have had good relations with Cuba.[26]

For similar reasons, beginning in 1959, the Cuban government actively promoted high culture, reaching out to artists and writers the world over to relish in the vibrancy of a cultural renaissance in Cuba and, in exchange, to defend the Cuban experiment from hostile attacks. Casa de las Américas—the Cuban regime's premier cultural institution for international affairs—evolved into an influential place taken seriously by people in arts and letters. Though the Nicaraguans surely learned these lessons by themselves, the Cuban leaders urged Sandinista leaders to avoid the intellectual repression that had been typical in the Soviet Union and, instead, to seek to wed the vanguard to the avant-garde.

In due course, policies begun in Latin America were extended, though on a more modest scale, to Cuban relations with Lusophone Africa. The partial intelligibility between the Spanish and Portuguese languages facilitated many of these contacts. Responding to the African context, moreover, the Cuban regime rediscovered the Africanness of its own people as one justification for its military activities (e.g., the claim was the need to repay historical debts to Africa for the foundation of Cuba's nationality). In turn, by the late 1970s this awareness led the Cuban regime to be more relaxed in its toleration of Afro-Cuban religions and to welcome such expressions as one more bond between African countries and Cuba.

In this way, Havana created its power to act in world affairs, combining the hard power of its armed forces with the soft power of its ability to lead, based in part on some attractive features of its people and society.[27] Cuba was not a sleepy giant waiting for a great awakening; it was not a country rich in natural resources or well-located geographically to launch military assaults on other places. In its impressive international accomplishments of the 1970s and 1980s, Cuba stands, instead, as an example of how people make their own history, even if Cuba's political and economic difficulties in the early 1990s also illustrate that the people do not make it just as they please.

Cuba's Strategy of Deterrence and Military Commitment

There are additional features of the behavior of Cuban leaders, and especially of Fidel Castro, aimed at deterring a US attack on Cuba. Above all, the Cuban government has sought to leave no doubt that the United States would suffer many casualties were war to break out with Cuba. It is unlikely that Cuban leaders had deduced this strategy in advance; it is likely, however, that they discovered it in the course of a day's work.

"The sophisticated negotiator," Thomas Schelling wrote over three decades ago, "may find it difficult to seem as obstinate as a truly obstinate man."[28] Schelling goes on to discuss the bargaining need to make self-binding commitments in order to convince the party whose behavior one seeks to influence of one's willingness to act and of one's inability or irrevocable unwillingness to change one's behavior in response to changes in the other's behavior.[29] Fidel Castro, though a highly "sophisticated negotiator," has cultivated the image of obstinacy to improve his international leverage. Asked in early 1990 by Mexican journalist Martha Anaya whether he was obstinate, Castro replied, "What is obstinacy? Were the child heroes of Chapultepec obstinate because they did not surrender the Mexican flag and chose to hurl themselves from the castle [defending Mexico City in 1847 against invading US forces]? . . . Then God bless the obstinate of the world, those who are capable of defending their country and their flag." One purpose of this portrayal of obstinacy is to lend credibility to his oft-repeated view that "those who think they can survive by making concessions to the enemy are lost; only the brave survive, those who resist, those who struggle."[30]

One's bargaining leverage can also be enhanced by cultivating a certain image of irrationality. In the face of a mugger who behaves as a madman, we are more likely to give up our wallets. So, too, the United States may be deterred from attacking Cuba by the concern that in his irrationality, Castro might absorb higher casualties than those a rational leader could sustain. Castro would be unlikely to surrender before those huge casualties were incurred, and a conflict of greater duration means more casualties for the United States. A hint of madness, therefore, may serve the rational purpose of deterrence. Castro told an interviewer: "Don Quixote's madness and the madness of revolutionaries are similar to the spirit of the knight-errant, of righting wrongs everywhere, of fighting against giants."[31]

In late 1990, the Cuban government declassified parts of the October 1962 Castro-Khrushchev correspondence to communicate and update Castro's commitments, obstinacy, and hints of madness (as well as to respond to statements that made him appear irrational). Included was a letter in which Castro noted that he expected the United States to attack Cuba militarily within 72 hours, that he thought the attack might be an air strike or a full invasion, and that he considered a full invasion less likely. Should the less likely invasion occur, conscious that the tens of thousands of Soviet troops in Cuba would likely fight alongside the Cubans and thus place the United States and the Soviet Union at war, Castro recommended that the USSR launch a first-strike against the United States with nuclear weapons. He also insisted that his views and positions on these fundamental matters had not changed from 1962 to 1990.[32] Though he left ambiguous what this continuity of views might imply, it is a fair inference that he remains prepared to launch war on US territory and to use all defensive means available to Cuban leaders should the United States attack Cuba.

Mere words, of course, are not enough. At the critical junctures from late 1959 and continuing into the 1960s, Fidel Castro's personal public demeanor—the extraordinary length of his speeches, the fury of his words, the flashes of anger in his eyes, the aggressive body language on the podium—also raised doubts about his rationality and about the wisdom of challenging him. In fact, this personal political style was, at the time, well within the range typical for politicians in Cuba and in some other

Latin American countries. The difference is that Castro proved more effective in employing the style and in consolidating power.

Castro's public behavior had two advantages for Cuba's policy of deterrence in a context where US-Cuban relations had already been gravely damaged and both governments were on the path to confrontation. First, it was inexpensive: there were no budget commitments, and no acts of war were required beyond the leader's words and demeanor. Second, it communicated effectively the Cuban government's will to the United States. Fidel Castro thus publicly pledged his reputation to resist the United States, making "any retreat dramatically visible" in a manner, again according to Schelling, that makes a leader appear to have become "visibly incapable of serious compromise" and, as a result, likely to gain an ability to change his adversary's behavior instead.[33]

Cuban leaders have demonstrated an always present and occasionally flawed, but typically improving, level of understanding of the need to communicate one's intentions and capabilities clearly for the sake of deterring one's adversaries. The issue arises in part from what Schelling called a "tantalizing dilemma inherent in a choice of secrecy or revelation. If in order to prove that one is committed to a threat, or that one is in fact capable of fulfilling the threat, one must display evidence of the commitment or the capability to the other party, the evidence may be of a kind that necessarily yields information helpful to the second party in combating the threat."[34]

At the time of the 1962 missile crisis, Cuban leaders understood that their interests would be best served if the USSR and Cuba were to announce publicly that the Soviet Union had deployed ballistic missiles and nuclear weapons to Cuba. Cuban leaders wanted to make public the agreement in August; Soviet leader Nikita Khrushchev wanted to wait until the deployment was completed in November. A public agreement, as Philip Brenner has noted, would have served Cuban interests in two ways:[35] First, it would have deterred the United States because a public Cuban-Soviet agreement would make a US attack on Cuba equivalent to an attack on the Soviet Union. Second, it would have paralleled US defensive agreements with countries around the USSR, making it harder politically for the United States to compel the withdrawal of Soviet missiles from Cuba. Moreover, Cuba did not entirely trust the USSR to defend it. A public alliance would have pledged Moscow's reputation, making "any [Soviet] retreat dramatically visible" and thus, Cuban leaders hoped, less likely. Cuba's interests in deterrence did not require the deployment of missiles and nuclear warheads as much as they required a public Soviet pledge to go to war with the United States, with weapons based anywhere, for the sake of Cuba's defense.

Cuba's fury at the US-Soviet settlement of the missile crisis revealed, however, a misunderstanding of aspects of communications among adversaries. Cuba opposed any means of international inspection of its territory. And yet, after 1962 such inspection was necessary for the United States not to invade Cuba. Cuba's continuing security required tacit collaboration with US intelligence services.[36] It took some time, but Cuban leaders eventually learned this lesson.

In the late 1970s, the Cubans began to display publicly the submarines and advanced combat aircraft they had recently received from the Soviet Union to communicate to the United States that Cuba did, indeed, have these weapons. These displays also enabled the United States to count the armaments and verify that they lacked the capability to deliver nuclear warheads. In private, the Cuban leaders communicated that they understood that the United States had the means to verify Soviet and Cuban activities by means of airplanes, satellites, and electronic intelligence; they also knew they could not stop this surveillance. By the mid-1980s Castro signaled in public that he no longer objected to US reconnaissance flights around Cuba; he objected only to those directly over Cuba. For these reasons, in late 1984, the Tenth Plenum of the Cuban Communist Party's Central Committee recognized that its national security required that "Pentagon and CIA strategists . . . know that we are strong in every respect"—such knowledge, they believed, would deter a US attack.[37]

Of course, this discussion of communications presupposes the existence of a substantial capability. That is one reason why the Cuban government has built a large military establishment. At issue is not Cuba's ability to defeat the United States militarily but, instead, Cuba's ability to inflict such severe casualties on invading US forces that the United States would be deterred from attacking—pipsqueak power in deterrence. In early 1991, the US government again demonstrated its concern for minimizing US casualties in its conduct of the war against Iraq, thereby lending added intellectual support to this basis for Cuba's military policy.

One important dimension of the construction of Cuba's military power has been the military utility and effectiveness of Cuba's reservists, as demonstrated as early as the mid-1970s by their participation in wars in Angola and in Ethiopia.[38] In the late 1970s and in the 1980s, Cuban reservists served continuously and in large numbers in Ethiopia and especially in Angola. Perhaps the most public demonstration of the role of Cuban reservists occurred in 1983 during the US and Anglophone Caribbean intervention in Grenada. Cuban forces on Grenada fought so bravely that, at first, US commanders thought that there were many more Cubans on Grenada than the actual 784, of whom 92 percent were engaged in civilian activities, mainly as construction workers. Once Cuban officers made the decision to surrender, none of the Cubans defected to the United States. This demonstration of fighting will, and of political loyalty, served Cuban government policies well.

The quality of the Cuban officer corps was poor, however. Colonel Pedro Tortoló, commander of Cuban forces in Grenada, later described his own behavior in an interview in Cuba, where he was first received as a hero. Tortoló said that he expected only a US rescue mission (a number of US citizens, most medical students, were in Grenada at the time); he was asleep when the full-scale invasion began. He had not issued enough ammunition to those who received weapons. Therefore, "the US troops captured several of our comrades who had run out of ammunition along with another group that was unarmed."

A key factor in Cuba's response to the US intervention in Grenada was the need to impress the United States with Cuba's commitment to, and capacity for, combat in the event that the United States were to attack Cuba. Cubans would fight even in the face of apparently impossible odds. For this reason, Cuban personnel had been ordered not to withdraw from Grenada as the United States prepared to attack. Withdrawal would be a "dishonor and could stimulate aggression not only in Grenada but also in Cuba and elsewhere." Once the battle for Grenada began, the Cubans there were ordered not to surrender. The fact that they did thus posed a strategic problem for the Cuban government. To set an example, Tortoló and other Cuban officers serving in Grenada were eventually demoted for conduct unbecoming officers.[39]

In short, the Cuban government, and Fidel Castro in particular, have pursued a strategy of deterrence that is characteristically rational and quite consistent with strategic thought in the United States. This is not to say that every dimension of Cuban policy can be defended as equally necessary to advance these rational purposes. Castro's willingness to threaten collective suicide in 1962, and to order and fully expect it from a few hundred Cubans in 1983, were rational and necessary for a strategy of deterrence. His apparent actual willingness to commit the country to collective suicide is not rational, for it is incompatible with a strategy for national survival. These nonrational instances of Castro's behavior may, it should be clear, strengthen his government's rational bargaining position with the United States by conveying credible evidence of his "madness."

Cuba's Tactics

Within the overall strategic rationale already described, three specific Cuban tactics deserve mention: the utility of war, the utility of talk, and the prudent limitations self-imposed on Cuban military activities.

The Cuban government believes that war is a useful instrument of national policy. Cuban conventional forces crossed the Atlantic to fight on Algeria's side against Morocco in 1963, to fight as insurgents in the Congo (today's Zaire) in 1965, to fight for Angola's Luanda government in 1975–1976 and for fifteen years thereafter, and in 1977–1978 to fight for Ethiopia against Somalia (remaining until the end of 1989 to assist the Ethiopian government). Whereas US government officials understand the 1988 Southern African settlement as a victory for US diplomacy, Cuban leaders and scholars claim, not without reason, that the particular outcome cannot be explained without reference to Cuba's successful military actions in 1987–1988 to stop South Africa's military incursion into Angola at Cuito Cuanavale and, then, to force a South African retreat from Angola.

Consider Castro's explanation of the turn of events in Angola in 1987–1988: it was the increased deployment and firepower of Cuban troops that caused "this change in the balance of power" and that "was what paved the way to negotiations." He cast doubt on the efficacy of the US government's mediation: "While these supposed [US-brokered Angolan-South African] negotiations were taking place . . . the South Africans had intervened and tried to solve the Angolan situation militarily, and perhaps they would have achieved it if it had not been for the effort our country made." With the deployment of over 50,000 Cuban troops with tanks, artillery, MiG-23 combat aircraft, and antiaircraft equipment, "the conditions were created that made possible the negotiations."[40] Armed Forces Minister General Raúl Castro was more straightforward: "Only South Africa's military defeats on the battlefield demonstrated to the racist South African government the end of its superiority in that conflict and the unforeseen consequences for them from the continuation of their aggression [and] compelled Pretoria's representatives to sit at the negotiating table and the US government to accept the reality that without Cuba's participation next to Angola's in the talks no agreement could be reached."[41]

War is not, of course, the only useful instrument of national policy. In the same speech in which he extolled the utility of Cuba's military contribution to the Southern African settlement, President Castro praised not only the efficacy of Cuban diplomacy but also the "positive aspect" of the US role as a mediator. In December 1988, at the time of the settlement, Castro certainly did not feel that his government had backed down in the face of a US government success or Soviet pressure. Instead, he said that "in this case our interests coincide, our wishes coincide with the interests and the wishes of the United States." From his view, the settlement was what Cuba wanted. On the eve of its signing, he argued: "A political solution that gives Angola guarantees, that opens the road to Namibia's independence, that moves the South African troops away from Angola's borders and forces them to remain within their own borders would be highly positive and highly convenient for us." Then, "upon the causes that led to the presence of the Cuban troops in Angola really disappearing," Cuban troops, mission accomplished, could return home.[42]

This is, of course, the most favorable description that a Cuban official could place on Cuba's withdrawal from Angola, and one that has received support from the president of Angola and from scholars who otherwise disagree.[43] And yet, it is incomplete. During the negotiations, for example, Cuba and Angola had to agree to a quicker schedule for Cuban troop withdrawal than the two governments had proposed. Cuba also had to change its preference not to withdraw all its forces from Angola while the civil war was still under way between the Luanda government and the UNITA insurgency.[44] Cuban and Angolan proposals prior to 1987 had emphasized that Cuban troops could remain in northern Angola indefinitely. More important, once the settlement was signed in December 1988, the UNITA insurgency remained free to continue, and the US government remained at liberty to support it.

With the reduction in Soviet economic assistance to Angola because of the collapse of the Soviet economy and the withdrawal of Cuban troops, UNITA has been able to pressure the Luanda government; important changes have been occurring in Angolan politics and economics and more may yet occur. In short, though Cuba's military successes were a necessary ingredient in the Angolan settlement, the Angola that Cuba saved has already become rather less "Marxist-Leninist" than Cuba had hoped and may become even less so. Moreover, the role of the US government as a negotiator and as a continuing presence in the southern cone of Africa looms large indeed.

The central feature of Cuba's foreign military policy, however, is the Cuban leaders' belief in the utility of both war and diplomacy. Coercion is at times necessary for successful diplomacy, just as diplomacy is useful to minimize the costs of war. In 1988, still during the Cuban–South African confrontation, President Castro argued that "our objective was not to achieve a humiliating and destructive victory over our enemy" because "we were looking for a political, just solution to the conflict."[45] This speaks more generally to the limits Cuban leaders have imposed on their overseas military activities.

Cuba's tactical prudence may have prolonged conflicts, but this would not invalidate the proposition that in the 1970s and 1980s degrees of self-restraint have typically been a component of Cuba's foreign military policy. Consider again the Angolan question in Castro's words. By the late 1970s Cuban troops had settled "about 250 Kilometers from the border with Namibia" while the South Africans operated "between our lines and the border. . . . This situation lasted for years. . . . Our forces were large enough to defend that line but not to prevent South African incursions in part of Angola." The reasons for this Cuban self-restraint varied. One reason was the wish to minimize Cuban casualties. Another was the desire to leave the fighting between the Luanda government and UNITA to the Angolans themselves—a policy more restrained than the more intrusive Soviet presence in that civil war. Yet a third was the on-again–off-again quality of the Angolan–South African negotiations, about which Cuba had mixed feelings, but which it typically (though not always) respected.[46]

Similarly, Cuba's military role in the Horn of Africa showed elements of tactical prudence. Cuban armed forces powerfully assisted the Ethiopian government in its defeat of Somalia's invasion in 1977–1978 and remained to guard the boundary. They also performed a variety of military tasks, including providing crews to operate Soviet-supplied tanks in order to help the Ethiopian government conduct its counterinsurgency campaigns in Eritrea and other parts of the territory over which it claimed sovereignty. But Cuba did not agree at any time to a full-scale deployment of its combat forces in Eritrea.

As in Angola, so too in Ethiopia: the Soviet behavior was more intrusive in Ethiopia's internal affairs. Never was this clearer than in 1990. Though all Cuban military forces had withdrawn from Ethiopia, hundreds of Soviet military specialists remained. As in the past, such Soviet assistance was justified to enable the Ethiopian government to fight various insurgencies. Though Soviet military personnel had pulled out from combat zones and from outlying areas, some Soviets still argued that "it would be irresponsible to call for the unthinking severance of existing alliances and the breaking of established ties. No self-respecting state would take such a step." Cuba just had; the USSR had not. Cuba's decision was surely the more prudent, even if there is some intellectual merit to a collapsing superpower's effort to cling to its commitments.[47]

These three Cuban tactics—war, talk, and self-imposed limits—have been a "package" in Cuban foreign policy since at least the mid-1970s, but commentators have usually focused on only one tactic. Thus Cuba's first major deployment to Angola in 1975 was undertaken at the same moment that the first serious talks between the United States and Cuba were underway. Similarly, Cuba's first major deployment to Ethiopia in 1977 was undertaken at an important moment for US-Cuban talks, which had just reconvened. And Cuba's major deployment to Angola in late 1987 occurred when the US and Cuban governments had reactivated a migration agreement, until then the first and only diplomatic accomplishment between them in the 1980s. The Cuban government did not see these actions as inherently contradictory, but, quite the contrary, as part of its tactical package. It was entirely reasonable, however, for the United States to reject the proposition that Cuba could expect to deploy forces worldwide while presuming that US-Cuban diplomatic negotiations would remain unaffected.

For Cuban leaders, coercive diplomacy is at the heart of their thinking about the world. They know that others have in the past used coercive diplomacy against them, and some still will. Thus in the defense of their perception of their interests, they act accordingly. Tactical prudence is but a necessary ingredient to temper the use of force by a small country far from its shores. Consistent with this perspective, the Cuban government has typically counseled its allies engaged in war to talk and fight. That was their recommendation to Angolan, Ethiopian, and Nicaraguan leaders, for example. Thus there is reason to suppose that Cuban leaders would continue to behave internationally in this way.

Consequences for Bilateral and Regional Settlements

These features of Cuba's foreign policy have in part affected Cuban agreements that relate to some regional disputes also involving the superpowers. One example may help explain the wider pattern: Even at the height of the 1962 missile crisis, US and Cuban weather bureaus continued their cooperation.[48]

This cooperation, of course, hardly matches the terror of having the world in 1962 come closer to the edge of nuclear war than at any time since 1945. Yet this limited cooperation between weather bureaus is noteworthy for a number of reasons. Cuba and the United States are so close geographically that some cooperative arrangements, however modest, can readily be described as being in their joint interest. Such collaboration can and has saved lives and property over the years, thus meeting a high test of moral worth. The record of weather bureau cooperation is sustained, having occurred even at times of confrontation between the two countries over other issues. As in 1975, 1977, and 1987, cooperation over some issues can be decoupled from confrontation over other issues. The technical skills in this area in both the United States and Cuba are of a high order; mutual professional respect has been essential. Finally, both parties meet their commitments once they have agreed to them; both can and do deliver.

Other instances of US-Cuban collaboration include formal and informal air and maritime piracy agreements to prevent such piracy and to ensure punishment of those guilty of piracy. As a result, piracy, which reached epidemic proportions in the late 1960s and early 1970s, is now quite rare; passengers, crews, and airplanes are better protected. A formal agreement existed between 1973 and 1976, negotiated by conservative US politicians, President Richard Nixon and Secretary of State Henry Kissinger. Neither this collaboration nor that between weather bureaus could be thwarted by right-wing Cuban-American politicians.

These two modest examples contain many of the following factors evident in the agreements reached in late 1988 on Southern Africa:

1. The settlement met the test of moral worth because it was intended to save lives and property; it has already accomplished much of that goal.

2. Cooperation was possible on a given issue by decoupling it from other still conflicting issues in the relationship. The settlement in Southern Africa was reached even though the United States and Cuba

continued to back opposite sides in the internal and international wars in Nicaragua and El Salvador.

3. Both the United States and Cuba engaged in coercive diplomacy. Just as Cuba increased substantially its deployment of conventional forces to Angola, the United States continued its funding and other support of UNITA. Although the origins of US funding for UNITA are best explained as the result of congressional pressure imposing such funding on the US State Department, this use of force was an integral ingredient of the negotiations.

4. Just as conflict does not necessarily spill over into all areas of possible cooperation, so too cooperation over functionally specific issues need not spill over into other areas in need of pacification; however, it could. Governments that agree to cooperate over particular issues still need to decide, separately, whether or not to improve other aspects of their relations. Instances of specific cooperation may, but need not, commit the two governments in other areas of policy.

5. The technical skills brought by the United States and Cuba to the Southern African negotiations were necessary, effective, and successful. Without such skills on both sides, the settlement would not have been reached. US and Cuban negotiators developed a professional regard for each other.

6. Both the United States and Cuba have met their commitments under the settlement. In particular, when in April 1989 the settlement seemed about to unravel in Namibia, the US and Cuban governments collaborated to pressure South Africa and SWAPO, respectively, to abandon renewed confrontation. Thus the settlement succeeds because the key parties have the capacity to enforce it.

7. The Southern African settlement was reached during the tenure of conservative politicians: Ronald Reagan as president and George Bush as vice-president (then in the midst of a presidential election campaign), neither having warm feelings for the Cuban leadership. Personal likes and dislikes are irrelevant to these forms of collaboration.

8. The settlement could not be prevented by right-wing Cuban-American politicians.

There are also two important negative lessons in the pattern of Cuban involvement in settlements that illustrate some of the differences between settlements in Southern Africa in 1988 and in Nicaragua in 1990. First, Cuba is unlikely to negotiate with the United States for the purpose of reshaping the domestic politics of a Cuban ally. In the Southern African settlement, the future of Angolan domestic politics was near the negotiating table but not on it, and the international settlement left the Angolan civil war unsettled. In Central America, the Esquipulas agreement, first brokered by Costa Rica's President Oscar Arias, focused directly on the need to reshape the domestic politics of various signatories,

Nicaragua in particular. Cuba was not a party to that agreement, and it was concerned that the Sandinistas were making too many concessions. In similar fashion, in 1983, Cuba did not negotiate with the United States over Grenada's domestic politics; even though Cuba strongly disapproved of the coup that overthrew Grenada's Prime Minister Maurice Bishop, Cubans died defending Grenada in the face of external invasion.

Second, Cuba rarely gains a role at a negotiating table unless it has material strength directly pertinent to the issues. In Southern Africa no settlement could have been reached without taking into account the role of Cuba's armies. In Nicaragua, there were Cuban military advisors but no Cuban troops, so consequently Cuba was not taken into account to the same degree. This observation reinforces the Cuban leaders' belief in the utility of coercive diplomacy and in the dangers of diplomacy without force to back it up.

The Hell of Success and Other Hells

Cuba entered the 1990s with impressive international successes to its credit. It could claim victory over South Africa in Angola, and it could claim a major contribution to Namibia's independence from South Africa, with long-standing ally SWAPO winning power in Namibia through internationally supervised elections. Fidel Castro once asserted that Cuban troops were ready to remain in Angola until the apartheid regime collapsed in South Africa. As the Cuban withdrawal from Angola was completed, apartheid was ending in South Africa for various reasons, including the consequences of South Africa's setbacks in Angola and Namibia. Cuban troops returned home with honor.

In the Horn of Africa, Cuban troops helped to defeat Somalia's invasion of Ethiopia. Cuba even had the pleasure of witnessing the collapse of President Siad Barre's regime in Somalia a few months after the completion of Cuba's troop withdrawal from Ethiopia. In Nicaragua, despite substantial US support, the resistance (the contras) were unable to overthrow the Sandinista government; Cuba's military advice and support to the Nicaraguan government was efficacious. Indeed, on the eve of Nicaragua's February 1990 national elections, the contras had been defeated militarily. The Sandinistas had won the war, though they went on to lose the peace.

And yet, the very fact of success in Southern Africa made the continued presence of Cuban troops unjustifiable; their withdrawal was a necessary part of the settlement even though the Luanda government was far from consolidated. Military victory against the Somalis also rendered the continued presence of Cuban troops in the Horn of Africa unwarranted; the troops withdrew even though the Ethiopian government was in serious domestic difficulty. In Nicaragua military victory over the contras could not ensure an electoral victory for Cuba's allies, but military victory made it more difficult for the Sandinistas not to hold open national elections.

Cuba's military successes overseas have shown, therefore, the limits of military power. Some goals have been attained, but other, perhaps more important, goals cannot be achieved by force of arms. Cuba's allies no longer govern Ethiopia, Grenada, or Nicaragua; the fate of Cuba's allies in Angola is in grave doubt.

Perhaps more important, as Cuban troops return, Cuba necessarily becomes less influential internationally. If it is the case that Cuban diplomacy has been influential mainly when it can be backed by specific capabilities, including military force, then the repatriation of Cuban troops severely impairs Cuba's capacity to project power. That is the hell of success.

Even if guerrillas in El Salvador were to continue to demonstrate staying power in the battlefield during a classic talk-and-fight strategy, and even if Cuba continues to support that insurgency, the changes in Central America and worldwide may reduce the significance of that projection of power. The quandary for Cubans, in short, is to live on an island, just an island, surrounded by a sea that creates violent hurricanes year after year. One is certain of the existence of threats of the worst sort, but uncertain about when they will come. Hurricanes require permanent preparedness to address an insolvable problem. There is no better metaphor for Fidel Castro's view of the US government, and no better way to describe the predicament of a leader who in the 1990s may have become just a pipsqueak, no longer capable of projecting military power overseas.

Notes

I am grateful to the coeditors, to the coauthors, and to the participants in this project's two conferences for their suggestions and criticisms of earlier versions. Errors are mine alone. Much of my earlier work related to Cuban international relations was made possible by funding from the Ford Foundation, the Heinz Endowment, and the World Peace Foundation.

1. *Granma Weekly Review*, 17 Dec. 1989, 2.

2. On this and other points, I draw on historical material in my *To Make a World Safe for Revolution: Cuba's Foreign Policy* (Cambridge, Mass.: Harvard University Press, 1989).

3. For one Soviet's justification of a continued post–Cold War role for Cuba in Soviet intelligence-gathering efforts, see Sergei Tarasenko, "Azúcar que sabe a amargo o respuesta a Andrei Kortunov," *América Latina*, no. 4 (1990): 32.

4. *Granma Weekly Review*, 17 Sept. 1989, 1; *Current Digest of the Soviet Press* 42, no. 13 (2 May 1990): 31–32.

5. *Granma Weekly Review*, 18 March 1990, Special Supplement; 1 Apr. 1990, 1; and 27 Jan. 1991, 4.

6. *Granma Weekly Review*, 8 Apr. 1990, 2.

7. *Granma Weekly Review*, 10 Dec. 1989, 3; and 10 Feb. 1991, 1.

8. Bruce Allyn, James G. Blight, and David A. Welch, "Essence of Revision: Moscow, Havana, and the Cuban Missile Crisis," *International Security* 14, no. 3 (Winter 1989–1990): 136–172; and Philip Brenner,

"Cuba and the Missile Crisis," *Journal of Latin American Studies* 22: 115–142.

9. For an oft-dissenting participant's overview, see Wayne S. Smith, *The Closest of Enemies* (New York: Norton, 1987).

10. For the best intellectual defense of that US policy, see David Ronfeldt, *Geopolitics, Security, and US Strategy in the Caribbean Basin*, R-2997-AF/RC (Santa Monica: Rand Corporation, 1983), 1–87.

11. See James G. Blight, janet M. Lang, and Bruce J. Allyn, "Fidel Cornered: The Soviet Fear of Another Cuban Crisis," *Russia and the World* (Fall 1990): 21–25, 39–40; see also Fidel Castro's remarks in *Granma Weekly Review*, 14 Oct. 1990, 2.

12. I am grateful to Wayne Smith for calling this distinction to my attention.

13. On Castro's early initiatives, see testimony from the USSR's first envoy to Cuba, Alexandr Alexeev, "Cuba después del triunfo de la revolución: Primera parte," *América Latina*, no. 10 (October 1984): 56–67.

14. Cuba's policy toward Third World countries cannot, and should not, be explained solely in terms of Cuban relations with the United States and the Soviet Union, much less solely in terms of a strategy of deterrence. The Cuban government's motives have been far more complex. Exploring the totality of Cuban policies toward Third World countries is, however, beyond the scope of this chapter.

15. A turning point in achieving this consensus was the publication of the memoirs of Soviet defector Arkady N. Shevchenko, *Breaking with Moscow* (New York: Knopf, 1985), 272.

16. See the Cuban government's official explanation of its policies in *Granma Weekly Review*, 2 Dec. 1990, 2–4.

17. Quoted in Juan Sánchez, "Crisis de Octubre," *Bohemia* 81, no. 6 (10 Feb. 1989): 74.

18. *Granma Weekly Review*, 23 Apr. 1989, 8.

19. *Granma Weekly Review*, 15 July 1990, 1; 23 Dec. 1990, 3; and 10 May 1990, 3.

20. For a retrospective, see *Current Digest of the Soviet Press* 42, no. 13 (2 May 1990): 31–32.

21. See, for example, "Meeting at the Ministry of Communications," 9 Nov. 1982, 3. Mimeo.

22. Raúl Castro, "Graduación del III curso de la escuela básica superior 'General Máximo Gómez,'" *Ediciones al orientador revolucionario*, no. 17 (1967): 21.

23. *Granma Weekly Review*, 4 Feb. 1985, 2.

24. *Granma Weekly Review*, 7 Aug. 1988, 4.

25. Pedro Prada, "El puñetazo de Stevenson," *Verde olivo*, no. 12 (1989): 30–43; González Herrero, Roger, "Con el escudo y los laureles," *Bohemia* 81, no. 4 (27 Jan. 1989): 20–25; *Granma Weekly Review*, 18 Dec. 1988, 3.

26. Domínguez, *To Make a World Safe for Revolution*, Chapter 6.

27. See Joseph S. Nye, Jr., *Bound to Lead: The Changing Nature of American Power* (New York: Basic Books, 1990). I am grateful to Thomas G. Weiss for this suggestion.

28. Thomas C. Schelling, *The Strategy of Conflict* (London: Oxford University Press, 1960), 22.

29. Though many besides Schelling have written about the strategic issues under discussion, it seems best to illustrate Cuban strategic behavior in subsequent pages with reference to the arguments posed by someone like

Schelling, who has come to symbolize the field well beyond his own impressive contributions.

30. *Granma Weekly Review*, 22 Apr. 1990, 3–4.

31. "Playboy Interview: Fidel Castro," *Playboy* 32, no. 8 (August 1985): 183.

32. *Granma Weekly Review*, 14 Oct. 1990, 2; and 2 Dec. 1990, 2–4.

33. Schelling, *The Strategy of Conflict*, 29.

34. Ibid., 176n.

35. Brenner, "Cuba and the Missile Crisis," 128.

36. For a similar point, see Schelling, *The Strategy of Conflict*, 148.

37. Discussion and citations in Domínguez, *To Make a World Safe for Revolution*, 58–59.

38. Jorge I. Domínguez, *Cuba: Order and Revolution* (Cambridge, Mass.: Harvard University Press, 1978), Chapter 9.

39. Domínguez, *To Make a World Safe for Revolution*, 168–169.

40. *Granma Weekly Review*, 18 Dec. 1988, 3.

41. *Bohemia* 81, no. 3 (20 Jan. 1989): 22–23.

42. Ibid.

43. See Jaime Suchlicki, "The United States Loses in Angola," in Sergio Díaz-Briquets, ed., *Cuban Internationalism in Sub-Saharan Africa* (Pittsburgh: Duquesne University Press, 1989); Armando Entralgo and David González López, "Cuban Policy for Africa," in Jorge I. Domínguez and Rafael Hernández, eds., *U.S.-Cuban Relations in the 1990s* (Boulder, Colo.: Westview Press, 1989); and José Eduardo dos Santos, "There Will Be Peace in Southern Africa," *World Marxist Review* 32, no. 10 (October 1989): 13–15.

44. *Granma Weekly Review*, 14 Sept. 1986, 9; and 21 Sept. 1986, 9–10.

45. *Granma Weekly Review*, 7 Aug 1988, 5.

46. *Granma Weekly Review*, 7 Aug. 1988, 5; and 18 Dec. 1988, 3–4; for a thoughtful discussion of various Cuban unsuccessful endeavors, see Olga Nazario, "Cuba's Angolan Operation," in Díaz-Briquets, ed., *Cuban Internationalism in Sub-Saharan Africa*.

47. Domínguez, *To Make a World Safe for Revolution*, 159–162; *Current Digest of the Soviet Press* 42, no. 13 (2 May 1990): 32; *Granma Weekly Review*, 10 Jan. 1990, 1.

48. Gordon Dunn, "The Hurricane Season of 1963," *Monthly Weather Review* 92, no. 3 (March 1964): 135–136.

■ 4 ■

South Africa in
Angola and Namibia

NEWELL M. STULTZ

The Angola-Namibia accords of December 1988 are examined in this chapter in the light of a supposed relationship between superpower rivalry or cooperation and regional conflict in the so-called Third World. The overarching notion is that just as unrestrained competition between the two superpowers can, and often does, fuel regional conflicts, superpower cooperation, when it appears, can have an opposite, conflict-dampening effect—within particular regions as well as in general. The perspective here is especially concerned with the views of the government in Pretoria.

The central task is to try to account for the apparent reversal of Pretoria's foreign policy toward the Angola-Namibia subregion (as I will call the area) in the middle of 1988 and in particular to estimate the degree to which this reversal can be linked to changes in Soviet policy toward the Southern African region as a whole that occurred at about the same time. Subsidiary questions addressed en route, or at the end, include (1) the nature of Soviet influence on Pretoria's Southern African regional policy, (2) the historic uniqueness of the December 1988 agreements, (3) the contribution of the US policy of "constructive engagement" to this outcome, (4) the degree to which this recent experience could spill over and influence ongoing political confrontations within South Africa itself, and (5) the generalizability of the present case to other instances of regional conflict in the Third World.

The End of Neutralization/Destabilization

For most of the decade of the 1980s, the Republic of South Africa pursued "an aggressive, multipronged campaign to weaken and dominate its neighbors."[1] The specific goals of this campaign varied, but there was always the overriding objective of protecting white minority rule within

South Africa. In certain cases the intention of the South African government was to alter through economic pressures and/or military action (the latter euphemistically called "forward defense" by Pretoria) the policies of particular neighboring governments. Robert Price has termed this strategy "neutralization," in contrast with the goal of replacing particular neighboring regimes altogether, which he calls the strategy of "destabilization."[2]

But whatever its name or proximate purposes, the consequences of this campaign were catastrophic for the region. Chris Brown cites figures prepared for the Commonwealth committee of foreign ministers that indicate that the costs of South African neutralization/destabilization for the nine countries of the SADCC may have been as high as $35 billion in property damage and one million lives lost, not to mention the displacement of perhaps another million refugees. Quoting UN statistics, *The Economist* recently put the cost of South Africa's military aggression toward its neighbors at $60 billion for 1980–1988. And within the republic itself, apart from South Africans killed or injured in various kinds of armed encounters, defense expenditures in the middle of the 1980s were 5.5 times larger than a decade earlier, and a staggering 52 times larger than they had been at the time of the founding of the republic in 1961.[3]

Then in the middle of 1988, things changed in the Angola-Namibia subregion. In the words of Clough and Herbst, South Africa's "confidence in the power of guns and ideology" appeared suddenly to dissolve before the promise of serious bargaining with the country's external opponents.[4] Ten rounds of formal negotiations ensued, beginning in early May in London, and these discussions, together with two sets of secret or informal talks, finally resulted in the signing by Cuba, Angola, and South Africa of the so-called Angola-Namibia accords in New York City on December 22, 1988.[5] These accords, which ended more than thirteen years of military conflict in the area, stipulated that the three parties agreed to:

1. A timetable for Namibian independence (pursuant to Security Council Resolution 435), the process itself to begin on April 1, 1989, and to be supervised by a UNTAG;
2. Elections for a Namibian constituent assembly, to be held on November 1, 1989;
3. Withdrawal of all South African troops from Namibia within one week of the announcement of the results of the aforementioned elections; and finally,
4. The phased departure of all Cuban troops from Angola, to be completed by July 1991.[6]

Different Interpretations

Three different assessments of the reasons for Pretoria's seeming turnaround concerning Angola and Namibia have been put forward. Brown believes that South Africa was simply forced out of Angola and Namibia by military and economic pressures mounted against it—that is, by "naked power,"[7] and for him no other explanation for Pretoria's volte-face is needed.

On the other hand, Chester Crocker, who is at an advantage over other commentators because of his own role in the 1988 negotiations as assistant secretary of state for Africa, posits quite a different assessment: "The decisive ingredient [in the Angola-Namibia negotiations] was not the level of pain; the parties decided to preempt the pain. The key factors were the existence of a realistic framework of negotiations, the availability of a suitable forum, and a basic equilibrium of power that made it possible for every party to gain."[8] In short, effective diplomacy was coupled with some changes of conceptual orientation among the parties.

The analysis by Clough and Herbst lies somewhere between. They hold that South Africa's destabilization strategy collapsed in 1988 because of a number of factors, some of them pressures in a conventional realpolitik sense. Among other considerations were a growing feeling among South African whites that the danger to the country of a Soviet-backed guerrilla war coming from beyond South Africa's borders had been greatly exaggerated, and a new appreciation in Pretoria of the value to all states in Southern Africa of economic cooperation and good neighborliness.

The views of Clough and Herbst on the contribution of national "pain" to the agreements of December 1988 are more convincing than Crocker's. Surely there is evidence that the objective circumstances "on the ground" in Angola in the middle of 1988 constituted, as even Brown himself suggests, a "hurting stalemate" involving Angola, South Africa, and Cuba.

But not all hurting stalemates turn into what William Zartman, the originator of this idea, calls "ripe moments" for the resolution of international disputes. He states, "People [can] learn to live with stalemates, even unpleasant ones." What is additionally needed, he says, for such conflicts to be resolved is the discovery by each party of "a way out." This is a new approach for a state toward its adversaries, one that promises to reduce the costs of a particular ongoing encounter with those adversaries while concurrently achieving "an acceptable number of the goals and interests originally sought."[9] Brown fails to see any such discovery in Pretoria's decision in 1988 to leave Angola and Namibia, while for Clough and Herbst, and clearly for Crocker too, a conceptual change of some sort was significant.

An Outline of the Basic Facts of the Case

The core facts of this case are not in serious dispute. We begin with the date April 25, 1974, when the government of Portugal was overthrown in Lisbon. Among the consequences was the collapse of Portugal's overseas empire, and following from this, a significant breaching of the *cordon sanitaire* that had protected apartheid against the fury of independent black Africa since the early 1960s. Scholars now identify 1974 as a critical turning point in the politics of Southern Africa,[10] though at the time the event took many of them by surprise. In Pretoria, government analysts were caught no less unawares, and the 1974 Portuguese coup produced a fundamental rethinking of the country's basic foreign policy assumptions.[11] Subsequently, on October 23, 1975, several thousand troops were sent deep into Angolan territory—ultimately nearly to Luanda itself.

October 1975 was not the first time since the end of World War II that SADF soldiers had crossed international frontiers. In August 1966, SADF troops attacked a guerrilla training camp in Namibia, and by 1972 these same forces, now in far greater numbers, were broadly engaged within the territory in a far-reaching counterinsurgency campaign. This campaign was directed against SWAPO, the territory's principal liberation group, which was recognized by the United Nations in a 1973 General Assembly resolution as the "sole authentic representative of the Namibian people." But Pretoria always considered Namibia a special case because of its status as a League of Nations mandate given to South Africa in 1920. Namibia had for decades been treated as virtually a fifth province of the country, and in Pretoria's view this made it exempt from the republic's long-standing and frequently enunciated regional policy of noninterference in other countries' internal affairs.[12] This exemption was extended to cover SADF incursions into southern Angola in pursuit of SWAPO guerrillas.

The 1975 invasion of Angola by South African troops reversed this noninterference policy. Prime Minister John Vorster justified this invasion in parliament by stating it was required by the "excessive" stockpiling by Cuba and the Soviet Union of war materials in Angola.[13] This stockpiling, thought to have begun in March 1975, was far beyond Angola's own military needs, and, therefore, South African military analysts concluded that South Africa itself was the goal of Soviet intervention in the region.

However, one well-informed observer cautions against the easy assumption that South African policy in the Southern African region has been coherent, well coordinated, and the product of, as it were, a single "rational actor" sitting in Pretoria. Notwithstanding traditions of political authoritarianism in South Africa, even within the white community, Annette Seegers, a military policy analyst at the University of Cape Town, points out that like most governments, the South African regime embraces a great many different interests, bureaucratic and otherwise, many having their own divergent or competing agendas. The reconciliation of these interests at the level of state policy has often been incomplete and confusing, military policymaking included.[14]

Pretoria's strategy of destabilization/neutralization had emerged by the late 1970s and thereafter underwrote a presumptive right of the country to exert economic and military pressure on any of its regional neighbors if they were thought to be harboring guerrillas intent on terrorist action against the republic or its citizens. Even so, Seegers reports that specific decisions were sometimes made at operational levels without prior reference to civilian authority.

Excluding Angola itself, from which South African troops were temporarily withdrawn at the end of January 1976, it is widely believed that the first military effort at neutralization occurred early in 1981, when South African uniformed commandos raided a supposed ANC headquarters in Maputo, Mozambique, killing 12. Throughout the remainder of the decade, only conservative Swaziland among South Africa's immediate neighbors escaped organized SADF assaults, and even Swaziland complained publicly in 1986 of periodic cross-border violations of its sovereignty by armed South African "operatives."[15] SADF troops also reentered Angola in 1981 (twice), 1982, 1983 ("Operation Askari"), and finally again in September 1987, each time engaging militarily MPLA government forces.[16]

The last of these incursions involved some 3,000 South African troops, augmented by another 1,500 to 2,000 black soldiers of the South West African Territorial Force. The mission of these units was to help UNITA rebel forces thwart a Soviet-planned offensive by government MPLA troops against UNITA strongholds, an offensive that was then already under way at Mavinga. A month later this MPLA offensive was finally blunted and turned back.

Gerald Bender writes that at Mavinga the MPLA suffered its greatest military losses of the war,[17] losses that Robert Jaster reports may have been as high as 2,000 dead and perhaps 4,000 wounded.[18] But the South Africans' victory at Mavinga tempted them to pursue MPLA forces to Cuito Cuanavale, 100 miles to the north, and here, aided by Cuban reinforcements, the government forces held firm throughout a protracted four-month siege. This battle at Cuito Cuanavale is sometimes referred to as Angola's Stalingrad, marking a turning point against South Africa's military fortunes in the subregion. Yet in strict military terms, this battle was more a standoff than a rout.

The military significance of the battle at Cuito Cuanavale lay in the number of white South African casualties. For the first time, this number was great enough to jeopardize the capacity of the republic's regime to deal with the domestic political consequences of such losses. After years of having fought a low-level "bush war" in Angola, in which casualties were largely confined to black troops, South Africa found itself involved in a major military engagement, one that would produce in time the largest tank battle in Africa since World War II. Such an escalation represented for Pretoria a psychological-political threshold, one which the Cubans readily appreciated and sought increasingly to turn to their own advantage.

In December 1987 Cuba increased its troop strength in Angola to about 45,000, and later to 50,000. Concurrently, 15,000 of these soldiers were moved south toward the Namibian border, where, in Pretoria's view, they threatened South Africa's military position in northern Namibia. Jaster reports that Defense Minister Magnus Malan later admitted his government's worry in early 1988 that SWAPO guerrillas might push straight through into Namibia "behind a Cuban shield."[19] In April, following their heaviest war losses ever, the South Africans began withdrawing from their positions around Cuito Cuanavale, and concurrently through diplomatic channels the Pretoria government "signaled [its] willingness to enter into serious negotiations with Angola and Cuba."[20]

Meetings for this purpose were held in London and Brazzaville in May, and in Cairo in June, but at all of these gatherings, South Africa offered no significant concessions. Then just two days after the Cairo meeting ended, two apparently unplanned clashes occurred between Cuban and South African forces in the vicinity of the Calueque dam in Angola near the Namibian border. An estimated 150 Cubans died in the first of these encounters, but more important from a strategic point of view was that 12 South Africans perished in the second, an air attack on the dam. The results of this air attack demonstrated that in consequence of Angola's recent acquisition of ultramodern air defense equipment from the Soviet Union, South Africa had lost the air superiority over southern Angola it had once enjoyed. In the ensuing days, a South African counterattack appeared imminent. US analysts felt that the South Africans "had the capacity to crush the joint Angolan-Cuban force along the [Angola-Namibia] border."[21] But the attack never came. Instead, on July 13, 1988, on Governor's Island in the New York harbor, the republic agreed "to a set of principles for a settlement and, then, in early August, it undertook to withdraw all of its forces from Angola."[22]

Zero-Sum Perceptions

Robert Price highlights the cognitive framework that foreign policymakers brought to their work in the United States and the Soviet Union during the Cold War. Where such officials approach the world with an orientation that is "zero-sum," where every Soviet gain is assumed to entail a US loss and vice versa, "international politics," Price writes, "will inevitably move in a precarious, tension-oriented, and conflict-generating direction." But should these same policymakers "approach the world with a very different set of assumptions, ones that allow for situations of non-zero-sum relations . . . then the potential for conflict [is] substantially reduced."[23]

If only implicitly, other analysts have suggested that over the decade ending in 1988, South Africa's regional policy *was* heavily influenced by zero-sum perceptions, especially of the role and intentions of the Soviet Union vis-à-vis the republic. Accordingly, subsequent abandonment of this perspective in favor of a more "positive-sum" outlook might explain the change in South African regional policy that occurred in 1988.

The best summary of South Africa's 1975 intervention in Angola is provided by Robin Hallett, who lived in South Africa while he was on the faculty of the University of Cape Town. His study, based on mostly "non-secret" material, is highly detailed and his sources rich and varied. Hallett describes the situation in Angola as seen by policymakers in Pretoria at the beginning of August 1975 as "massive military support flowing from the Soviet Union, Cuba and Eastern Europe to the MPLA; increasing alarm in Zambia and Zaire; a bitter debate over Angola in the American State Department culminating in a decision to counter the Russian threat by supporting the FNLA and UNITA; and finally increasing tension on the Angolan–South West African border. *It was a situation that could be interpreted in almost apocalyptic terms by some influential South African observers.*"[24] It is hard to imagine a better example than this of zero-sum thinking in official South African circles.

Tied directly to current happenings on the ground in Angola, these attitudes do not, at least in Hallett's description, appear to have owed much to enduring anticommunist prejudices among South Africa's white leaders at the time.[25] The codification of these sentiments into a coherent policy doctrine for South Africa, having itself possible explanatory value, appears to have come a bit later. Indeed, the experience in Angola in 1975–1976 seems to have been an important impetus to that codification, especially to the belief that South Africa had been deserted on the Angolan field of battle by the United States in December 1975.[26]

Total Onslaught/Total National Strategy

The doctrine that developed in time had two interrelated parts. The first, an estimate of the international challenge to South Africa, was called "total onslaught." The phrase itself was not in the late 1970s an original one: Seegers notes that these same words appeared in a South African police report as early as 1964. The second part was the republican government's response to total onslaught, called "total national strategy."

Total onslaught referred to the alleged global campaign of malevolence toward South Africa, and indeed the West generally, orchestrated centrally from Moscow and implemented primarily within South Africa or on its borders by guerrillas of the banned ANC. General Magnus Malan, the republic's defense minister after 1981, stated: "The total onslaught is an ideologically motivated struggle and the aim is the implacable and unconditional imposition of the aggressors' will on the target state. . . . [Within South Africa its goal is] the overthrow of the present constitutional order and its replacement by a subject communist-oriented black government."[27]

Fears of "international communism" were scarcely new within Pretoria's governing circles. While these fears came to be articulated by officials with a frequency and intensity that even some regime sympathizers found laughable at times,[28] one of the several objectives of Soviet policy in Southern Africa was in fact "the gradual development of a strong united front for armed struggle in and against South Africa, including communists within the ANC."[29]

Total national strategy was first mentioned in an April 1977 white paper on defense, where it was referred to as a comprehensive plan, applicable at all levels of the South African government, "to utilize all the means available to [the] state, according to an integrated pattern, in order to achieve [the country's] national aims."[30] While the idea was not actually implemented until the beginning of the next decade, during the interim Pretoria experimented with two quite different proposals for its own international relations. One was a declaration by Prime Minister P. W. Botha in August 1979 of a qualified neutrality for South Africa in future conflicts between East and West. The second was the suggestion that a peaceful constellation of states be created for Southern Africa, each of whose members would respect the cultures, traditions, and ideals of the others.[31]

Against the background of Pretoria's long-standing and well-known anticommunist and anti-Soviet rhetoric, the first of these two proposals simply lacked credibility. It struck many observers as mere pique at mounting criticisms of apartheid abroad, especially from Washington, or alternatively a deliberate threat to Western capitals intended to reestablish

Pretoria's diplomatic value in their eyes. The idea of a constellation of states fared little better; it was immediately seen at home and abroad as a transparent effort to gain regional acceptance for apartheid, especially for the government's "homelands" policy, and it was readily dismissed as such. With the victory of Robert Mugabe and his ZANU party in Zimbabwe in March 1980 and, as Price notes, mounting international pressure "for a similar result involving SWAPO in Namibia," Pretoria soon scaled back the "constellation" idea to include only South Africa and its "independent" African homelands.[32] At this point, the Botha government prepared to implement its total national strategy in earnest.

Total national strategy had three goals. Militarily, Brown writes, it was meant to keep the armed wings of the ANC and the PAC "weak and at bay" and altogether out of the region. At the same time, Pretoria hoped to preempt the possibility of an attack on the republic by the armed forces of any of its neighbors. Economically, it maintained the dependence of the SADCC states on South Africa, protecting the republic from international sanctions. And politically, the aim was to undermine the governments of the SADCC states to keep them weak, while suggesting that black Africans were incompetent to govern themselves.

The signing of the Nkomati Mutual Non-Aggression accords by Mozambique and South Africa in March 1984 seemed to signify a dramatic success for this overall strategy. Marxist Mozambique was forced to capitulate to South African power. Another kind of success occurred in January 1985 when the government of Chief Leabua Jonathan in Lesotho was overturned in a military coup that had been precipitated by the republic's closing its land frontier with Lesotho a few days earlier.

A Realist Assessment

Chris Brown notes that less than three years later, the politics of the region, certainly the Namibia-Angola subregion, seemed entirely different,[33] though even he toys with an argument that the December 1988 signing of the Angola-Namibia accords in New York actually confirmed the republic's position as "an exploitative-hegemonic regional power." This surprising suggestion rests on his observation that the withdrawal of both Cuban troops and ANC guerrillas from Angola, provided for in the accords, realized long-held South African aims, and it rests on his belief that, notwithstanding the agreements, "South Africa [has in fact] managed to position itself well for the [future] 'neo-colonization' of Namibia." But Brown's central and more important position is that South Africa was actually forced against its will to agree to the accords because of the "altered military and economic equation." In particular, he writes that "the peace accords do not represent a sudden infusion of norms into the southern African conflict, but rather a reaffirmation of the primacy of power in explaining regional outcomes." Brown's analysis refers to "international regime theory," but his argument can be expressed adequately in four linked statements:

1. The current South African regime is incorrigibly wedded to white minority rule in the republic (apartheid), notwithstanding its periodic protestations of interest in policy reform.
2. The SADCC states are "implacably opposed to apartheid."
3. This opposition will cause these states to take action and to support the action of others, which South Africa will inevitably regard as threatening.
4. Accordingly, so long as apartheid exists, South Africa will be driven to pursue aggressive policies against its neighbors and to deny their legitimacy.

The last point, Brown says, makes South Africa a "revolutionary power." This is a state "whose domestic ideology leads [it] to define the international status quo as unacceptable." Brown concludes: "Third parties . . . should not seek accommodation among the existing states of southern Africa; instead, they should seek to overthrow apartheid."

Agreements and Disagreements

No analyst has disputed the importance of military and economic considerations in bringing South Africa to the bargaining table in mid-1988. South Africa's setbacks at Cuito Cuanavale and Calueque during the first half of 1988, following closely the victory at Mavinga, seem certain to have persuaded Pretoria that the military situation in Angola/Namibia was stalemated and that it would likely remain so even with an increased commitment of forces. All agree that the government of President P. W. Botha thereafter favored a negotiated settlement, all the more so because of the mounting numbers of white casualties in Angola.[34] Meanwhile, within the South African government, the fact of military reversals in Angola revived, it is said, the influence of the Department of External Affairs, which had long favored diplomacy over the use of military force.[35]

By 1988, fourteen years after it began, the war in Angola/Namibia was costing more than $1 million a day, clearly more than the country could afford.[36] The South African economy had been in recession for some years, and even without the war, Pretoria would have been hard pressed to fund its program of domestic racial reform. Jaster notes that throughout the 1980s South Africa's gross domestic product grew at a paltry 1 percent a year, consistently lagging behind the African birthrate, which averaged about three times this figure. Servicing the country's $21 billion of foreign debt was another problem, especially at a time of falling international gold prices. Finally, Pretoria worried that the US Congress might impose even tougher US economic sanctions than those legislated in 1986.[37] Military and economic factors, then, were strong incentives for Pretoria to leave the battlefields in Angola in mid-1988.

But were these the only considerations that mattered? Brown's analysis seeks to dispel the idea that a normative consensus on international cooperation and accommodation could grow in the region sufficient to support a "security regime" in Southern Africa: "After repeated interventions in their countries, and the violation of the Nkomati Accord, SADCC leaders simply have not trusted anything that Pretoria says," he writes.[38] But the issue, from Pretoria's vantage point, would seem to be less trust than capacity, for as Price observed in 1984, "Since they will not in the near future have the capability to defeat Pretoria's defense force, South African insurgent groups, or liberation movements, which are . . . provided . . . territorial sanctuaries by neighboring states in southern Africa, represent little immediate threat to the survival of white political power."[39]

What has worried South African planners, Price continues, is the prospect of Soviet and Cuban military assistance to "economically strong and politically viable" black African states bent on attacking South Africa. If the prospect of this assistance within the region is eliminated convincingly, South Africa's belligerence should also be reduced. Admittedly this would not usher in a security regime for Southern Africa, or remove altogether the ability of guerrilla groups to carry out sabotage in the republic. But arguably it could in time herald an important step away from the anarchistic "war of all against all" that increasingly characterized politics in the region only a decade ago.

Positive-Sum Perceptions

Charles Freeman, Jr., Chester Crocker's deputy at the time of the 1988 negotiations, makes the following observation: "There are [in diplomacy] at least two basic approaches to an apparently intractable problem if a frontal assault seems unlikely to work: one can either disaggregate the problem and attack it piece by piece, or one can link the problem to issues that open the possibility of trade-offs between an expanded list of parties."[40]

Theoretically, the latter course opens the possibility that all parties to a dispute can gain something of value from its resolution. In the eyes of his deputy, it was because of Crocker's diplomatic genius that, after having made "a realistic appraisal of the ultimate interests of [all] the parties," the assistant secretary perceived that an initially politically unpopular *linkage* of diverse issues in the area "could promote a broader peace in the southern African region."[41] G. R. Berridge lists other aspects of this multilateral diplomacy as it unfolded that he sees contributing to its success, including Crocker's personal efforts at mediation of the dispute; the use by both South Africa and Angola of generals and senior officials as negotiators; the choice of negotiating sites that gave "extra incentives to one or more of the parties to negotiate"; and the practice of setting deadlines, publicly suggesting from time to time that success in the negotiations was near and providing superpower or third-party guarantees for some of the agreements reached.

Berridge argues that Crocker's ability to link separate or loosely related issues—to negotiate "on a broad front," in Henry Kissinger's words—was also a key element in the success of negotiations.[42] This element alone made it possible to redefine the diplomatic problem in Angola-Namibia as a positive-sum game.

Freeman enumerates the benefits that each of the parties received from the Angola-Namibia accords. Both Angola and South Africa gained extra security. Cuba increased its international prestige by compelling Pretoria at long last to accede to Namibian independence. The Soviet Union obtained "relief from the expense of financing a seemingly endless war" in a part of the world of no vital interest to it, though there were other Soviet considerations as well. And in an election year, the US administration obtained a hard-won diplomatic triumph together with the satisfaction of seeing the Cubans agree to leave this part of Africa.

How is it that an agreement most specialists felt would inevitably result in a SWAPO-led government in Windhoek could be understood in Pretoria as enhancing South Africa's own security? The explanation is doubtless related to the passing of superpower rivalry in the region, and indeed throughout in the world, in the mid-1980s. The concept of total onslaught presupposed global superpower competition and a Soviet strategy of resource denial to the West. With these specters diminishing, the credibility of total onslaught among the public was inevitably undermined. Some believe that this undermining was well advanced before the mid-1980s as a result of demographic and generational changes particularly within the Afrikaner ruling group. However and whenever this conviction came to pass, the idea of a Namibian government dominated by SWAPO had apparently became no more abhorrent to white South Africans than the reality of the FRELIMO government already installed in Mozambique.

A new appreciation of Soviet intentions in the region did not materialize overnight, of course, although as recently as early 1987 the director of the Institute for Political and Africa Studies at the University of Potchefstroom wrote that "no change in the foreign policy of the Soviet Union can be foreseen at present."[43] But at about the same time, a deputy director of the respected Africa Institute in Moscow provided an early hint of a fundamental change in official Soviet thinking concerning Southern Africa. In June 1986, Gleb Starushenko allowed publicly that resolution of the South African problem might require constitutional guarantees for whites in the country similar to those agreed to for independent Zimbabwe at the Lancaster House conference in 1979.[44]

Similar unconventional declarations on other politically sensitive issues, including the ANC's allegedly misguided "insistence on a decidedly dogmatic socialism,"[45] and the improbability of revolution in the republic followed from various sources within the Soviet hierarchy, including Boris Asoyan, deputy director of the Southern African department in the Ministry of Foreign Affairs.[46] In time these sources included Mikhail Gorbachev himself. Thus in only two years a prominent academic Sovietologist in South Africa, Philip Nel of Stellenbosch University, could write that Soviet leaders had now accepted the need for stability in Southern Africa; they did not relish the prospect of a racial war in South Africa; and they would prefer to see a negotiated settlement to outstanding difficulties in the region. In short, Nel concluded, "There are interesting conceptual changes taking place in Soviet assessments of South Africa."[47]

Freeman reports that at about the same time—early 1988—Assistant Secretary Crocker himself became persuaded of the same view,[48] and this interpretation was later confirmed.[49] Accordingly, Crocker took a bold step. He invited the Soviets to become associated as external "counselors"—available to talk with the participants outside the meeting rooms—at a London meeting he was organizing on the subregion on May 3. The Soviets accepted Crocker's invitation and later agreed to continue this form of participation during the subsequent meetings over the next seven months. Freeman reports that this gave the Soviets and the South Africans the unprecedented opportunity to convince each other that a settlement acceptable to all parties with interests in the region was in fact feasible.[50]

Crocker has written that Pretoria now heard directly a "new policy line from Moscow," including characterizations of the ANC's armed struggle against apartheid "as if it were a relic of a bygone era." The Soviet Union and Cuba also perceptively gave "Pretoria a stake in regional peace-making by their decision to join with it in the work of the Namibia-Angola Joint Commission,"[51] which oversaw implementation of the 1988 accords. South Africa, Cuba, and the Soviet Union therefore became allied in this one respect. Berridge's conclusion that "superpower cooperation [had] a decisive impact on the settlement in southern Africa," as it had earlier in Afghanistan, thus seems plausible.[52] J. E. Spence calls this process one of "superpower midwifery,"[53] and Klaus Freiherr von der Ropp makes the same point when he writes that the ability of the two superpowers "to agree on a common policy [on Southern Africa] around the turn of the year 1987/88 was a critical 'breakthrough.' "[54]

Conclusions

It is not possible on the strength of available evidence to substantiate the claim of Clough and Herbst that a change, beginning in the mid-1980s, in the way white South Africans in general understand long-term Soviet intentions in the subregion was an important factor contributing to the December 1988 Angola-Namibia accords. This is not to deny that some such change in Pretoria's perceptions of the Soviet threat may have begun to appear publicly during this period. But it seems unlikely that the republic's decisionmakers could have so quickly altered fundamental strategic calculations, as they appear to have done in late 1988, on the basis merely of verbal assurances given in conversations by various Soviet officials, unprecedented as those encounters were.

The eventual willingness of both Havana and Luanda, responding to what Fen Hampson describes as behind-the-scenes pressures from the USSR, to agree to the December 1988 settlement, and in particular to accept the controversial linkage of Cuban troop withdrawal from Angola and South African troop withdrawal from Namibia, was probably far more critical to South Africa and promoted their willingness to sign the accords. Had Cuba not agreed in 1988 to withdraw its troops from Angola, Pretoria would likely have chosen to stay in Namibia, and perhaps even in southern Angola in defensive positions.

In all likelihood this conclusion will distress those analysts who contend that linkage originated with US rather than South African negotiators, and that the idea was thereafter taken up by Pretoria as a convenient but wholly disingenuous rationale for failing to comply with various United Nations' resolutions on Namibia. But while this latter accusation was probably correct prior to the 1987–1988 battles at Cuito Cuanavale and Calueque, after those battles a new consideration emerged. Unilateral South African withdrawal from Angola and Nambia at this point would have necessarily carried with it the stigma of defeat and the appearance of having been forced out of the subregion by superior military power. This is precisely Brown's interpretation of South Africa's withdrawal, but the evidence suggests that the military position of the

SADF in Angola in the middle of 1988 was not desperate, and that therefore a concurrent face-saving (for Pretoria) removal of Cuban troops was necessary if the South African troops were themselves to depart. In short, the battles in 1987 and 1988 at Cuito Cuanavale and Calueque highlighted Pretoria's inability to tolerate substantial white casualties as well as the ability of the Cuban troops to inflict casualties on the SADF. This realization moved South Africa generally in the direction of a negotiated settlement in the region, but the battles did not require South African acquiescence in *any* kind of settlement. From this perspective, then, the settlement that did occur need not be taken as indicating a dramatic reversal in traditional South African foreign policy, although, in fact, some limited change in these attitudes may have been occurring.

It is easy in 1991 to forget the political context that existed at the time of the signing of the Angola-Namibia accords in December 1988. The most recent happenings described took place fully ten months before the accession of F. W. de Klerk to the South African presidency and at a time when de Klerk's subsequent policy differences with his predecessor, P. W. Botha, were still not widely appreciated. December 1988 was still one full year before Eastern Europe's watershed winter of 1989–1990. From the perspective of peacemaking, which is how Chester Crocker characterizes the Angola-Namibian settlement process, the second half of 1988 was certainly a less hopeful time within Southern Africa than it is today.[55]

Even so, the changing political context since early 1989 can also suggest that had the negotiations of 1988 actually collapsed rather than succeeded, subsequent developments in Southern Africa and the world might well have produced essentially the same results. However much the Angola-Namibia accords constitute a turning point in the international politics of the subregion, they probably should not be seen to have signified a unique moment in the contemporary history of this area. Rather it is probably more correct to see the accords as largely the tangible expression of the virtually inevitable convergence of a great many separate and often deeply rooted developments—some political, such as changes in South African leadership; some military, such as the loss of South African air supremacy in southern Angola; and some, such as growing turmoil in the Soviet empire, having little to do with events in Southern Africa at all.

For his part, Crocker clearly saw in the Angola-Namibia accords a gratifying, if eleventh-hour, validation of the Reagan administration's controversial policy of constructive engagement, a policy for which Crocker was both the principal architect in 1980–1981 and later its chief agent. "As a result of our efforts," Crocker wrote in the fall of 1989, "a new regional order is emerging in southern Africa."[56] But Brown, among others, has drawn exactly the opposite conclusion, namely, that third parties should not try, as constructive engagement clearly had tried, to manage the Southern African conflict "if by management is meant promoting grounds for co-operation and accommodation among the existing parties to the dispute."[57] US efforts at constructive engagement, these critics hold, may actually have *delayed* South Africa's recognition of the bankruptcy of its policies in the subregion; when finally this awareness did arrive, it alone was decisive in redirecting Pretoria's foreign policy quite apart from any conceptual reorientation that may or may not have been occurring among high-level policymakers in Pretoria.

This later argument might be tenable if it could be shown that after its losses at Cuito Cuanavale and Calueque, South Africa was prepared in the middle of 1988 to withdraw unconditionally from Angola and to grant Namibia independence—to surrender the fields of battle of the subregion, as it were, to the country's real or imagined enemies. It seems, however, that a more plausible case can be made for a different view, namely that Cuban withdrawal from Angola was necessary for South Africa to agree to depart from Angola-Namibia. Ultimately the weight of the evidence on either side of this argument is less persuasive than the somewhat larger number of putative authorities (Spence, Berridge, Jaster, Freeman) who appear to hold that alleged battlefield reverses in Angola in 1987–1988, important as they were, are alone an insufficient explanation for South Africa's new willingness to strike a diplomatic deal concerning the subregion in the second half of 1988.

Effecting an acceptable multilateral deal for Southern Africa was of course the central goal of the proponents of constructive engagement in the heyday of that policy, a goal seemingly vindicated by the events of 1988. Yet at the same time, constructive engagement was entirely a US formulation, and at its outset the policy itself certainly did not assume as a requisite for its success the cooperation of the Soviet Union. Indeed, in his well-known article advocating a "strategy for change" in South Africa, Chester Crocker scarcely mentioned the Soviet Union at all. When he did, it was in conventional Cold War terms.[58] Thus while there is an undoubted conceptual congruence between the diplomatic thrust of constructive engagement as it was originally formulated and the State Department's role in advancing the Angola-Namibia accords in 1988, the success of the latter effort can reflect only in the most general way on the sagacity of the underlying policy. How different, one might ask, would the results of the 1988 negotiations have been if the Cold War had then been intensifying instead of beginning to wind down?

But there is, to this writer at least, a musty or passé quality to this debate over whether or not constructive engagement succeeded in this case. The important thing now would seem to be that the accords were signed and were implemented, however achieved. Yet in the writings of both Brown and Crocker, the stakes of this continuing debate on past policies include not just the content of the historical record leading up to December 1988 or the reputations of various commentators, but also the lessons that should be drawn from this experience by those seeking to shape the future of domestic affairs in South Africa itself. Crocker writes that the Angola-Namibia accords can hopefully provide South Africans and presumably others as well with an example and "a tangible basis of hope in . . . the politics of negotiation."[59] Meanwhile, for his part, Brown urges continued efforts to overthrow apartheid rather than accommodating the interests of those who support it.

In 1990, after Brown and Crocker had written their essays, Nelson Mandela was released from prison and the outlawed ANC and other antiapartheid groups were sanctioned. Today the interventionist premise that underlies both essays, if it is not out of date, appears at least undermined by recent events. Even the ANC now talks openly of the need for negotiations with the South African government. But neither the ANC nor the regime itself appears willing, let alone anxious, to have these negotiations, when they occur, be orchestrated in any way by non–South Africans. There will, both Mandela and de Klerk insist, be no Lancaster House conference for South Africa. The direct relevance of the 1988 accords for future political events in South Africa is therefore probably minimal. Nonetheless, the loss of enthusiastic Soviet support for the ANC's onetime armed struggle presumably did help nudge that organization to the negotiating table in 1990, much as international sanctions in the West have moved Pretoria itself toward genuine negotiations.

There is, finally, the question of the degree to which the present case confirms a general estimate—"model" may be too pretentious a word—of the impact of superpower collaboration on the Third World. At the outset one is forced to concede a considerable uniqueness to the case of Angola-Namibia, most noticeably the absence of symmetry between the roles of the two superpowers. The Soviets pressured Havana to agree to a negotiated settlement of the Angola conflict, including withdrawal of Cuban troops. But nothing comparable is known to have been required of the United States, either with respect to its renewed support of UNITA within Angola (though two years later even that at last appears to be ending), or regarding South Africa within the region. Rather than "wallets" or "muscle," Crocker writes that the United States provided diplomatic skills in the multilateral discussions leading up to the December 1988 accords.[60] In particular, the United States and South Africa succeeded in getting the Cubans out of Angola without apparently having to give any parallel undertakings to end their support for UNITA. The

Angola-Namibia settlement thus fell short of providing for a general regional settlement. In fact, in Angola the civil war has continued, at least through April 1991.

The last point seems to confirm Neil MacFarlane's finding that "superpower cooperation on Third World conflict does little to address the fundamental problems which conduce to conflictual behavior,"[61] though this was decidedly not true in 1988 concerning long-standing conflicts among Namibians, or for that matter among South Africans. However, there is no evidence as yet that the removal of Soviet influence from the subregion has served to rekindle enduring political divisions in the area that were somehow suppressed during the Cold War. The significance of the Angola-Namibia accords would appear to be a confirmation of the following proposition: Where global superpower competition has sustained conflicts and impeded their resolution, the end of that rivalry should provide the opposite effect.

There is one last point that would seem to modify this proposition. The ending of superpower rivalry in Southern Africa was not a straight-line development. Both Cuba and the Soviet Union actually increased their military support to the MPLA government during the second quarter of 1988 only shortly before beginning negotiations during the second half of that year. And it was this sequencing of divergent images that appears to have particularly influenced South African thinking, emphasizing first the *need* and then almost immediately the *opportunity* for an exit for Pretoria from the subregional imbroglio to which it had become party. All of this would seem to confirm Zartman's idea, cited earlier, of the necessity of there being both a "hurting stalement" *and* a perception of a "way out" if an international conflict such as the one we have considered is to be made "ripe for resolution." The specialness of the case we have described is that it appeared in the second half of 1988 to provide South Africa with both.

Notes

1. Michael Clough and Jeffrey Herbst, "South Africa's Changing Regional Strategy—Beyond Destabilization," *Critical Issues 1989*, no. 4 (New York: Council on Foreign Relations, 1989): 7.

2. Robert M. Price, "Pretoria's Southern African Strategy," *African Affairs* 83, no. 330 (January 1984): 21. For a discussion at some length of the "destabilization" policy, see Deon Geldenhuys, "The Destabilization Controversy: An Analysis of a High-Risk Foreign Policy Option for South Africa," *Conflict Studies*, no. 148 (1983): 11–26.

3. Chris Brown, "Regional Conflict in Southern Africa and the Role of Third Party Mediators," *International Journal* 45, no. 2 (Spring 1990): 343–344; "Survey South Africa," *The Economist*, 3 Nov. 1990, 22; Philip H.

Frankel, *Pretoria's Praetorians: Civil-Military Relations in South Africa* (Cambridge: Cambridge University Press, 1984), 72; *Race Relations Survey 1984*. (Johannesburg: SA Institute of Race Relations, 1985), 738.

4. Clough and Herbst, "South Africa's Changing Regional Strategy," 5. Pretoria's parallel wish for negotiations with the country's internal black opposition was not persuasive for yet another year and a half, if then—that is, until Nelson Mandela's release from the Victor Verster prison in early February 1990.

5. G. R. Berridge, "Diplomacy and the Angola/Namibia Accords," *International Affairs* 65, no. 3 (Autumn 1989): 467. Robert Jaster identifies two other meetings in this series, those listed in the chronology for August 24–26, 1988, and for November 22–24, 1988.

6. J. E. Spence, "A Deal for Southern Africa?" *The World Today* 45, no. 5 (May 1989): 80. The last of these points was an agreement between only Havana and Angola, Pretoria not being involved.

7. Brown, "Regional Conflict in Southern Africa and the Role of Third Party Mediators," 337, 349.

8. Chester A. Crocker, "Southern Africa: Eight Years Later," *Foreign Affairs* 68, no. 4 (Fall 1989): 155.

9. A "hurting stalemate" is a deadlock among adversaries, with high or rising costs, that offers all parties to it "no prospect of escape through escalation of the conflict." I. William Zartman, "Ripe Moment, Formula & Mediation" in Diane B. Bendahmane and John W. McDonald, Jr., eds., *Perspectives on Negotiation* (Washington, D.C.: Foreign Service Institute, Department of State, 1986), 21–22.

10. See for an example of this belief the papers appearing in John Seiler, ed., *Southern Africa Since the Portuguese Coup* (Boulder, Colo.: Westview Press, 1980).

11. Deon Geldenhuys, "South Africa's Regional Policy," in Michael Clough, ed., *Changing Realities in Southern Africa: Implications for American Policy* (Berkeley: Institute of International Studies, 1982), 134–135.

12. Ibid., 132.

13. Ibid., 139. See also Robin Hallett, "The South African Intervention in Angola 1975–76," *African Affairs* 77, no. 308 (July 1978): 356–357.

14. Oral commentary by Dr. Annette Seegers upon an earlier draft of this chapter delivered at a Brown University conference in April 1991. I am indebted to Dr. Seegers for this assistance and also for the similar help of Dr. Robert Jaster.

15. Price, "Pretoria's Southern African Strategy," 21; *Africa South of the Sahara, 1990* (London: Europa Publications, 1990), 985.

16. Robert Jaster, "The 1988 Peace Accords and the Future of Southwestern Africa," *Adelphi Paper 253* (London: International Institute for Strategic Studies, 1990), 14, 17.

17. Gerald J. Bender, "Peacemaking in Southern Africa: The Luanda-Pretoria Tug-of-War," *Third World Quarterly* 11, no. 2 (April 1989): 26.

18. Jaster, "The 1988 Peace Accords and the Future of Southwestern Africa," 17.

19. Ibid., 21.

20. Clough and Herbst, "South Africa's Changing Regional Strategy—Beyond Destabilization," 21. Jaster, in "The 1988 Peace Accords and the Future of Southwestern Africa," 18, estimates South African casualties at Cuito

Cuanavale to have been about 150. Clough and Herbst, "South Africa's Changing Regional Strategy—Beyond Destabilization," 21.

21. Bender, "Peacemaking in Southern Africa: The Luanda-Pretoria Tug-of-War," 29.

22. Clough and Herbst, "South Africa's Changing Regional Strategy—Beyond Destabilization," 21.

23. Michael Clough, ed., *Reassessing the Soviet Challenge in Africa* (Berkeley: Institute of International Studies, 1986), viii–ix.

24. Robin Hallett, "The South African Intervention in Angola 1975–76," *African Affairs* 77, no. 308 (July 1978): 356–357 (emphasis added).

25. I wrote of the existence of these perceptions in an article entitled "The Politics of Security: South Africa Under Verwoerd, 1961–66," *Journal of Modern African Studies* 7, no. 1 (April 1969): 3–20.

26. Hallett, "The South African Intervention in Angola 1975–76," 380; James Barber and John Barratt, *South Africa's Foreign Policy: The Search for Status and Security 1945–1988* (Cambridge: Cambridge University Press, 1990), 260.

27. Quoted in ibid., 253–254.

28. Deon Fourie, "The Climate of Security," in Gideon Jacobs, ed., *South Africa—The Road Ahead* (Johannesburg: Johnathan Ball, 1986), 188.

29. Seth Singleton, "The Natural Ally: Soviet Policy in Southern Africa," in Michael Clough, ed., *Changing Realities in Southern Africa: Implications for American Policy* (Berkeley: Institute of International Studies, 1982), 207.

30. Barber and Barratt, *South Africa's Foreign Policy: The Search for Status and Security 1945–1988*, 255.

31. South African Institute of Race Relations, *Survey of Race Relations in South Africa, 1980* (Johannesburg: SA Institute of Race Relations, 1981), 10.

32. Price, "Pretoria's Southern African Strategy," 16.

33. For citations, see Brown, "Regional Conflict in Southern Africa and the Role of Third Party Mediators," 335, 353–354, 358–359.

34. Jaster, "The 1988 Peace Accords and the Future of Southwestern Africa," 18. P. W. Botha was prime minister of South Africa from 1978 to 1983 and president of the country from 1983 to 1988. The title of his position was changed by constitutional amendment in 1984.

35. Spence, "A Deal for Southern Africa?" 80.

36. Berridge, "Diplomacy and the Angola/Namibia Accords," 465.

37. Klaus Freiherr von der Ropp, "Peace Initiatives in South West Africa," *Aussenpolitik* 11 (1989): 188.

38. Brown, "Regional Conflict in Southern Africa and the Role of Third Party Mediators," 356.

39. Price, "Pretoria's Southern Africa Strategy," 12.

40. Charles W. Freeman, Jr., "The Angola/Namibia Accords," *Foreign Affairs* 68, no. 3 (Summer 1989): 130.

41. Ibid., 130–131.

42. Berridge, "Diplomacy and the Angola/Namibia Accords," 464, 470.

43. Chris Maritz, "Pretoria's Reaction to the Role of Moscow and Peking in Southern Africa, *Journal of Modern African Studies* 25, no. 2 (1987): 328.

44. Daniel R. Kempton, "New Thinking and Soviet Policy Towards South Africa," *Journal of Modern African Studies* 28, no. 4 (December 1990): 549.

45. von der Ropp, "Peace Initiatives in South West Africa," 189.

46. Kempton, "New Thinking and Soviet Policy Towards South Africa," 549.

47. Philip Nel, "The Earnestness of Being Unimportant," *Leadership* 7, no. 4 (1988): 26.

48. Freeman, "The Angola/Namibia Accords," 134–135.

49. Stephen Larrabee, "Lessons for the USSR and the USA in the Third World," *International Affairs* (June 1990): 29.

50. Freeman, "The Anglo/Namibia Accords," 135.

51. Crocker, "Southern Africa: Eight Years Later," 153.

52. Berridge, "Diplomacy and the Angola/Namibia Accords," 466.

53. Spence, "A Deal for Southern Africa?" 80.

54. von der Ropp, "Peace Initiatives in South West Africa," 186.

55. Chester A. Crocker, "Southern African Peace-making," *Survival* 32, no. 3 (May/June 1990): 221–232.

56. Crocker, "Southern Africa: Eight Years Later," 147.

57. Brown, "Regional Conflict in Southern Africa and the Role of Third Party Mediators," 358.

58. Chester A. Crocker, "South Africa: Strategy for Change," *Foreign Affairs* 59, no. 2 (Winter 1980/1981): 323–351.

59. Crocker, "Southern Africa: Eight Years Later," p. 153.

60. Ibid., 1.

61. Neil S. MacFarlane, "Superpower Collaboration: The Impact on the Third World," in Thomas G. Weiss and Meryl A. Kessler, eds. *Superpowers and Third World Conflict in the Post–Cold War Era*, (Boulder, Colo.: Lynne Rienner, 1991).

■ Part 3 ■
Third Parties and
Conflict Resolution

■ 5 ■

Conflict Management
in the Caribbean Basin

WAYNE S. SMITH

The world revolution, and with it the Cold War, are over. In the resulting dramatically changed circumstances, the two superpowers, rather than fueling regional conflicts, will more often than not find it in their interests to work together to defuse or resolve them. In many cases, this working together may even involve agreements stipulating restraint on both sides, and in almost all cases it will reduce the likelihood of superpower intervention.

The region likely to be the least affected by these developments is the Caribbean Basin, the oldest and most central US sphere of influence. Here the Monroe Doctrine lives on as a unilateral policy statement. The United States will not hesitate to demand Soviet restraint and outright concessions in the region, but it will be most reluctant to enter into any agreement or take any other step that could be interpreted as legitimizing a Soviet presence in the area. It will be even more reluctant to tie its own hands; rather, for the foreseeable future, the United States will want to retain the full flexibility to intervene in the area if it believes intervention is necessary, with or without the approval of the UN or the OAS.

The Concept of Strategic Denial

Not at any other time in this century has the world seen such hopeful change as that opened up by the end of the Cold War. For US policy in Latin America—and most especially in the Caribbean Basin—the implications of that change go far beyond the Cold War, and even beyond this century, for the two governing assumptions for US policy in the region date back almost to the beginnings of the republic. For some two hundred years, the first and most basic of these assumptions has been what Lars Schoultz of the University of North Carolina has called the imperative for strategic denial.[1] Simply put, this concept flowed from the historical observation of US leaders that while no other state in the Western Hemisphere was powerful enough to threaten the security of the United States, their very weakness rendered them vulnerable to the penetration and control of other great powers. Americans had a deeply ingrained appreciation of the advantages of insularity. From the earliest days of the republic, the Atlantic Ocean stood between the United States and those who would do it harm. Then, as it became a continental power with two seaboards, two great oceans protected it. The one danger was that potential enemies might overcome or avoid those natural barriers by taking advantage of the weakness of the states to the south to position themselves close under US guns. Thus, one of the earliest and most enduring US objectives in Latin America—and most particularly the Caribbean Basin—has been to keep other powers out.

Initially, two European powers were already positioned to the south: Spain and Portugal. Portugal was never viewed as capable of mounting a military threat. By the early nineteenth century, the Spanish Empire was in decline, giving the United States little reason for concern. Precisely for that reason, the United States made it clear on several occasions that it would not accept the transfer of Spanish territory to other European powers. For example, in 1811 the US Congress passed the No-Transfer Resolution, which applied to the Floridas. In 1825, Secretary of State Henry Clay asserted that "we could not consent to the occupation of those islands [Cuba and Puerto Rico] by any European power other than Spain under any contingency whatever."[2]

Strategic denial is also reflected in the great US shibboleth of the Monroe Doctrine. One need only examine President James Monroe's words to confirm this: "We owe it, therefore, to candor and to the amicable relations existing between the United States and those powers," he warned the European states in 1823, "to declare that we should consider any attempt on their part to extend their system to any portion of this hemisphere as dangerous to our peace and safety."[3]

Monroe was not concerned with the deleterious implications that European encroachment might have for the Latin American states; rather, he concentrated on the threat that encroachment might pose to the peace and security of the United States itself. After 1803, this concern of US leaders was most sharply centered in the Caribbean Basin. With the Louisiana Purchase of that year, the United States acquired the immense territory that emptied through the Mississippi River into the Gulf of Mexico, and the port of New Orleans became the US interior's window on the rest of the world. Control of the Gulf, and of the Caribbean, through which the Gulf sea-lanes fed, was therefore perceived to be a vital need.

The importance of the Caribbean Basin was further enhanced in the middle of the nineteenth century with the discovery of gold in the recently acquired California. The Central American isthmus quickly became the indispensable link between the two US seaboards, which the United States could not afford to see under the domination of any other power. The linkage took on new and more dramatic dimensions with the construction of the Panama Canal. Thus, by early in the twentieth century, control of the Caribbean Basin, which guarded both the entrance to the Gulf and access routes to Panama, was perceived as one of the greatest priorities of US foreign policy.

During the years immediately after the enunciation of the Monroe Doctrine, the United States did not have the military capability to exclude other powers at will from the Caribbean Basin. Except for the irritating presence of the British on Nicaragua's Mosquito Coast, there were few serious challenges to the doctrine during that period. But by mid-century, newly emerged from its war with Mexico and now a continental power, the United States was prepared to assert itself in defense of the doctrine. Thus, when Spain briefly reannexed Santo Domingo in 1862, the United States, describing the act as a violation of the Monroe Doctrine, warned Spain to withdraw. The United States was soon caught up in its own civil war and did not immediately follow up with military action; however, the marker had been put down. Thus, in 1865, facing a popular uprising and realizing that the United States would soon be in a position to use military force, Spain withdrew. Indeed, in 1864 when Spain, in a dispute with Peru, temporarily seized the Chincha Islands off that country's coast, the usual US protest had been answered not only with Spanish assurances that it had no intention of holding the islands, but also acknowledgment that it recognized and would respect the Monroe Doctrine. As far as is known, this was the first European acceptance of the doctrine.[4]

A more serious affront began in 1862, when Napoleon III of France intervened in Mexico and in 1864 imposed Archduke Maximilian, brother of Emperor Franz Josef of Austria, on a Mexican throne of Napoleon's creation. This act was a clear and blatant violation of the doctrine. As the intervention began, the United States was embroiled in its civil war. By 1866, however, it was free to turn its attention to the French puppet state in Mexico—with a huge Union army ready to move to the frontier, as the US minister in Paris pointed out to Napoleon III. The French immediately acceded to US demands and by 1867 all French troops had been withdrawn. The unlucky Maximilian, choosing to remain, was soon captured and shot by Mexican forces under Benito Juárez.

The Monroe Doctrine was enforced again in 1895 when Great Britain and Venezuela were in dispute over the border between that country and British Guiana. The United States insisted that it would study the two claims and itself appoint a commission to decide where the border lay. President Grover Cleveland made it clear that he was prepared to go to war if Great Britain refused. It did not. Indeed, most Englishmen seemed to regard what amounted to US arbitration as a welcome way out of a nettlesome situation.[5]

Having sensed in the Venezuelan case that it now had the upper hand, the United States moved to rid itself of the Clayton-Bulwer Treaty of 1850, a document which had stipulated, among other things, that a canal built across the isthmus would be jointly constructed and controlled by Great Britain and the United States. Many in the United States regarded the treaty as an infringement of the Monroe Doctrine and as an embarrassing reminder of past US weakness—a reminder that needed to be wiped away. Certainly the United States was no longer weak. On the contrary, it had emerged in 1898 from war with Spain as a recognized world power. The United States was unwilling, therefore, to share a canal or anything else in the region with Great Britain. Accordingly, the United States negotiated a new agreement, the Hay-Pauncefote Treaty of 1890, abrogating the Clayton-Bulwer Treaty and signaling the unquestioned preeminence in the region of the United States.

Now firmly in command, the United States began to react not just to actual foreign interventions but to situations that might invite such incursions. For example, if a country covered by the doctrine did not pay its debts to Germany, for example, it might find itself pressured by the United States to do so, lest nonpayment invite German intervention. This new dimension was formalized in 1904, when President Theodore Roosevelt enunciated what came to be called the Roosevelt corollary to the Monroe Doctrine: because the United States would not permit outside powers to intervene to redress wrongdoing in the region, it had the responsibility to step in itself to set things right.

The United States wasted no time in taking up its new duties as regional police. The United States intervened in the Dominican Republic in 1905 and in Nicaragua in 1912 and 1915 to establish customs collection operations to pay off those countries' debts to several European creditors. During the early years of the century, in fact, the United States landed troops in the area no fewer than 14 times. By 1927, US domination of Central America was so nearly total that Under Secretary of State Robert Olds could say, "Central America has always understood that governments we recognize and support stay in power, while those we do not recognize and support fall."[6]

The Drive for Hegemony

The Monroe Doctrine was a direct assertion of hegemony and led to the second assumption that has long guided US policy: the conviction that as the preordained regional hegemon whose flag would probably one day fly from the Bering Straits to Tierra del Fuego, the United States had the right to arrange things in Latin America to suit its own purposes. What the countries of the region thought of this was of little consequence. Thus, in 1848 the United States absorbed half of Mexico's territory. A few years later, it gave unofficial sympathy and support and, finally, official recognition to William Walker in his filibustering expeditions in Central America. As the twentieth century began, it took Puerto Rico and turned Cuba into a virtual protectorate. And, taking quick advantage of the Hay-Pauncefote Treaty, it engineered Panama's separation from Colombia in the early 1900s and immediately acquired rights to build a canal across the newly created state.

President John Quincy Adams had predicted in 1819 that the United States would absorb all the lands to the south. This, he said, was as certain as the fact "that the Mississippi flows to the sea."[7]

The cost of absorbing so large an area against the wishes of its inhabitants, however, was simply too high. Further, by the end of the nineteenth century it was clear to most US leaders that actual sovereignty over the area to the south was of little importance. What counted was the ability to exercise control when necessary, and, of course, to deny the area to other powers. Secretary of State Richard Olney was confident enough of US capabilities to do both that in 1895 he declared openly that the United States "is practically sovereign on this continent, and its fiat is law upon the subjects to which it confines its interposition."[8]

Olney's statement and others like it exaggerated the degree of control actually enjoyed by the United States. It may never have been "practically sovereign" in this hemisphere (though it came close in the Caribbean Basin). As the century turned, nonetheless, most Americans believed that in the rightful order of things their country enjoyed and had a duty to exercise certain hegemonic rights.

The Good Neighbor Policy

Near the end of the 1920s, the role of regional police began to clash with a growing idealism in the United States. Certainly many Americans had qualms about the continued occupation of a number of countries against the clear wishes of their citizens. This was especially so in Nicaragua, where a fiercely nationalist leader, General Augusto Sandino, fought US marines from 1927 until 1932, eventually winning the grudging admiration not only of many US citizens but of the marine officers themselves.

In any event, the pendulum began to swing against interventionism.

During the presidency of Herbert Hoover (1929–1933), marines were withdrawn from every country except Haiti. Deploring the whole concept of intervention, Hoover ordered a review of its historical and legal underpinning. The response in 1930 was the now-famous Clark memorandum, a study authored by Under Secretary of State J. Reuben Clark, which held that in fact the Monroe Doctrine had never given the United States the right to intervene anywhere in Latin America. Mindful of the need for strategic denial, Clark noted that there might be cases in which the United States must intervene to protect itself, but it could not claim to do so under the umbrella of the Monroe Doctrine.[9] The Clark memorandum left the Roosevelt corollary null and void and cast doubt on the legitimacy and even the wisdom of the military interventions carried out under its mandate.

President Franklin Delano Roosevelt continued the trend begun by Hoover. Calling for a Good Neighbor Policy, he stressed strong economic ties rather than political domination, and he favored collective security over unilateral actions by the United States. At the 1933 Pan-American Conference in Montevideo, Uruguay, he pledged the United States to abide by a resolution prohibiting the intervention of one state in the affairs of another. In 1934, the last marines left Haiti. Neither Roosevelt nor Harry S Truman again dispatched troops to any Latin American country. In fact, the United States did not again unilaterally send troops into any Latin American country until President George Bush ordered the invasion of Panama in December 1989.

Roosevelt encouraged hemispheric collective security during World War II. In 1947, under President Truman, the Rio Pact made defense of the Western Hemisphere the responsibility of all member states. This was followed in 1948 by the creation of the OAS, which provided for the adjudication of disputes among members and for collective peacekeeping measures. It became the joint responsibility of all members to prevent the intervention of foreign powers. The intention, as noted by US political leaders and scholars at the time, was to render the Monroe Doctrine multilateral.[10]

The intention did not prevail. Initial indications that the United States would commit itself without reservations to the charter of the OAS were taken as encouraging signs that it no longer saw itself as "practically sovereign" on the continent or held itself above the law. But even as the OAS was being formed, the Cold War was growing in intensity. The concept of strategic denial took on a new and more passionate dimension as the United States sought to exclude the Soviet Union from the region. Excluding France and Great Britain had been a strategic need. Excluding the Soviet Union was more on the order of a religious crusade.

To his credit, President Truman resisted the temptation to go to extremes in his efforts to block Moscow abroad, just as he tried to restrain the hysteria of McCarthyism at home. He refused to intervene in Guatemala, where a nationalist revolutionary government had come to power in 1944—a government that, among other things, had permitted the open organization of a Communist Party and announced an agrarian reform to nationalize lands belonging to the United Fruit Company. Truman also refused to suggest the incorporation of an anticommunist resolution in either the Rio Pact or the charter of the OAS, pointing out that this might simply be used by dictatorial governments to suppress any opposition at all.[11]

The Cold War Years

Truman's moderation was undone by the Eisenhower administration and Secretary of State John Foster Dulles, who brought the Cold War to Latin America with a vengeance. In 1954, he flew to Caracas, Venezuela, to attend the Tenth Inter-American Conference and promoted a resolution declaring that the domination by international communism of hemispheric political institutions was incompatible with the inter-American system, exactly what Truman had resisted. What the United States intended, Dulles explained to other members of the Eisenhower administration, was to extend the Monroe Doctrine "to include the concept of outlawing foreign ideologies in the American Republics."[12]

This was an unprecedented expansion of President Monroe's message that had warned the European powers against attempts to extend their systems to this hemisphere. He made no pretense of outlawing extrahemispheric ideas, or even ideologies, so long as their adoption was not linked to the projection into the hemisphere of some European power's political or military sway. The United States objected to a French-imposed monarchy in Mexico in the 1860s but would probably not have protested an indigenous one. The United States did not protest the existence of the Brazilian monarchy (1822–1889). The Monroe Doctrine aimed to prevent extrahemispheric powers from seizing control or otherwise gaining some strategic position. The United States did not repudiate adaptation by hemispheric governments of foreign political ideas per se or even to alternative systems of government.

Latin Americans had grave reservations about the Dulles resolution, but US economic leverage won out. The anticommunist resolution was adopted in Caracas, and Dulles's interpretation of the Monroe Doctrine gained some credence at home. Dulles advanced the idea that with the commitment of the members of the OAS to stand united against communism, the Monroe Doctrine had indeed become a multilateral instrument.[13]

The United States did not, however, choose to work through the OAS, or even multilaterally, in addressing problems in Guatemala. Shortly after the Caracas conference, Dulles and his brother Allen, director of the CIA, engineered the overthrow of Guatemala's president Jacobo Arbenz, whom Dulles insisted was a communist. Arbenz was in fact an army officer who did not have a single Communist Party member in his cabinet. Only four party members served even in the national legislature. Arbenz had accepted communist support in his agrarian reform program and listened to the advice of several key Communist Party leaders who were experts in that field, but his government was never remotely communist in nature. This was a nationalist revolution, not one engineered in Moscow. On the contrary, the Soviets made no effort to position themselves in Guatemala or even take advantage of Arbenz's progressive attitudes. They sent no advisors, no economic or military aid; they never even opened an embassy. Members of the Guatemalan Communist Party begged Moscow at least to establish a consulate, but Moscow was not sufficiently interested to do even that.

None of this mattered in the slightest. Arbenz was tolerant of the communists, which to John Foster Dulles was unacceptable. US actions in Guatemala went beyond preventing an extrahemispheric power from positioning itself in the area, as envisaged by the Monroe Doctrine. Prevention was unnecessary because Moscow had made no effort whatsoever to move into Guatemala. US actions also went beyond even Dulles's anticommunist resolution. No one had adopted the communist system in Guatemala, and there was no evidence that the Arbenz government had any intention of doing so. Perhaps there was a communist idea or two implicit in the agrarian reform law. That apparently was enough.

The unilateral intervention in Guatemala set a pattern. The United States would work through the OAS when it sensed that the other members were amenable to its security needs. If, however, the other members were reluctant to use force or if working through the OAS seemed inconvenient, the United States would act alone. As it had reacted in Guatemala in 1954, so would it react at the Bay of Pigs in 1961; in Chile in 1973, when the CIA helped engineer the overthrow of President Salvador Allende; and in Nicaragua in the 1980s, with the contra war against the Sandinista government. In short, the Monroe Doctrine had not been multilateralized at all. The United States still decided for itself when and how to intervene.

During the Cold War, strategic denial had one focus: the Soviet Union. "The Russians are coming" was the cry, and all US efforts were aimed at stopping them. Virtually everything Washington did in Latin America between 1945 and 1985 was geared to its rivalry with the Soviet Union. Any new proposal put forward had to be justified in terms of its relevance to that rivalry. If the State Department desk officer for, say, Ecuador, wished to argue for a new economic assistance program or new terms of trade, he had to demonstrate how the innovation would contribute to the overall effort against Soviet penetration—if only by arguing that if the United States did not provide the assistance, the Soviets might.

Not all the US Cold War initiatives in Latin America were punitive. During the administration of President John F. Kennedy, a program of economic assistance on a hemispheric scale, called the Alliance for Progress, was introduced, avowedly to deny Moscow targets of opportunity by furthering the development of healthy societies and economies. It accomplished little, but its methods were at least constructive and its objectives honorable.

The same could not be said of CIA operations in Guatemala in 1954, in Cuba in 1961, or in Nicaragua during the 1980s. As a result of the latter, the United States was for the first time in its history condemned by the World Court for illegally mining Nicaraguan harbors.

These operations were, however, at least indirect, and supposedly clandestine. From 1934 to 1965, the United States did not intervene in any country with its own troops. In 1965, President Lyndon B. Johnson sent troops into the Dominican Republic, allegedly to prevent a communist takeover. No evidence was ever produced that a takeover was indeed imminent—or even planned. Rather, Johnson would seem to have reacted more on the basis of the Cold War atmosphere than in response to hard evidence and careful analysis.

On the other hand, Johnson did at least go through the motions of consulting with the OAS and securing its endorsement for outside forces to maintain order. Several OAS members even provided troops. The facade was thin, but technically this was not a unilateral intervention; it was one carried out under the aegis of the OAS.

President Ronald Reagan's invasion of Grenada in 1983 was also carried out under a multilateral umbrella, though the facade was even thinner. In this case, the countries of the eastern Caribbean supposedly asked the United States for assistance in addressing a Soviet-Cuban–inspired threat to their security articulated through the revolutionary government in Grenada. And the British governor-general had allegedly invited the United States to send in troops. However, the Caribbean countries had been consulted only after the United States had already decided to invade, and the governor-general's "invitation" had come two days after the troops were ashore. Even Prime Minister Margaret Thatcher of Great Britain, normally a strong supporter of almost anything Reagan did, condemned the invasion, as did most other governments. The Reagan administration's drummed-up international support fooled no one outside the United States, but it did at least show some concern for legal niceties and for international public opinion. Even so, the invasion was condemned by the OAS, which had not been consulted.

The Case of Cuba

All these interventions and clandestine operations were presented by the United States as responses to Soviet challenges to US national security. In fact, some were not East-West conflicts. The situation in Guatemala in 1954 certainly was not, nor that in the Dominican Republic in 1965. With the exception of the 1962 missile crisis, in no case was there any serious threat to US security. The Reagan administration's efforts to paint Grenada as a threat were little short of absurd. Without amphibious or sea-lift capacity, its tiny army could not be brought to bear against even its closest neighbors. And as to the airfield Reagan warned so much of, it was being constructed at the suggestion of the United Nations with a view to the expansion of tourism. British firms were participating in its construction, and it was wide open to tourists and anyone else who wished to roam about taking pictures—a strange way to proceed, surely, had it been the secret military facility portrayed by Reagan. Significantly, after the invasion, the new government continued its construction, now with the help of the United States.

Nicaragua was hardly more of a threat. Without an air force or a navy, it had no means of striking the Panama Canal, or nearby sea-lanes, let alone the United States. Its large army was an obvious worry to its neighbors, although it offered to sign regional treaties providing for the reduction of armed forces on all sides and halting arms shipments to irregular forces, both subject to stringent verification procedures. The United States consistently opposed these treaties and continued the contra war, thus suggesting that it was more determined to topple the Sandinistas than to address any potential threat they might pose. As to any Soviet threat through Nicaragua, there were no Soviet bases, missiles, or submarines operating out of Nicaraguan ports or long-range aircraft operating from Nicaraguan airfields. Nicaragua also gave assurances on several occasions that there would be none, and it was willing to sign formal agreements to that effect. The United States ignored the offers.

Cuba, then, was the single case in which the Soviet Union presented a threat to the United States itself and to neighboring states. It has been said that Castro's relationship with the Soviet Union violated the Monroe Doctrine. His adoption of Marxism/Leninism did not, but it did violate

John Foster Dulles's interpretation of the doctrine. On the other hand, the growing Soviet-Cuban military alliance and the introduction of Soviet missiles in 1962 were close to a direct infringement of the doctrine's intent to prevent any other power from mounting a military threat to the United States from nearby areas to the south. Once threatened, the United States reacted strongly and effectively, with President Kennedy declaring a naval blockade of Cuba and demanding that the missiles be withdrawn. The crisis was defused by an understanding between Kennedy and Khrushchev that both sides have subsequently respected. Under the terms of this understanding, the Soviet Union cannot reposition offensive weaponry in Cuba, and the United States is pledged not to invade Cuba.

The Kennedy-Khrushchev understanding effectively eliminated any security threat to the United States from Cuba. Even so, the bitter global rivalry between Moscow and Washington dictated that the alliance between Cuba and the Soviet Union remained a concern to US leaders, who analyzed Cuban initiatives and policies in terms of how they might advance the cause of the Soviet Union.

The End of the Cold War

But the Cold War is now over. The fear of a threat to US security mounted through Cuba or through any other country in the Caribbean Basin can be put aside. Moscow has no further interest in mounting such a threat, and Havana, even if it had the wish, does not have the capability.

Not only is the Cold War over, but the concept of strategic denial itself has become, after almost two centuries, obsolete. The other superpower is out of contention and there is no other power on earth with reason and capability to threaten the security of the United States by intervening in Latin America. Japan, the European Community, and the People's Republic of China compete economically, but they have nothing to gain from strategic thrusts in the area.

For the first time since the United States became a nation, the inherent security concerns that gave rise to the Monroe Doctrine and to the deep-seated impulse to control the areas to its south have dissipated. Is it possible, then, that the United States will begin to move beyond the mind-set of the Monroe Doctrine? Will it, for example, become more disposed to cooperate with the Soviet Union in the prevention or resolution of conflicts in the area, or will its focus remain exclusion of the other superpower from the region? Even more basically, can it overcome its own instincts toward hegemony? With no need to exercise even minimal control over the countries to its south, is it in a position to commit itself fully to rule of law, to respect scrupulously the sovereignty of its neighbors, and to conduct its policies strictly within the precepts of the charters of the UN and of the OAS? Is it, in other words, willing to place clear limits on its own actions in the Caribbean Basin?

Cooperation with the Soviet Union?

While it would of course be premature to draw any conclusions about long-term US response, the evidence indicates no willingness to negotiate with the Soviet Union on security issues in the Caribbean Basin under the Reagan administration, and very little under President George Bush.

For its part, the Reagan administration began by blaming the turmoil in Central America squarely on the Soviet Union. Even before taking office, Reagan told the *Wall Street Journal* that "the Soviet Union is behind all the unrest that is going on. If they weren't engaged in this game of dominoes, there wouldn't be any hot spots in the world."[14] The Santa Fe Committee Report of 1980, on which so much of the Reagan administration's early Latin America policy was based, had asserted that "Latin America . . . is being penetrated by Soviet power. . . . The Soviet Union is now ensconced in force in the Western Hemisphere."[15]

The republics of the Caribbean Basin, said the report, faced "the dedicated, irresponsible activity of a Soviet-backed Cuba to win ultimately total hegemon."[16] Secretary of State Alexander Haig picked up where the Santa Fe Committee Report left off by accusing Moscow of "being responsible for international terrorism." What Washington faced in Central America, according to Haig, was nothing less than "Soviet expansionism" aided by Moscow's Caribbean surrogate, Cuba.[17]

These assertions represented the administration's call to arms. It was the mind-set behind them that led to supporting the contras and then to circumventing Congress and defying the World Court to keep it going. Whether the administration really believed its own alarmist rhetoric or simply used it to justify the hard-line policy is moot. It put them forward as its rationale and then acted on them. Perhaps the president was simply trying to reverse the so-called Vietnam syndrome by intervening on the cheap. The US people had to assume their president meant it when in 1986 he warned that unless we aided the contras, "the Soviets and Cubans can become the dominant power in the crucial corridor between North and South America." These two powers, he went on, intended to "threaten the Panama Canal, interdict our vital sealanes, and ultimately, to move against Mexico."[18]

There was never evidence of any such Soviet blueprint for conquest. The unrest in Central America stemmed from economic underdevelopment, political instability, and social injustice, not from external aggression. The Soviets and Cubans had their own friends and allies in the region and doubtless wished to see an outcome different from that preferred by the United States. To suggest, however, that it was Moscow and Havana that had unleashed the conflict as a plan for hemispheric conquest was a gross exaggeration. Further, despite its insistence that the root of the problem was Soviet expansionism, the Reagan administration was rigidly opposed to negotiations that involved the Soviets or Cubans.

The administration's reaction to the first Contadora draft agreements is a case in point. The United States had accused the Soviet Union of fueling a military buildup in Nicaragua, of supplying arms to the guerrillas in El Salvador, and of intending to position sophisticated weaponry in Central America—weaponry, it claimed, that could threaten the Panama Canal and even the United States. The Contadora agreements of 1984 addressed these concerns. They would have limited the size of armies in Central America, sent home all the foreign military advisors, prohibited foreign military bases as well as the importation of sophisticated weaponry, and halted cross-border support for guerrilla groups operating in any country in the region. Given US concerns about Soviet and Cuban involvement, the Contadora negotiators feared the draft agreements would be unacceptable to the United States without some device to preclude that involvement. Hence, a protocol was added to the original draft under which extraregional powers were to commit themselves to adhere strictly to all the provisions of the agreements. This would have had the result of prohibiting Soviet bases, sophisticated weaponry, supply of arms to guerrillas, and dangerous military buildups.

The Contadora negotiators thought that they were responding to Washington's concerns, so they were surprised when one of the points the Reagan administration rejected was inclusion of the protocol. The United States, said Washington, would not accept any document that might be signed by Moscow and Havana because to so include those two powers in the diplomatic process would be tantamount to confirming for them a political role in Central America.[19]

The idea of a protocol was abandoned. Even so, the administration never accepted the Contadora agreements—neither the draft put forward in 1984 nor any subsequent version. It also continued to eschew anything that smacked of negotiations with the Soviet Union. During the December 1987 summit conference in Washington, Reagan failed to respond to General Secretary Mikhail Gorbachev's suggestion that the two sides show mutual restraint on military shipments.[20] According to subsequent clarifications by Soviet officials, what Gorbachev proposed was an agreement between the two superpowers that would lead to the eventual transformation of Central America into a demilitarized zone.[21] Foreign

Minister Eduard A. Shevardnadze raised the question of mutual restraint again during his March 1988 visit to Washington.

One can understand why the idea of mutually halting all military assistance was unacceptable to the United States. With the civil war continuing in El Salvador, the United States wished to retain the flexibility to continue military assistance there. But might it not have been possible to work out useful mutual reductions? If Washington were indeed so concerned with Soviet military involvement in Central America, surely it might have found ways to take advantage of the Gorbachev-Shevardnadze overtures. Moscow was suggesting that the two superpowers support the new Central American peace plan (launched in June 1987 by President Oscar Arias of Costa Rica) by agreeing to limit mutually their arms shipments to the region. Did the Reagan administration not even wish to explore the possibilities?

Washington was certain it could topple the Sandinistas through the indirect use of force. It had no interest in a negotiated settlement, and especially not in one that might have appeared to acquiesce to a Soviet role. The only response was to label the Soviet proposal ludicrous. As one State Department officer put it, "Neither reciprocity nor mutuality has any place here. This is our backyard. The Soviets must halt their military assistance to Nicaragua, but we aren't going to halt our own to the other Central American countries."[22]

Despite US recalcitrance, the Soviet Union unilaterally suspended any major shipments of military equipment to Nicaragua in 1988. Even so, the Bush administration's attitude toward negotiations, like Reagan's, was suspicious of the Central American peace plan and determined to exclude the Soviets from any but bilateral talks, at which US diplomats demanded unilateral concessions of their Soviet counterparts. It made virtue of necessity in 1989 by postponing any further request for military aid to the contras because Congress would have refused. On February 14, 1989, the five Central American presidents met and agreed to a scenario in which Nicaragua would advance the date of its elections and permit international monitoring of its respect for human rights and democratic processes in return for the near-term demobilization of the contras; the Bush administration expressed only deep reservations. Vice-President Dan Quayle, for example, described the new agreement as nothing more than a ruse to keep Nicaragua under a Marxist/Leninist dictatorship.[23]

In contrast, the Soviet Union was quick to issue a statement applauding the Central American agreement. In referring to the Arias plan's call on all outside powers to halt assistance to irregular forces in the area, the Soviet statement repeated assurances that the Soviet Union had not given and would not give such aid to those forces.[24]

Notwithstanding its own virtual embargo on arms shipments to the area, Moscow kept hammering away at the idea that the only way to reach a lasting solution was through multilateral negotiations. During Gorbachev's April 1989 visit to Havana, he publicly called for such a process to work out phased, reciprocal arms reductions. As Georgi Shakhnazarov, one of his foreign policy advisors, put it, cuts in military aid "should be addressed in a package, across the board, in negotiations where we can reach agreements to reduce the overall military presence." He stressed, however, that "military assistance cannot be resolved on a unilateral basis."[25]

To US complaints that despite Soviet reductions, overall Soviet bloc shipments to Nicaragua, principally from Cuba, continued apace, the Soviets noted that they could undertake no commitment for the Cubans. If the United States were concerned over Cuban actions in Nicaragua, it should talk directly to the Cubans. "That," said a Soviet diplomat in Washington, "was precisely one of the reasons multilateral talks were needed."[26]

For its part, Havana had already sent a clear message to Washington that it was prepared to sit down and discuss such issues as outside arms supply to Central America in the same constructive way the talks on Southern Africa had been conducted—talks that resulted in December 1988 in a tripartite agreement under which, among other things, Cuban troops began to withdraw from Angola.[27]

In late 1989, moreover, the Cubans indicated that they would be guided by the wishes of the Sandinistas in suspending military shipments to Nicaragua in the period prior to the elections. Beyond that, Cuban officials stressed that while they considered it a duty to help Nicaragua meet its defense needs as long as necessary, they were perfectly prepared to help work out security arrangements in Central America satisfactory to all sides. As a Cuban Foreign Ministry official summed it up in November 1989, "We have indicated to the U.S. our willingness to hold substantive discussions of the arms-supply question, but we have received no reply from the Bush Administration."[28]

Nor did they ever receive one. There was a new flurry of accusations against Cuba and the Soviet Union in November 1989 when a light plane crashed in El Salvador and was found to be carrying surface-to-air missiles from Nicaragua. The missiles, however, had not been manufactured in the Soviet Union and in any event had been received by the Sandinista army weeks before that year's guerrilla offensive in El Salvador and weeks before the Cuban overture mentioned previously.

The Bush administration has consistently rejected the idea of negotiations with the Soviet Union, either by saying that the United States does not negotiate things in its backyard or by maintaining that the Soviets have no legitimate security interests in the area whereas the

United States does.[29] It has, to be sure, talked to the Soviets, but always to demand concessions—for instance, that they halt military shipments to Nicaragua, that they force the Cubans to halt shipments anywhere in Central America, and that they cut off all assistance to Cuba itself. Never has it been a matter of sitting down to work out some form of cooperative effort to resolve conflicts. Rarely have any quid pro quos even been on the table.

Certainly the negotiated settlement in Nicaragua culminating in elections there in February 1990 was not the result of some deal between the two superpowers, or even of a cooperative effort on their part. The credit for the settlement must go to the Central Americans themselves. The United States opposed it almost to the last moment. Finally, after so much momentum had built up toward elections, it saw its way clear to urge the contras to abide by the terms set forth in the Central American plan. The Soviets, who had from the beginning supported the Central American plan, urged the Sandinistas to accept it.

This was far from being a resolution made in Washington and Moscow.[30] Nonetheless, there was no clash of interests between the two to wreck the plan, and both Assistant Secretary of State Bernard Aronson and his Soviet counterpart, the director of the Latin American department of the Soviet Foreign Ministry—first Yuri Pavlov, then, beginning in mid-1990, Valery Nikolayenko—seemed to find their periodic "talks" useful. To the extent that this suggests some positive change, it is welcome. We are, however, a long way from US-Soviet cooperation in problem solving in the Caribbean Basin.

Perhaps nowhere is the lack of collaboration more apparent than in Cuba. The United States has flatly rejected any improvement in relations with Cuba and refuses even to begin a negotiating process to address the disagreements between the two countries. It insists that the Soviet Union should halt its assistance to Cuba—especially military assistance[31]—but it offers to take no conciliatory steps of its own.

The Soviet Union, on the other hand, emphasizes that this is a two-way street. They will not abandon Cuba, they say, so long as it is threatened by the United States. As Nikolayenko stated in November 1990, "The nature and scope of our military assistance to Havana will depend on the degree to which this threat will decrease, on whether the normalization of Cuban-American relations will begin."[32]

The United States seems to understand that Cuba no longer constitutes any kind of security threat, and even that its foreign policy is no longer of particular concern. In the past, foreign policy issues were always at the head of the list of conditions put forward for more normal relations with Cuba—led by the demand that Cuba reduce its ties with the Soviet Union. But Cuban troops are already out of Africa,

Cuba's involvement in Central America is not of crucial importance, and its links to the Soviet Union no longer pose any threat to US national security. Hence, the latest set of condition for improving ties, enunciated by Bush in March 1990, do not even mention foreign policy issues or Cuba's ties to the Soviet Union; rather, what is now demanded is that Cuba give up its present politico-economic system and adopt a market economy.[33]

This goes beyond even the needs of the Monroe Doctrine. It would seem to harken back to the earlier hegemonic instinct to insist on internal arrangements in the countries to our south that suit the tastes and purposes of the United States. Given the dramatic changes in the world around it, Cuba will almost certainly undergo change also, probably gradually moving from the Marxist/Leninist state it is today to a social democracy. It could make the transition more smoothly, however, if US policy toward the island were to reflect the end of the Cold War. It is usually futile to put forward long-term objectives as preconditions for talks. This is no exception.

US Willingness to Place Limitations on Its Own Actions?

Rather than reacting to the end of the Cold War by committing itself now fully to respect the UN and OAS Charters, the Bush administration has become more assertive and has given less rather than more attention to international law. The invasion of Panama in December 1989, for example, represented a virtual resuscitation of the Roosevelt corollary. The United States made no effort to consult with the OAS or with individual Latin American governments, nor did it take its case to the UN Security Council prior to the invasion, as required by Article 51 of the UN Charter. The latter provides for the right of self-defense, but only until the Security Council itself can act on the matter. The state claiming to be defending itself obviously must report the action against it to the Security Council so that the latter can act. President Bush's claim that he had acted under Article 51 was inadmissible. Accordingly, the UN strongly deplored the invasion by a vote of 75 to 20, with 40 abstentions.

None of the other four reasons the president gave for the invasion met the standards of international law. These reasons were (1) to protect US citizens, (2) to arrest Panamanian strongman Manuel Noriega, (3) to defend democracy, and (4) to defend the Panama Canal.[34] No nation has the right under either the UN or OAS Charters to use force against another nation to defend democracy or any other political system. Nor do the charters stipulate any right to invade to protect one's citizens. In the case of Panama, moreover, US citizens could have been more effectively protected if they had been confined to US military installations; as it was, a number were killed during the invasion.[35]

Certainly under international law the United States had no right to arrest Noriega. To claim such a right was in effect to assert a form of extraterritoriality. Noriega is, to be sure, a thug and a scoundrel. He doubtless was engaged in criminal activity and his armed forces had indeed harassed US personnel. But none of that conferred any right to intervene. Panama is, after all, a sovereign nation.

Finally, the Panama Canal treaties themselves did not give the United States the right to invade. On the contrary, the treaties specifically state that nothing in them shall be interpreted as giving the United States the right to intervene in Panama's affairs. The United States had an obligation to defend the canal, but there was no evidence that it was threatened. Noriega had been careful not to give the United States such a pretext. Furthermore, even if the canal had been threatened, US forces could have defended it from their own installations without invading Panama.

As suggested earlier, the invasion of Panama marked the first time since the days of "big stick" diplomacy that the United States has sent in its own troops without some veneer of multilateral sanction. The United States did not claim to be invading to prevent a communist takeover or to thwart a plot made in Havana or Moscow. After giving the OAS a few weeks to accomplish the US goal of getting rid of Noriega, Washington took matters into its own hands, ignored the OAS Charter, and was unanimously condemned by the OAS.

Latin Americans wonder if the end of the Cold War means the return to the tactics of an earlier era. Now that the United States is no longer concerned about retaliatory action by the Soviet Union, will it resort to imposing its will by force in the Caribbean Basin whenever it chooses?

Certainly the invasion was an inappropriate way to react to the end of the Cold War. Former US ambassador to the United Nations Jeane Kirkpatrick had argued that the United States would conduct its foreign policy according to the UN Charter if the Soviet Union would too. Since 1987, the Soviet Union has vowed to do precisely that, but the response of the Bush administration has been the exact opposite of that imagined by Kirkpatrick in the Caribbean Basin: it has paid less rather than more attention to the charter. Only time will tell whether the invasion of Panama was an anomaly or the portent of things to come.

Conclusion

The present is indeed a hopeful moment. The two superpowers are no longer automatically on opposite sides in regional conflicts. They worked together in the Gulf crisis, as they had in Afghanistan, Cambodia, and Angola, areas over which the Monroe Doctrine never cast its shadow. Close superpower cooperation is likely to come last to the Caribbean Basin, the oldest US sphere of influence.

The United States needs to realize that the assumptions on which it based past policies in the area are outmoded. There is no threat and therefore no need for the concept of strategic denial. Even less is there any need to assert hegemony. The nations of the world are moving toward a more interdependent system, and Washington should adapt its policies in Latin America to that new spirit. What it needs is not the control, but rather the cooperation, of the Central Americans—indeed, of all Latin Americans—in addressing such new challenges as halting drug trafficking, protecting the environment, and redressing the imbalance between North and South.

The Soviet Union is far less involved and interested in the Caribbean Basin than in Afghanistan and the Middle East. However, there should also be room for superpower cooperation here as well. Could not the two, for example, encourage a nuclear-free Caribbean Basin—indeed, a nuclear-free Latin America—through a joint commitment of their own? The Soviet Union could pledge to never again place nuclear weapons of any kind in the area, and the United States could pledge to exclude nuclear devices of any kind from its bases in Guatánamo Bay, Puerto Rico, Panama, and other sites in the region. These pledges might provide the incentive for such holdouts as Argentina, Brazil, and Cuba to sign the Tlatelolco nuclear nonproliferation agreement. Surely Moscow has no intention of returning such weaponry, and why would Washington have any need for them in Guantánamo Bay or Roosevelt Roads?

And could not the two pool their technology in a joint effort to protect the disappearing rain forests and encourage the Latin Americans to do so? A massive international effort is required. Would not a joint US-Soviet commitment to that effort be an inspiring way to begin?

Such cooperation, however, will depend on a change of Washington's attitude. But policies toward this region will change slowly; it is the region where the great shibboleth of the Monroe Doctrine has most clearly shaped US responses for two centuries.

Notes

Portions of this chapter are adapted from "The United States and South America: Beyond the Monroe Doctrine," *Current History* (February 1991).

1. Lars Schoultz, "Inter-American Security: The Changing Perception of U.S. Policymakers," unpublished paper, presented at a Latin American Studies Association roundtable discussion in April 1990.

2. Quoted in Julius W. Pratt, *A History of U.S. Foreign Policy* (Englewood Cliffs, N.J.: Prentice-Hall, 1955), 165. For a discussion of the no-transfer concept, see John Arthur Logan, *No Transfer: An American Security Principle* (New Haven, Conn.: Yale University Press, 1961).

3. Pratt, *A History of U.S. Foreign Policy*, 169.

4. Ibid., 339.

5. Richard W. Leopold, *The Growth of American Foreign Policy: A History* (New York: Alfred A. Knopf, 1962), 163–165.

6. Quoted in Wayne S. Smith, "Will the U.S. Again Send in the Marines?" in *World Paper*, November 1983, 1.

7. Leopold, *The Growth of American Foreign Policy*, 225–226.

8. Pratt, *A History of U.S. Foreign Policy*, 164.

9. Ibid., 398.

10. J. Reuben Clark, *Memorandum on the Monroe Doctrine* (Washington, D.C.: US Government Printing Office, 1930).

11. In their *The Organization of American States* (Dallas: Southern Methodist University Press, 1963), Ann Ven Wynen Thomas and A. J. Thomas, Jr., concluded that "the Rio Treaty is the final step to date in the multilateralization of the Monroe Doctrine" (see p. 356). See also Samuel Guy Inman's account of Republican Senator Arthur Vanderberg's conclusion that this would be the effect of bringing into being the OAS. In Inman's *Inter-American Conference, 1826–1954: History and Problems* (Washington, D.C.: University Press of Washington, 1965), 221–222.

12. Stephen G. Rabe, *Eisenhower and Latin America: The Foreign Policy of Anti-Communism* (Chapel Hill: University of North Carolina Press, 1988), 15–18 and 48–49.

13. Ibid., 51.

14. See the interview with Reagan in the *Wall Street Journal*, 1 May 1980, 1.

15. Committee of Santa Fe, *A New Inter-American Policy For the Eighties* (Washington, D.C.: Council for Inter-American Security, 1980), in the introduction.

16. Ibid., in the foreword.

17. See quotes in the *New York Times*, 26 Feb. 1981, 1; and 19 Mar. 1981, 1 and 10.

18. Text of President Reagan's speech of March 16, 1986.

19. See *Contadora: A Text for Peace*, a pamphlet published by the Center for International Policy, Washington, D.C., November 1984.

20. See Wayne Smith, "The 'March of Folly' in Further Contra Aid," the *New York Times*, 29 Jan. 1988, 35.

21. Based on a conversation in March 1988 with a Soviet Embassy officer who asked to remain anonymous.

22. See Wayne S. Smith, "Curbing the Arms Flow," in the *Christian Science Monitor*, 31 Mar. 1988, 10.

23. See the *Washington Post*, 23 Feb. 1989, A17.

24. Press release issued by the Soviet Foreign Ministry on February 21, 1989.

25. *Washington Post*, 8 Apr. 1989, A14.

26. Based on the statement of a Soviet Embassy officer who asked to remain anonymous.

27. The Cuban delegation, on instructions, made this proposal to the US delegation near the end of the negotiations on Southern Africa. That the United

States never responded has been confirmed by members of the delegation as well as by those in the Cuban delegation.

28. Statement of an officer of the Cuban Foreign Ministry who asked to remain anonymous.

29. See the *Washington Post*, 6 Apr. 1989, A30.

30. See *Time*, 4 June 1990, 38–41. The thrust of the article is that the United States and the Soviet Union did cooperate closely in ending the war in Nicaragua. A careful reading of the article, however, makes clear that it is simply reporting the same old thing, namely the United States insisting that the Soviet Union take measures to address our security concerns in Central America while the United States offers to take no such steps in return. It is interesting to note, however, that in their interviews, Assistant Secretary of State Bernard Aronson and Soviet Foreign Ministry official Yuri Pavlov go out of their way to stress their cordial working relationship. That in itself marks a change from the attitudes of the Reagan administration.

31. See the text of the unpublished speech by Michael G. Kozak to the Cuban-American National Foundation on October 11, 1990.

32. Comment by Nicolai at 10 Nov. 1989 conference at the Johns Hopkins University School for Advanced International Studies.

33. See the *Washington Times*, 16 Mar. 1990, 3.

34. For a detailed discussion of the illegality of the invasion, see Charles Maechling, "Washington's Illegal Invasion," *Foreign Policy*, no. 79 (Summer 1990): 113–131.

35. US authorities in Panama did try to confine all US citizens to US military reservations, but many refused to be confined—thus suggesting that they did not share the conviction of the authorities that there was any general danger to them.

■ 6 ■

Winding Down Strife in Southern Africa

FEN OSLER HAMPSON

The 1989 resolution of the conflict in Namibia and the country's subsequent achievement of full independence on March 21, 1990, closed an important chapter in the history of Southern Africa. For SWAPO, formed in 1958, and its leader, Sam Nujoma, who was sworn in as the country's first president, independence marked the triumphant conclusion of a 24-year struggle that had begun in 1966.

For many years, Namibia had been the scene of one of the forgotten conflicts in international relations. The territory had been controlled by South Africa under a League of Nations mandate when Germany lost the colony after World War I. In 1968, however, the United Nations changed the name of the territory from South-West Africa to Namibia, and in 1973, the General Assembly, after the ICJ ruled in 1971 that South Africa's presence in Namibia was illegal, recognized SWAPO as the "sole authentic representative of the Namibian people." However, it was not until December 22, 1988, when representatives of Angola, Cuba, and South Africa formally signed an agreement calling for implementation of Security Council Resolution 435 (1978), that concrete plans for peace in the region—of which Namibian independence was the central element—were set in motion.

This chapter explores the reasons a negotiated settlement was reached in 1988 and not earlier, and whether coordinated US-Soviet diplomacy with the ending of the Cold War was a necessary precondition for the settlement of this particular regional conflict. It is the argument of this chapter that this was not the only factor but that a combination of variables, separately and together, affected the process of settlement. These variables include domestic political forces within the countries at war as well as within the countries of the third parties who attempted to participate in the resolution, the structural evolution of the conflict itself, and the international context of the conflict. As illustrated by this particular case, the prospects for resolution in other ongoing (and future)

Third World regional conflicts may well depend on factors and forces that are both intrinsic and extrinsic to the conflict in which superpower cooperation may be a necessary but insufficient condition to achieve a peaceful settlement.

The first section of this chapter briefly reviews analytical lenses that have been identified in the examination of the Angola-Namibia settlement: constructive engagement, "ripeness" and third-party mediation, and systemic change. The origins and background of the Southern African conflict are then recounted. The modalities of US-led mediation efforts under the Carter and Reagan administrations respectively are summarized. US initiatives and the settlement are finally analyzed in terms of the following questions: Were the accords a validation or repudiation of constructive engagement? To what extent was successful third-party intervention in this particular conflict related to the nature of the issues under dispute, the timing of the intervention, the qualities and skills of the intervener, and the methods used? To what extent did the presence or absence in the conflict of a "hurting stalemate," which, in this case constituted ripeness, facilitate a negotiated settlement? What role did coordinated US and Soviet diplomacy (and pressure) in the context of lessening Cold War tensions play in facilitating the achievement of a negotiated settlement?

Alternative Explanations

Constructive engagement, "ripeness" and third-party mediation, and systemic change have been offered by various scholars as analytical tools for investigating events surrounding the settlement of the Angola-Namibia conflict. As will be demonstrated in this chapter, these three appear superficially to be separate processes, ranging from bilateral negotiation to disinterested intervention to contextual change. However, each had a part separately and jointly in the settlement.

A Triumph for Constructive Engagement?

The United States was intimately involved in the Namibian peace settlement, and US-led mediation efforts eventually helped resolve the conflict. These efforts had been under way since the early days of the Carter administration, first as part of a multilateral approach to mediation through the WCG, established by Carter and including the United States, the Federal Republic of Germany, France, Canada, and the United Kingdom. They continued as a bilateral initiative introduced under the Reagan administration's policy of constructive engagement toward South Africa.

Some observers, like former Assistant Secretary of State for African Affairs Chester Crocker, who was the principal architect of constructive engagement, view the settlement as a vindication of the Reagan administration's policies and bilateral approach to the problem.[1] Others argue that the policies of the Reagan administration only delayed a timely resolution of the conflict by lending support to South Africa and other interests intent on thwarting Namibia's search for independence and national self-determination. In particular, it is argued that Reagan's embrace of linkage between Namibian independence and a withdrawal of Cuban troops from Angola played right into the hands of the South African government and its interests in delaying a settlement as long as possible. These critics take issue with the Crocker thesis that the United States had limited leverage over the parties to the conflict; instead, they believe that the United States could have brought about a settlement to the conflict earlier had it opted to flex its bargaining muscle over South Africa. Thus, a key question is whether the accords represented victory or failure for the Reagan administration's policy of "constructive engagement."

Ripeness and Third-Party Mediation

A broader analytical question that is raised by this case is whether third-party intervention facilitated movement toward dispute resolution and, if so, how.[2] One puzzle is why third-party mediation, first by the WCG and then by the United States acting on its own initiative, through constructive engagement, took so long to resolve the dispute in Angola-Namibia. Chester Crocker's arguments support the thesis that conditions surrounding US-led mediation efforts were not conducive to "mediation with muscle,"[3] that is, to exercising special leverage over the parties to the conflict by having the ability to impose penalties or sanctions for recalcitrant behavior, or to offering rewards or side payments as positive inducements.[4] Instead, Crocker argues, the United States had to rely on its "wits," "relevance," and "special diplomatic possibilities" rather than on its "wallets" and "muscle" to bring about a settlement to the conflict.[5] Thus a key consideration is whether Washington's bargaining power and leverage were indeed limited as Crocker indicates, and whether this in turn frustrated negotiations and delayed a settlement, or whether the United States in fact had more leverage or "muscle" than it chose to exercise.

Structural characteristics of the conflict itself and the absence of a "hurting stalemate" to force the parties to the bargaining table may have delayed a resolution. Three possibilities in this area exist. Perhaps the Angola-Namibia conflict lacked not a shortage of skilled mediators or "resolving formulas" but "ripeness," the point at which the parties no

longer felt they could win the conflict and both sides perceived the costs
and prospects of continued confrontation to be more burdensome than the
costs and prospects of a settlement.[6] Prospects for a negotiated settlement
may have been enhanced by war-weariness, creating a plateau or hurting
stalemate that obscured the possibility of unilateral advantage.
Alternatively, a looming catastrophe or the sudden emergence of a secure
way out may have eliminated delay as an option to concessions required
for de-escalation of the conflict. Finally, the presence of large grey areas
may have posed problems for potential third parties who, prior to any
intervention, needed a rough measure of the common ground between
parties.[7]

Systemic Explanations

At a systemic level, great-power relationships and the changing dynamics
of East-West competition have been identified as having an impact on the
possibilities for diplomacy and resolution of Third World conflicts. When
competition has been viewed as a zero-sum game, the superpowers have
relied on military instruments to achieve their aims, limiting the
prospects for achieving a negotiated settlement in regional conflicts.[8]
Conversely, détente in superpower relations has been associated with the
settlement of many disputes and the promotion of security cooperation at
the regional level. Many see a strong link between improvements in East-
West relations in the late 1980s and the settlement of some major regional
conflicts, including the Iran-Iraq war, Afghanistan, and Angola-Namibia.[9]

The superpowers have been able to facilitate conflict resolution and
settlement processes by bringing pressure to bear on client states and other
parties to conflict and by working toward joint solutions based on a non–
zero-sum view of their respective interests. Thus, the settlement of the
Angola-Namibia conflict is arguably part of a more general trend toward
détente in superpower relations and the settlement of regional conflicts
that emerged in the late 1980s throughout the Third World.

The use of force and the changing politico-military balances of power
in international relations may explain bargaining outcomes. Realist and
neorealist writers on international relations see military strength and
diplomatic resolve as the crucial ingredients of state power. In this view,
wins and losses in international politics are determined by the relative
power resources that state actors can bring to bear on particular issues and
problem areas.[10] Declining Soviet hegemony in the face of US strength,
power-projection capabilities, and ability to demonstrate resolve may,
therefore, best explain the outcome of the conflict over Namibia-Angola.

Underlying all systemic-level explanations—be they of the
"superpower détente bringing peace" or the "United States prevailed"

variety—is the assumption that East-West rivalries lie at the heart of Third World regional conflicts. Thus, according to this assumption, systemic level change will bring about subsystemic change, and regional actors will alter their behavior in response to shifting power balances at the geostrategic level. This view sees regional conflicts largely driven by external factors and forces. Internal or subregional forces will be refracted through the prism of superpower competition and global politics. The prospects for conflict resolution at the regional level will thus depend significantly on two factors: the ability of the great powers to accommodate their divergent preferences, or one great power's ability to prevail over the other.

Origins and Background of the Conflict in Southern Africa

Civil strife in Southern Africa has a long history. The separate conflicts in Angola and Namibia were linked when, in 1981, the South African government, with US support, included the withdrawal of Cuban forces from Angola in the Namibian peace process. However, informal linkage between these two conflicts was established much earlier by South Africa's destabilization activities against Angola and by the overlapping dynamics of civil war and regional conflict.[11]

Warfare erupted in Angola in 1975 when the country obtained its independence from Portugal as competing tribal interests, centered on the Ovimbundu, Kimbundu, and Bakongo tribes, fought for control of the central government. An accord, negotiated with the help of Portugal, sought to establish a tripartite government among the three major political factions in Angola. The agreement disintegrated almost as soon as the ink was dry, and, in the ensuing struggle, the MPLA formed a government and sustained its preeminence with the help of Cuban troops. An opposition guerrilla group known as UNITA eventually became the major opposition force, receiving assistance from South Africa, China, and the United States. In 1987 the civil war in Angola reached a stalemate as Cuban and Soviet aid to the MPLA was matched by South African and US assistance to UNITA. By 1989, over 100,000 Angolans had died in the civil war and over one million required emergency food and other aid because of the war.

On June 22, 1989, at a summit in Zaire of 18 African heads of state, Angola's President José Eduardo dos Santos and UNITA rebel leader Jonas Savimbi agreed to an immediate cease-fire. However, negotiations on the status of Savimbi in the Angolan government broke down shortly afterward, with the government accusing the rebels of violating the cease-fire. Following direct negotiations between the United States and the

Soviet Union, in early April 1990, the Angolan government agreed to direct peace talks with UNITA in Portugal and Cape Verde.

SWAPO began as a guerrilla movement for Namibian independence in 1966. It enjoyed strong support from the Ovambo, who constitute approximately 50 percent of Namibia's estimated 1.5 million population and had been designated in 1973 as the sole representative of the Namibian people. SWAPO established bases in southern Angola and enjoyed the political support of the Frontline States and the OAU. In 1978, Security Council Resolution 435 called for a cease-fire, a UN peacekeeping force, and UN-sponsored elections. Resolution 435 ultimately became the basis for the peace settlement and independence for Namibia in 1989–1990.

A bewildering array of state and nonstate actors and interests have been involved at one time or another in this conflict and subsequent peace negotiations. In addition to the United States, South Africa, Portugal (as the former colonial power in Angola and Mozambique), the United Kingdom (another colonial power with close ties to South Africa), and the Soviet Union, the other key actors include Cuba, several key Frontline States—Angola, Zambia, Mozambique, and Zimbabwe—and the OAU. Leading nonstate actors include various antigovernment guerrilla groups, including the ANC, SWAPO, UNITA, and the MNR of Mozambique. United Nations involvement took the form of successive resolutions of the Security Council and direct mediation efforts by the UN secretary-general and the WCG.

From Carter to Reagan: Multilateral Versus Bilateral Diplomacy

Almost 11 years passed from the time the United States first began in earnest to attempt a negotiated resolution to the conflict in Namibia until an actual agreement was concluded in December 1988. Under the Carter administration, the United States essentially pursued a multilateral approach to mediation through the WCG. Under Reagan, the policy shiftcd to a bilateral negotiating strategy between Washington and Pretoria as part of the administration's new doctrine of constructive engagement, premised on the notion that South Africa would be more willing to make concessions if the United States adopted a less confrontational approach that was sensitive to South Africa's security interests. A brief chronology of these negotiations follows.[12]

By 1976 the Namibian situation was proving to be increasingly costly to the South African government at a time when it was trying to improve its relations with the rest of Africa and the West. The Turnhalle Constitutional Conference, held in Windhoek, Namibia, was an attempt to dampen growing external pressure for sanctions against South Africa by setting in motion political reforms for an "internal" solution that might eventually lead to independence on terms that would be in South Africa's interest and subject to South African control. The goals of the conference were to draft a constitution for Namibia and establish an interim government on terms that would exclude nonethnic parties, like SWAPO, from any involvement in these deliberations. South Africa's neighbors objected and began to call for a mandatory arms embargo and cessation of new loans to South Africa.

On April 5, 1977, in an effort to head off an internal settlement, the Western powers launched their own diplomatic initiative in the form of the WCG. The group was initiated by President Jimmy Carter, who was concerned about mounting civil violence in South Africa following clashes in the township of Soweto. The WCG started negotiations with South Africa and its neighbors with a commitment to the creation of a Namibian settlement, free elections of an independent government, and the appointment of a special representative to ensure that elections would take place.

The WCG's objective was the creation of a representative government in Namibia without reference to ethnic or racial quotas. The group made some progress in getting South Africa to agree to Namibian independence. Outstanding issues in these negotiations included the timing of withdrawal of South African troops from Namibia, an agreed timetable for elections, and the question of ownership of the port of Walvis Bay, which South Africa claimed as part of its territory. SWAPO was unhappy about the direction of these discussions but came under pressure from the OAU to encourage the efforts of the WCG. By September 1977 negotiations had advanced to the most difficult issues.

The WCG's formula called for South Africa to reduce its forces to one or two army bases prior to UN-supervised elections in Namibia, with the understanding that South African security forces would then be replaced by UN peacekeeping and observer forces. Although South Africa was unhappy with this arrangement, it agreed on condition that both sides of the Angola-Namibia border be monitored to prevent guerrilla infiltrations.

The issue of when to hold elections proved to be more thorny. South Africa favored early elections in 1978 in order to give the advantage to pro-Turnhalle parties; the WCG favored later elections to allow other groups time to organize. At the same time, South Africa indicated that it would agree to a long-term treaty permitting future Namibian government use of the port at Walvis Bay.

In December 1977, there was a fourth round of inconclusive talks, which stalled on the matter of UN involvement in peacekeeping and monitoring of elections in Namibia. Threatened with the termination of oil exports from Iran (its principal supplier), South Africa subsequently agreed to reduce its military forces in Namibia under UN supervision and to allow the world organization's military forces to participate in monitoring elections for a Constituent Assembly, which would assume responsibility for drafting a constitution.

Early in 1978, the WCG elaborated a framework for all subsequent negotiations. The framework included provision for appointment of a special UN representative and a UN planning group to administer Namibia, a cease-fire followed by a three-month period during which both sides would redeploy their forces to specified locations, elections for a Constituent Assembly under UN auspices, and disbanding of local police forces in Namibia and release of all political prisoners.

While negotiations were still under way in New York, South Africa increased its military presence in Namibia and launched a series of attacks against SWAPO bases inside Angola. Following the Cassinga raid, SWAPO broke off talks for several months. In August 1978, Secretary-General Kurt Waldheim issued his report on Namibia, which was based on the report of UN commissioner for Namibia Marti Ahtisaari. The report, which was accepted by the Security Council in the form of Resolution 435 on September 29, 1978, became the internationally accepted framework for resolution of the conflict. South Africa voiced its objections to the report, complaining that the size of UNTAG in Namibia (7,500 military personnel and 1,500 civilians) exceeded the WCG's proposal and that the timing of elections in the plan would delay independence beyond the target date of December 31, 1978.

South Africa formally rejected the plan on September 20, 1978. On September 29, John Vorster announced his resignation as prime minister and was replaced by noted hard-liner P. W. Botha, the former defense minister. Not only did South Africa's new leadership reject all subsequent UN proposals for a cease-fire, but in March 1979 South Africa also began launching attacks against SWAPO bases in southern Angola. Negotiations were suspended but then resumed in June 1979 at just about the same time that South Africa was taking steps to increase its direct control of Namibia's internal affairs by appointing an administrator-general of Namibia.

On November 6, 1979, in a bid to rescue the stalled peace talks, Waldheim invited the South African government, WCG members, Frontline States, and SWAPO to attend a conference in Geneva to clarify demilitarization proposals. The purpose of these negotiations was to delineate a new WCG proposal for a demilitarized zone along the Angolan-Namibian border, which had been provisionally accepted by South Africa, SWAPO, and the Frontline States. However, South Africa continued to voice its objections to a number of technical points in the United Nations proposal while continuing to insist that the UN give a clear demonstration of its impartiality before any settlement could be reached.

During this period, it became increasingly difficult to focus the political attention of key WCG members on the talks. While Britain was busy with independence negotiations for Rhodesia/Zimbabwe, the United States was gearing up for the 1980 presidential elections. In the meantime, South Africa continued its efforts to establish an effective coalition of anti-SWAPO parties to install an internal administration with limited authority under the administrator-general. There were further rounds of negotiations throughout the summer and fall.

By the time pre-implementation discussions began under UN auspices in Geneva on January 7–14, 1981, South Africa had little incentive to make the necessary concessions that would lead to a settlement. Ronald Reagan was about to be sworn in as the new US president, and South Africa's hope that he would take a more favorable stance toward its interests was soon to be realized. The British government, under Margaret Thatcher, also made it clear that it was opposed to any attempt to impose sanctions against South Africa. The Geneva meeting broke up over the issue of representation and demands put forward by DTA leader Dirk Mudge to rescind UN recognition of SWAPO as "sole and authentic representative of the people of Namibia."[13]

The Reagan administration shifted course from the Carter administration's multilateral diplomacy to a bilateral approach, labeled "constructive engagement," which was based on the view that closer relations with South Africa would ease the way toward resolution of South Africa's disputes with its neighbors and the abolition of apartheid.[14] The WCG began to crumble with Pretoria's massive military strike into Angola (the so-called Operation Protea) and the US refusal to go along with other WCG members' condemnation of the raid and demand in the UN Security Council for immediate withdrawal of South African forces from Angola and reparations.

During the summer of 1982, apprehensions grew in the Reagan administration about the buildup of Cuban forces in Angola, apparently responding to a leaked State Department memorandum by Chester Crocker, who argued that Namibian independence should be tied "to a withdrawal of Cuban forces from Angola and a commitment by the Marxist leaders in Angola to share power with Western-backed guerrillas."[15] Pretoria indicated that it would not enter into implementation of an agreement on Namibian independence unless Cuban forces were withdrawn from Angola. US acceptance of this new demand, along with its increasingly direct role in negotiations between South Africa and the Frontline States, led to the WCG's eventual demise as the voice of Western diplomacy. Linkage was also rejected by SWAPO and the Frontline States, thus further compromising future negotiations.

In February 1984, the Angolan government negotiated the Lusaka accords with South Africa, under which Angola agreed to withdraw its support from SWAPO and the ANC if the SADF withdrew from Angola and ceased its support for UNITA. The accords created a Joint Monitoring Commission to oversee Angolan and South African forces in border areas. South Africa and Angola also agreed to the establishment of a USLO to monitor events in Namibia. The patrolled area covered roughly 400 to 450 miles of the border along SWAPO's main infiltration routes into Namibia. Almost as soon as the cease-fire went into effect, South Africa charged SWAPO with violations, using these as a further excuse to slow down its own withdrawal of forces from southern Angola.

The South African–Angola agreement in Namibia was followed by the Nkomati accords between Mozambique and South Africa. Both formed part of a coordinated South African strategy to force bilateral dealings with the Frontline States, weakening their solidarity. Subsequent talks between Pretoria, SWAPO, and other groups in Namibia proved to be fruitless because of Pretoria's insistence that a cease-fire precede implementation of Resolution 435. South Africa's insistence that Cuban withdrawal of forces from Angola precede implementation of the resolution also continued to be a sticking point, as did its installation of the interim central government in Namibia following the collapse of the DTA. The Angolan government rejected linkage, identifying continued Cuban involvement as an issue between Cuba and Angola; however, it pledged to consider Cuban withdrawal after South Africa agreed to implement Resolution 435.

In August 1984, the Reagan administration succeeded in getting Congress to repeal the Clark Amendment prohibiting US aid to UNITA. This was done in response to the reported Soviet buildup in Angola in 1983. With the repeal of the Clark Amendment, the United States gave $27 million in humanitarian assistance to UNITA. In April 1986 it was disclosed that in addition to humanitarian assistance, the United States was also supplying UNITA with Stinger missiles. This revelation shattered whatever credibility the United States enjoyed as a mediator in the dispute. In the eyes of SWAPO, the UN, the OAU, and the Frontline States, the United States was no longer a disinterested third party to the conflict. The Botha government's position was also hardening in response to its own domestic difficulties in which the ruling National Party had split with right-wing members, forming their own Conservative Party.

Discouraged by South Africa's lack of progress in abolishing apartheid, however, the US Congress, on October 2, 1986, overrode Reagan's veto to pass the Comprehensive Anti-Apartheid Act, which slapped economic sanctions on South Africa and effectively closed the window on the administration's policy of constructive engagement toward South Africa. This followed the decision taken by Commonwealth members to implement the 1985 Nassau sanctions package after the failure of the EPG mission to South Africa.

In 1987 the situation on the military front began to change. In September, South African forces went into Angola in support of UNITA rebel forces, which were in some danger of suffering defeat at the hands of a massive Angolan offensive. With Jonas Savimbi's troops, South African forces were engaged in the siege of Cuito Cuanavale, a town some 300 kilometers north of the Namibian border. However, South African forces failed to take Cuito, or to annihilate Angolan forces. Simultaneously, South African forces were engaged in fighting in southwestern Angola. Angolan government forces, substantially reinforced by Cuban troops, were able to push back the South African–UNITA offensive. By March 1988, South African forces had withdrawn from Angola.

Two months later, on May 3–4, 1988, regional peace talks had resumed between Angola, South Africa, Cuba, and the United States in London. There were further rounds of talks in Cairo, New York, Geneva, and Brazzaville. President Mobuto Sese Seko of Zaire organized the Angolan reconciliation talks, which enjoyed the widespread support of the African nations. There were six rounds of negotiations in the Congo, which led to the Brazzaville Protocol of December 1988, which immediately preceded the New York agreements on Namibia-Angola.

On December 22, 1988, high-level representatives of Angola, Cuba, and South Africa formally signed two agreements in New York, establishing the basis for peaceful transition in Namibia, cessation of hostilities between South Africa and Angola, and a timetable for withdrawal of Cuban troops from Angola. The first agreement called for the implementation of Security Council Resolution 435, while expanding its terms to reduce South African forces from approximately 50,000 troops to 1,500 troops in Namibia within six weeks of the agreement's implementation, and to confine these troops to two bases. The second agreement, signed by Cuba and Angola, set out a withdrawal timetable for the 50,000 Cuban troops, to begin with a 3,000-troop reduction on April 1, 1989. All Cuban troops were to be redeployed north of the fifteenth parallel (200 miles north of the Angolan-Namibian border) by August 1989. Twenty-five thousand were to be withdrawn from Angola, and the remainder moved north of the thirteenth parallel (350 miles north of the border) by November 1989. The Cuban departure from Angola was to be completed by July 1, 1991. Further provisions of the agreements signed in December 1988 included full independence for Namibia by April 1990, preceded by the election of a Constituent Assembly on November 1, 1989, to draft a constitution and organize a new government.

In December 1988, the Security Council unanimously voted to send a mission, UNAVEM, to Angola to verify the redeployment northward and the total withdrawal of Cuban forces from that country. This decision was the result of the December 1988 regional accord. The mandate of UNAVEM ran from January 1989 to January 1991. The verification team included 70 military observers and 20 civilians from Algeria, Argentina, Brazil, Congo, Czechoslovakia, India, Jordan, Norway, Spain, and Yugoslavia. In February 1989, UNTAG was created by the Security Council to monitor the Namibian peace plan agreements.

Sometime before dawn on April 1, 1989, the official cease-fire date and commencement of the Namibian peace process, more than 1,000 heavily armed SWAPO guerrillas entered Namibia from neighboring Angola, taking advantage of an ambiguity in the independence plan that failed to specify where SWAPO forces were to be stationed during the arranged cease-fire. They were attacked by South African security forces and over 300 SWAPO guerrillas were killed during two weeks of fighting. In May 1989, talks resumed between Angola, Cuba, and South Africa in order to put the Namibian independence process back on track. By July the conditions specified in the original timetable were being met, including the withdrawal of South African forces and the return of Namibian exiles for elections scheduled for November 1, 1989. However, the political atmosphere continued to be plagued by fear and intimidation on all sides, particularly by South Africa's Koevoet anti-insurgency forces. The UN threatened that continued action by South African troops as a matter of that country's policy might jeopardize the upcoming elections and called for a demobilization of the Koevoet forces. Elections were held from November 7 to 11 under international supervision and over 97 percent of Namibia's 701,583 registered voters cast their ballots. SWAPO obtained 57 percent of the votes cast and won 41 of 72 seats in the assembly. The DTA received 29 percent of the vote and 21 seats, the remainder going to 8 other minor parties. The Constituent Assembly immediately began drafting a new constitution in time for independence in March 1990.

Explaining Outcomes

The Role of Constructive Engagement: Bilateral Versus Multilateral Diplomacy

With hindsight, it is tempting to argue that bilateral diplomacy and constructive engagement succeeded where multilateral diplomacy under the WCG had failed. It is undeniable that Chester Crocker's persistence in narrowing and refining differences between the parties was important in reaching a settlement, as was Angola's acceptance of linkage. The departure of the Cubans was clearly a decisive condition for South Africa's military leadership to agree to the accord.

However, the achievements of the WCG should not be sold short. Much of the important groundwork for Namibian independence was laid by the group. Not only had it defined and packaged most of the issues, crystallized the negotiating agenda, and conferred international legitimacy on the key parties to the negotiation, the WCG had also identified the broad contours of what eventually became the final peace settlement or what William Zartman calls the "resolving formula." In a real sense, therefore, much of the important negotiating legwork had already been concluded by the time the Reagan administration arrived on the scene.

South Africa, however, complicated the smooth implementation of the WCG's plan by continually imposing new conditions as proof of UN impartiality. Further, from South Africa's perspective, the war against Angola was going well, and South Africa wanted to strengthen the internal coalition in Namibia before contesting the election against SWAPO. There was, therefore, little incentive for Botha to give in to the UN at that time, particularly when "Penelope's web" tactics in the talks were gaining additional concessions for South Africa. The successful continuation of the peace talks was also hindered by other factors: new leadership in South Africa that continued to be just as hard-line as its predecessor, the growing political weakness (domestically and internationally) of the Carter administration, British preoccupation with the Lancaster House negotiations over Rhodesia/Zimbabwe, and ultimately the election of Ronald Reagan.

The lesson to be drawn from this experience is not so much the failure of multilateral diplomacy. If anything, the WCG showed that it was essential for the Western powers to present a united front to bring South Africa to the bargaining table. The essential lesson is that any diplomatic initiative can be thrown off course by domestic political developments and events outside the negotiating arena that may nonetheless compromise the possibilities of achieving a negotiated settlement.

It would be a mistake to characterize constructive engagement and the bilateral approach to the problem adopted by the Reagan administration as a complete and unqualified success—unless an eight-year delay is part of one's definition of success. Not only did Pretoria successfully exploit its new relationship with Washington by playing the linkage card, thus capitalizing on the Reagan administration's Cold War sensitivities, but it was also able to press ahead with its own military and internal political solution in Namibia without incurring Washington's wrath. Linkage was a costly gift to South Africa, but it was crucial to keeping the South African military, which had an effective veto over any settlement package, on board. The eager embrace of linkage by the incoming Reagan administration limited Washington's leverage over South Africa. Had such support been withheld until 1985–1986, when the war was becoming more costly to South Africa, a negotiated settlement might have been achieved then.

Washington's limited ability to flex its negotiating "muscle" was further compromised by its own policies toward the region as well as internal administration politics. Chester Crocker had his own problems with the administration's right wing, which limited the amount of pressure he could apply to South Africa or the concessions he could offer to Angola. During the period of constructive engagement, the conflict escalated to new heights with South Africa's increasingly large military incursions into Angola and its buildup of security forces in Namibia. What ultimately brought South Africa back to the bargaining table was not constructive engagement per se. Rather, South Africa's own changing perceptions and growing concerns about the costs of the conflict, coupled with the new détente in US-Soviet relations, altered the international context of the conflict and created new outside pressures for resolution. To be sure, the US perceptions of the conflict in Southern Africa also changed over the course of eight years, but ultimately this change involved a repudiation of the premises behind constructive engagement, not an endorsement.

Ripeness and Other Explanations of Mediation Success

A structural account of the reasons why mediation failed would argue that the conditions of ripeness absent in 1980 were present in 1988. By 1988, a hurting stalemate had developed, and the parties began to perceive that the costs of continuing the conflict exceeded the benefits of a negotiated settlement.

The concept of ripeness is problematic insofar as the definition risks being a tautology if it is defined exclusively in terms of mediation success. Zartman argues that ripeness is a necessary but not sufficient condition for mediation success; not all students of international negotiation have been careful to make this distinction.[16] Others criticize the concept on the grounds that ripeness smacks too much of realpolitik, leaving conflict resolution up to the independent dynamics of the conflict, thereby denying the possibilities for third parties to introduce de-escalation alternatives that positively affect disputants' calculations and behavior in the direction of a peace settlement.[17] The perceived absence of ripeness can therefore become an excuse for third parties not to become involved in mediation on the self-fulfilling grounds that the situation is not ripe for resolution.

In this case, however, there was ongoing third-party mediation throughout much of the conflict. Moreover, it is arguably the case that in 1979–1980 the conflict was beginning to approximate the conditions of ripeness because it was becoming costly both politically and economically to South Africa. Western countries had earlier raised the stakes with the threat of an oil cutoff and South Africa's international image was being hurt. South Africa made a number of important concessions in response to these pressures. Moreover, there were only a few issues remaining on the negotiating table, though there were others lurking, including the linkage of Namibian independence to the withdrawal of Cuban forces in Angola.

It is interesting to speculate what the outcome would have been had the allies kept up the pressure by threatening economic sanctions against South Africa, or had the incoming Reagan administration sent clear signals that it did not intend to depart from the carrot-and-stick policy of the Carter administration. Would South Africa have responded to such pressures? Would South Africa have been able to play the linkage card had Washington not been so preoccupied with the presence of Cuban forces in Angola? Counterfactual history raises some interesting possibilities. As it was, Reagan moved quickly to distance himself from the policies of his predecessor by moving closer to South Africa. At the same time, UN sanctions were unlikely, given the proclivities of Margaret Thatcher and Britain's veto power in the Security Council.

The same factors that worked against a negotiated settlement in 1979–1980 worked for it in 1988. In the case of South Africa, there were growing economic and military costs from the conflict. As Chris Brown argues:

> Economically, by 1988 it was becoming increasingly difficult for South Africa to support the costs of a major war hundreds of miles beyond its borders. On the military side, in early 1988 South Africa suffered its first major defeat in Angola since the arrival of Cubans in 1975. In fighting around Cuito Cuanavale in south-eastern Angola, a combined Angolan-Cuban force first turned back a South African–UNITA offensive and then launched an attack of its own which, for the first time, raised the specter of Cuban and Angolan troops crossing the border into Namibia. Faced with this possibility, and the ever mounting financial and human costs of war, Pretoria was forced to the bargaining table.[18]

This argument raises the broader question that the resulting agreement may have also been the product of the combined Angolan, Cuban, and Soviet decision to escalate the conflict in the hope that increased military pressure on Pretoria would force it to the negotiating table and a settlement.

At the same time, the psychological impact that sanctions against South Africa had on domestic perceptions and attitudes, particularly within the South African business community and on white opinion, may have indirectly contributed to a more cooperative attitude on the part of the South African government and helped pave the way for the rise of the moderate faction of the National Party under Prime Minister F. W. de Klerk. These sanctions included the Nassau package of measures adopted by the Commonwealth in October 1985, the decision taken by the US Congress to override a presidential veto and enact its Comprehensive Anti-Apartheid Act, the modest show of solidarity subsequently demonstrated by the European Community, and the threat of enactment of the US Total Disinvestment Bill.[19] These measures were taken in response to growing domestic unrest within South Africa.

The combination of sanctions, the changing balance of forces in the military arena against South Africa, and growing disillusionment with the war within the white community of South Africa helped tip the scales toward a settlement in 1988. In this respect, the conditions much more closely approximated those of a hurting stalemate in 1988 than they had in 1979–1980. Nonetheless, this is not to say that, had the requisite political will been available earlier, the conflict could not have been ripened for resolution by outside third parties.

System Factors: Superpower Détente or Soviet Capitulation Under US Pressure?

Both superpowers were involved in the conflict in Southern Africa in a dual role: supplying arms to forces they supported and bringing diplomatic pressure to bear on the parties to the conflict. The Soviet Union's military involvement in the region in the late 1970s and early 1980s, however, was substantially greater than that of the United States. The Soviet Union contributed about $1 billion annually in arms to Angola during the 1980s, and Cuban forces were providing substantial assistance to MPLA forces against UNITA. Cuban and Soviet aid to the MPLA was subsequently matched by South African and US aid to UNITA, and the civil war had reached a virtual stalemate by 1987. The United States had no troops, bases, or alliances with any of the states in the region. Its opportunities for influence were therefore limited, although its decision to resupply UNITA forces after the repeal of the Clark Amendment may have prolonged the conflict and delayed a negotiated settlement.

The Angola-Namibia peace accords were unquestionably facilitated by the rise of Mikhail Gorbachev, changing Soviet interests not only in

Southern African but also elsewhere in the Third World, and the new climate and spirit of cooperation between the superpowers.[20] US mediators have acknowledged the positive role and the behind-the-scenes pressure the Soviets brought to bear on Angola and Cuba to accept the settlement and, in particular, the linkage of Cuban troop withdrawal with the independence of Namibia.

An alternative interpretation would argue that Moscow retreated under pressure from Washington, especially after the repeal of the Clark Amendment, and that the agreements affirmed the logic of the Reagan Doctrine. However, the evidence suggests that Moscow was increasing its support for the MPLA and Cuba in the period from 1985 to 1988 at the same time that the United States was resuming aid to UNITA and South African troops were actively intervening on UNITA's behalf. The Soviets also influenced Luanda with large aid packages, arguing that a settlement would bring about stability, reduced military expenditures, and Western aid.[21] Moscow also pressured Luanda to be forthcoming in the terms of a Cuban withdrawal and to negotiate a compromise with UNITA.[22] This action casts doubt on the claim that the Soviets knuckled under to US pressure.

Conclusion

The 1988 peace accords that gave Namibia its independence and led to the phased withdrawal of Cuban troops from Angola were neither an unqualified victory for constructive engagement nor an affirmation of the Reagan Doctrine. Rather, the accords represented the culmination of a lengthy and protracted negotiation that began with the Carter administration as a multilateral undertaking and was narrowed by the Reagan administration to a triangular one.

Multilateral diplomacy under the auspices of the United Nations played an important part in the eventual resolution of the conflict— protracted though the settlement was. As a third party to the conflict, the United Nations had special institutional advantages. Through the passage of resolutions, mediation, and sharpening definitions of the negotiating agenda, the UN helped move the parties to the negotiating table.

Whether a settlement to the conflict could have been achieved earlier had the members of the WCG maintained a united front and continued pressure on South Africa and had the dynamics of the conflict been closer to a hurting stalemate is a matter for continuing speculation. The WCG discontinued operations when it became apparent to its members that Washington supported Pretoria's intentions to negotiate details of a

Namibian peace process only if Cuban troops in Angola were withdrawn as part of a settlement. In this respect, it is undeniable that US portrayal of the conflict in terms of the logic of the Cold War set the peace process back and played into Pretoria's own strategy of delaying a negotiated settlement while pursuing an independent solution to Namibia. However, with the ascension of Gorbachev to power and improved US-Soviet relations in the late 1980s, this Cold War view of the conflict became less tenable. The changing tenor of East-West relations facilitated prospects for a peace settlement as Soviet interests in the Third World changed and a new climate and a tentative spirit of cooperation emerged between the superpowers.

Nonetheless, it would be a mistake to attribute the resolution of this conflict solely to superpower détente. Other factors that helped bring an end to the conflict included the shifting correlation of forces on the battlefield and South Africa's growing realization that the military option was no longer viable. At the same time, growing unhappiness with the war in South Africa and recognition that the situation was hurting the country abroad cleared the path to Namibian independence on internationally acceptable terms.

This point suggests that although US-Soviet cooperation may be a necessary condition for the settlement of regional conflicts—with the important caveat that this conflict might have been settled earlier had domestic circumstances in the United States and South Africa been different—it is not sufficient. The prospects for conflict resolution depend ultimately on the interests and perceptions of the parties to the conflict, the presence or availability of ripeness to the conflict, the nature of the issues under dispute, and methods, skills, and timing of the intervention by the mediator.

As this case suggests, domestic politics can have a decisive impact on the course of negotiations and the prospects for conflict resolution by closing or opening windows of diplomatic opportunity.[23] Furthermore, the context of diplomacy may be just as important as the substance of negotiations. This may be one of the lessons of superpower conflict resolution in Southern Africa. The other lesson is that multilateral diplomacy, with the United States acting in concert with other powers and interests under the auspices of the UN, was ultimately crucial to the overall settlement of the conflict.

Notes

The author would like to thank Robert Jaster and Doug Anglin, in particular, along with the coauthors of this volume and participants in the workshop on "Superpowers and Regional Conflict in a Post–Cold War World," at Brown University, April 9–10, 1991, for their extremely helpful comments in revising an earlier draft of this chapter.

1. Chester A. Crocker, "Southern Africa: Eight Years Later," *Foreign Affairs* 68, no. 4 (Fall 1989): 144–164.

2. Third parties can facilitate conflict resolution by restructuring issues, identifying alternatives, modifying adversaries' perspectives, packaging and sequencing issues, building trust, offering side payments, or threatening penalties and sanctions. See Jeffrey Z. Rubin, "Introduction," in Jeffrey Z. Rubin, ed., *Dynamics of Third Party Intervention: Kissinger in the Middle East* (New York: Praeger, 1981), 28–43; James Laue, "The Emergence and Institutionalization of Third Party Roles in Conflict," Marie A. Dugan, "Intervenor Roles and Conflict Pathologies," and Thomas Colosi, "A Model for Negotiation and Mediation," in Dennis J. D. Sandole and Ingrid Sandole-Staroste, eds., *Conflict Management and Problem Solving: Interpersonal to International Applications* (London: Frances Pinter, 1987), 17–29, 57–61, 86–99.

The intervention of a third party will transform dyadic bargaining into a three- or multi-cornered relationship in which the third party effectively becomes one of the negotiators in a now transformed multilateral negotiating system. See Saadia Touval, *The Peace Brokers: Mediators in the Arab-Israeli Conflict, 1948–79* (Princeton, N.J.: Princeton University Press, 1982).

The tasks of the third-party mediator typically involve meeting with stakeholders to assess their interests, helping choose spokespeople or team leaders, identifying missing groups or strategies for representing diffuse interests, drafting protocols and setting agendas, suggesting options, identifying and testing possible trade-offs, writing and ratifying agreements, and monitoring and facilitating implementation of agreements. See Lawrence Susskind and Jeffrey Cruikshank, *Breaking the Impasse: Consensual Approaches to Resolving Public Disputes* (New York: Basic Books, 1989), 143 *passim*.

3. The definition of success is, of course, problematic. To some, for the conflict termination process to be characterized as a success it must produce some set of arrangements that lasts for several generations or stands some other test of time to demonstrate robustness and permanence. Alternatively, as Christopher Mitchell argues, "Some processes never manage to get the parties into dialogue, let alone to agree to a cessation of fighting. Others reach dialogue but fail to find a possible agreement. Still others . . . achieve agreement only to see it repudiated. Still others rapidly break down at the implementation stage and the process ends in recrimination and accusation of bad faith." It is in the relative sense of a formal negotiated agreement to end military hostilities that the term "success" is used here. See Christopher R. Mitchell, *Conflict Resolution and Civil War: Reflections on the Sudanese Settlement of 1972*, Working Paper 3, Center for Conflict Analysis and Resolution, George Mason University, August 1989, 32.

4. Touval, *The Peace Brokers*; and Saadia Touval, "Biased Intermediaries: Theoretical and Historical Considerations," *Jerusalem Journal of International Relations* 1, no. 1 (Autumn 1975): 51–87.

5. Quoted in Touval, 146.

6. See Richard N. Haass, "Ripeness and the Settlement of International Disputes," *Survival* 30, no. 3 (May/June 1988): 232–251; Richard N. Haass, *Conflicts Unending: The United States and Regional Disputes* (New Haven, Conn.: Yale University Press, 1990); I. William Zartman, *Ripe for*

Resolution: Conflict and Intervention in Africa (New York: Oxford University Press, 1985); I. William Zartman, "Ripening Conflict, Ripe Moment, Formula, and Mediation," in Diane B. Bendahmane and John W. McDonald, Jr., eds., *Perspectives on Negotiation* (Washington, D.C.: Foreign Service Institute, US Department of State, 1986), 205–228; and Saadia Touval and I. William Zartman, eds., *International Mediation in Theory and Practice* (Boulder, Colo.: Westview Press, 1985), 251–268.

7. Other considerations for successful third-party intervention include the nature of the issues under dispute, the timing of the intervention, the qualities and skills of the intervener, and the methods used. The timing of third-party intervention in the dispute settlement process is a crucial, if understudied, variable. Scott Taylor, "The De-escalation of Regional Conflict and the Timing of Third Party Intervention," Master's research essay, The Norman Paterson School of International Affairs, Carleton University, Ottawa, January 1991.

Much of the literature on third-party intervention argues that conflicts are most amenable to resolution when issues are well defined and structured to permit confidence building to emerge over time. See, for example, Louis Kriesberg, "Timing and the Initiation of De-Escalation Moves," *Negotiation Journal* 3, no. 4 (October 1987): 375–384; and Loraleigh Keashley and Ronald J. Fisher, "Towards a Contingency Approach to Third Party Intervention in Regional Conflict: A Cyprus Illustration," *International Journal* 65, no. 2 (Spring 1990): 424–453.

When this is not the case, it may be difficult to identify a formula or any sense in which issues must be resolved first to lend momentum to risk taking. Conflicts that are not amenable to traditional forms and methods of conflict resolution are known as "protracted" or "intractable" international conflicts. See, for example, Edward E. Azar, "Protracted International Conflicts: Ten Propositions," in Edward E. Azar and John W. Burton, eds., *International Conflict Resolution: Theory and Practice* (Brighton: Wheatsheaf, 1986), 33–34; and Fred M. Frohock, "Reasoning and Intractibility," John Agnew, "Beyond Reason: Spatial and Temporal Sources of Ethnic Conflict," and Louis Kricsberg, "Transforming Conflicts in the Middle East and Central Europe," in Louis Kriesberg, Terrell A. Northrup, and Stuart J. Thorson, eds., *Intractable Conflicts and Their Transformation* (Syracuse, N.Y.: Syracuse University Press, 1989), 13–24, 41–52, 109–131.

8. David E. Albright, "East-West Tensions in Africa," in Marshall D. Shulman, ed., *East-West Tensions in the Third World* (New York: Norton, 1986), 116–157.

9. See Fen Osler Hampson, "Building a Stable Peace: Opportunities and Limits to Security Cooperation in Third World Regional Conflicts," *International Journal* 65, no. 2 (Spring 1990): 454–489.

10. For a theoretical discussion of these views see Robert Keohane, ed., *Neorealism and Its Critics* (New York: Columbia University Press, 1986), 1–97, 322–346; and Joseph F. Grieco, "Anarchy and the Limits of Cooperation: A Realist Critique of the Newest Liberal Institutionalism," *International Organization* 42, no. 3 (Summer 1988): 485–507. For various discussions about US interests and policies toward the Third World that, in varying degrees, reflect the realist/neorealist view, see Stephen M. Walt, "The Case for Finite Containment: Analyzing U.S. Grand Strategy," Steven R. David, "Why the Third World Matters," and Michael Detsch, "The Keys That Lock Up the World: Identifying U.S. Interests in the Periphery," *International Security* 14,

no. 1 (Summer 1989): 5–121. For a useful discussion about the limits of US military power in Third World conflicts see Steven van Evera, "The Case Against Intervention," *The Atlantic Monthly* (July 1990): 72–80.

11. For treatments of the history of this conflict, see Robert S. Jaster, "South Africa and Its Neighbours: The Dynamics of Regional Conflict," *Adelphi Papers No. 209* (London: International Institute of Strategic Studies, Summer 1986); and John A. Marcum and Hasu H. Patel, "Regional Security in Southern Africa," *Survival* 30, no. 1 (January/February 1988): 3–58.

12. The following discussion is based on the following sources: Robert S. Jaster, "The 1988 Peace Accords and the Future of South-western Africa," *Adelphi Papers No. 253* (London: International Institute of Strategic Studies, Autumn 1990); Vivienne Jabri, "The Western Contact Group as Intermediary in the Conflict over Namibia," in C. R. Mitchell and K. Webb, eds., *New Approaches to International Mediation* (New York: Greenwood Press, 1988), 102–130; Pamela Falk, "Namibian Independence and the Cuban Presence in Angola: Third Party Involvement in Southern African Conflict Resolution," in Report of the International Peace Academy, *Southern Africa in Crisis: Regional and International Responses* (Dordrecht: Martinus Nijhoff, 1988), 91–102; Gerald Bender and Witney Schneidman, "The Namibia Negotiations— Multilateral Versus Bilateral Approaches to International Mediation," Case No. 422, Pew Program in Case Teaching and Writing, Pittsburgh, 1988; Pamela S. Falk, "The U.S., U.S.S.R., Cuba and South Africa in Angola, 1974– 88: Negotiators' Nightmare, Diplomats' Dilemma," Case No. 405, Pew Program in Case Teaching and Writing, Pittsburgh, 1988; and Pamela S. Falk and Kurt M. Campbell, "The U.S., U.S.S.R., Cuba and South Africa in Angola, 1974–88: The Quagmire of Four-Party Negotiations, 1981–1988," Case No. 429, Pew Program in Case Teaching and Writing, Pittsburgh, 1988.

13. The United States offered to try to get SWAPO's role as the "sole and authentic representative of the people of Namibia" withdrawn if South Africa would agree to a date to implement Resolution 435. Dirk Mudge said no to the terms of the offer.

14. For discussions of US policies toward Southern Africa under Reagan, see Ben L. Martin, "American Policy Towards Southern Africa in the 1980s," *Journal of Modern African Studies* 27, no. 1 (1989): 23–46; Davidson Nicol, "United States Foreign Policy in Southern Africa: Third-World Perspectives," *Journal of Modern African Studies* 21, no. 4 (1983): 587–603; Michael Clough, "Southern Africa: Challenges and Choices," *Foreign Affairs* 66, no. 5 (Summer 1988): 1067–1090; Howard Wolpe, "Seizing Southern African Opportunities," *Foreign Policy* 73 (Winter 1988–1989): 60–75; and Robert E. Clute, "The American-Soviet Confrontation in Africa: Its Impact on the Politics on Africa," *Journal of Asian and African Studies* 24, nos. 3–4 (1989): 159–169.

15. Quoted in Ronald Dreyer, *Namibia and Angola: The Search for Independence and Regional Security (1966–1988)*, PSIS Occasional Papers No. 3/1988 (Geneva: Programme for Strategic and International Security Studies, Graduate Institute of International Studies, 1988), 31.

16. Zartman argues that there are four independent conditions for ripeness: a hurting stalemate to the conflict, a looming catastrophe, valid representatives, and a way out of the conflict, though not all conditions need be present for ripeness to occur. See Zartman, "Ripening Conflict, Ripe Moment, Formula, and Mediation," 217–218.

By contrast, Haass defines ripeness in terms of "the prerequisites for diplomatic progress" or the "circumstances conducive for negotiated progress or even a solution," which are based on the following conditions: "a shared perception of the desirability of an accord," willingness to reach a compromise, and compromises that are based on formulas in which the national interests of the parties are protected, and approaches or processes of dispute resolution that are acceptable to the parties. Haass's "conditions" come perilously close to defining ripeness in terms of the willingness of the parties to seek a negotiated compromise to settle their differences, i.e., equating parties' motivations and interests in a settlement (which may be difficult if not impossible to discern) with the negotiated outcome. See Haass, *Conflicts Unending*, 6, 27–28.

17. See, for example, John W. Burton, "The Means to Agreement: Power or Values?" in Diane B. Bendahmane and John W. McDonald, Jr., eds., *Perspectives on Negotiation* (Washington, D.C.: Foreign Service Institute, US Department of State, 1986), 229–242; and John W. Burton, *Resolving Deep-Rooted Conflict* (Lanham, Md.: University Press of America, 1987).

18. Chris Brown, "Regional Conflict in Southern Africa and the Role of Third Party Mediators," *International Journal* 65, no. 2 (Spring 1990): 352–353.

19. Douglas G. Anglin, "Ripe, Ripening, or Overripe? Sanctions as an Inducement to Negotiations: The South African Case," *International Journal* 65, no. 2 (Spring 1990): 368. Anglin points out, however, that the international banking community has taken the sting of sanctions on the South African economy by repeatedly bailing out the South African regime when foreign exchange crises forced it to default on its debts.

20. For discussions of Soviet foreign policies to the region, see Kurt M. Campbell, "Southern Africa in Soviet Foreign Policy," *Adelphi Papers No. 227* (London: International Institute of Strategic Studies, Winter 1987/88); Chi Su, "Moscow's Ideology and Policy in Southern Africa," *Issues and Studies* 22, no. 2 (February 1986): 99–110; Christopher Coker, "Moscow and Pretoria: A Possible Alignment," *The World Today* 44, no. 1 (January 1988): 6–9; Peter Clement, "Moscow and Southern Africa," *Problems of Communism* 34, no. 2 (March–April 1985): 29–50; Keith Somerville, "The U.S.S.R. and Southern Africa Since 1976," *Journal of Modern African Studies* 22, no. 1 (1984): 73–108; Peter Shearman, "Soviet Foreign Policy in Africa and Latin America: A Comparative Case Study," *Millennium: Journal of International Studies* 15, no. 3 (Winter 1986): 339–359; and Sam C. Nolutshungu, "Soviet Involvement in Southern Africa," *Annals, AAPSS* No. 481 (September 1985): 138–146.

21. Mark Owen Lombardi, "The Angolan-Namibian Peace Agreement and Superpower Foreign Policy: A Regionalist or Globalist Solution?" Paper presented at the International Studies Association annual meeting, Washington, D.C., 1990.

22. Neil S. MacFarlane, "The Soviet Union and Southern African Security," *Problems of Communism* 38, nos. 2–3 (March–June 1989): 85–86.

23. This reinforces the point made by Putnam that the structure of domestic coalitions and domestic bargaining strategies can significantly affect the prospects of agreement in international negotiations. See Robert Putnam in "Diplomacy and Domestic Politics: The Logic of Two-Level Games," *International Organization* 42, no. 3 (Summer 1988): 427–460.

■ Part 4 ■
Regional Conflicts and Their Resolution in the Post–Cold War World

■ 7 ■

Must the Grass Still Suffer?

JAMES G. BLIGHT & THOMAS G. WEISS

By the winter of 1989–1990, it was clear that momentous events were under way, events for which no student of international relations, no matter how clever or farsighted, could have been adequately prepared. The Cold War was drawing to an unexpected, dramatic conclusion. With its demise, the underlying assumptions of foreign relations for powers great and small had to be jettisoned. Everything we had been taught about the international system—East versus West, bloc versus bloc, containment of Soviet expansionism, struggling with Marxists for the minds of men and women—seemed suddenly in those months following the breaching of the Berlin Wall to acquire an antique aspect, even before the bulldozers could physically remove the structure that had symbolized the Cold War since 1961. Nowhere was this more obvious than in the regional conflicts of the Third World.[1]

There was a brief interlude between the symbolic demise of the Cold War and the Iraqi invasion of Kuwait several months later; leaders, particularly President George Bush, began somewhat prematurely to welcome in a new world order. Even before questions began to arise about a United Nations dominated by Washington, euphoria over the end of the Cold War had not extended to most Third World capitals.[2] Pessimism and fear surfaced, especially from regimes whose very existence owed much to playing the superpowers against each other.

Perhaps the most successful player in the Cold War game of superpower patronage had been Cuba's Fidel Castro, who had in various ways secured and maintained virtually a symbiotic relationship with the Soviet Union. Even before the final tumbling of the Berlin Wall, therefore, it was natural that Castro would feel himself to be vulnerable to abandonment by the Soviets, and by Cuba's other socialist trading partners. In July 1989, just days after the Hungarians opened their borders, initiating the chain reaction that led by the end of the year to the liberation of all of Eastern Europe, Castro shared his anxiety with the Cuban people in a nationally broadcast speech:

> Let's not be squeamish; we must call a spade a spade. There are difficulties in the world revolutionary movement. There are difficulties in the socialist movement. We cannot even say with certainty that the supplies that have been arriving with clockwork punctuality from the socialist camp for thirty years will keep arriving with the same certainty. . . . The problems of the Soviet Union are something of extreme concern to all Third World countries, to former colonies, to all those people who do not want to be colonized again; because in the USSR they found their fundamental and firmest ally.[3]

As would quickly become clear, Castro's rhetorical outburst was on the mark. Moreover, Cuba's situation differed from that of many other Third World countries only in the degree of that country's dependence on the Cold War's loser. The end of East-West tensions brought anxiety in other Third World capitals, not least in Baghdad, where Saddam Hussein seems to have drawn the conclusion that it was now or never concerning his designs on Kuwait. Moscow could not be relied on indefinitely to support its traditional allies in the Third World.[4]

Yet such anxious reactions at first struck many US observers as one-sided, even paranoid. Had not the Cold War been a euphemism in many regions of the Third World for just plain war, whose combatants on all sides had been supplied and encouraged by one or the other superpower? Had not Third World conflicts become ever bloodier and more costly in every way, primarily because of the interest taken in them by the two superpowers with their allies? Had not the denouement of the Cold War, beginning in the late 1980s, led to surprising and salutary resolutions to some of the most intractable and tragic of such conflicts, particularly in the Caribbean Basin and Southern Africa?[5] With peace breaking out in these former war zones of superpower proxies, why, many asked, be pessimistic about the post–Cold War Third World?

Two answers dominated, representing fears whose relative intensity differed from capital to capital in Africa, Asia, and Latin America. First, it was believed that with the waning of the Cold War, the great powers, neither of which had an intrinsic stake in the Third World, had no further reason to take a significant interest there. The United States would no longer feel obliged to contain communism; the Soviet Union would no longer believe in the world socialist revolution, in the name of which its connections and aid to insurgencies and governments in the Third World had been justified. Second, it was feared that the Soviet Union's inward turning, and its consequent uninterest in deterring US adventurism, would lead Washington to intervene with impunity in the Third World, perhaps under the ruse of collective security, as some held it had in the conduct of the Gulf War. Or perhaps the United States would return to an updated version of gunboat diplomacy, acting unilaterally as it had in Panama in December 1989, just weeks after the collapse of the Berlin Wall.

Thus, the feeling grew in the Third World that its governments and inhabitants were suddenly at risk: of being ignored and abandoned in the ruins of conflicts once maintained by Cold War animosities; or of being singled out by the United States, suddenly undeterred by Soviet power, for arbitrary intervention, conquest, and humiliation. It was in this context that we found fresh relevance in the Swahili aphorism: "Whether the elephants make war or make love, it is the grass that suffers." This adage seemed to capture the attitudes of many who had suffered disproportionately during, and in many ways because of, the superpowers' Cold War. Now, with the two Northern behemoths entering an unprecedented period of cozy relations, many in the South feared they would continue to suffer, for reasons directly related to the absence of the Cold War.

From Cold War's End to Unipolar Moment

From that winter of 1989–1990, in the midst of American euphoria and Third World paranoia, we undertook this research, whereby at least some of these fantasies and fears might acquire anchorage in empirical reality. At the outset of this exercise the fundamental fact of the new world order seemed almost universally to be the termination of the Cold War. It was this abrupt end to East-West tensions that had produced euphoria in the North and anxiety in the South. But before the chapters that make up this book could be drafted, improved, criticized, discussed, and revised again, it had become quite clear that embedded within the *end* of the Cold War was the undeniable fact that the Soviet Union had *lost* it.

Moreover, many factors indicated that the Soviet Union was itself on the brink of complete collapse. It could not keep its commitments to its own people, let alone its Third World allies. Marxism itself had been thrown into history's dustbin, and preventing the destabilizing collapse of the Soviet Union had become, incredibly, an important goal of Western democracies, which even involved expanding the G7, in London in July 1991, to include Moscow as an observer in the club of the most powerful industrial countries. This state of affairs was inconceivable, not only during the Cold War; it was also barely visible, if at all, in November 1989, when the Berlin Wall began to topple.

The implosion of Soviet society and the rapid disappearance of Soviet power assumed tremendous poignancy in the Third World during the year between the conception of this book and the completion of its central chapters. Iraq, a recipient of voluminous Soviet military assistance over the years, was abandoned to its lonely fate. The USSR fell in step behind Washington's leadership of the coalition that eventually forced the government of Saddam Hussein to withdraw from Kuwait. The Ethiopian regime of Mengistu Haile Mariam, long completely dependent on military assistance from the Soviets, was abandoned by them and overthrown by insurgents. Moscow began dramatically cutting back on aid to Vietnam, leading to what appears to be a turning point for that country's regime.

Finally, Cuba—the jewel of Soviet expansionism, whose armies had fought alongside Soviet advisers in Africa, and whose military assistance to insurgents and governments in the Caribbean Basin had led to important victories in the Cold War—now appeared to be on the brink of catastrophe. The worst fears of President Fidel Castro seemed to be coming true, as the Soviets simply lost their ability to keep their huge array of commitments to Cuba, which in turn had become so dependent on Moscow that it seemed unable to turn elsewhere for assistance in its hour of need.[6]

We summarize these familiar developments because they provided the unanticipated context for the two days of discussions for which the chapters in this volume were the literary stimulation. The exercise had begun as an inquiry into the possible effect of the end of the Cold War on the two regions in question. It evolved into a discussion of the impact of the collapse of the Soviet Union and the onset of what many observers began to call, following Charles Krauthammer, the unipolar moment.[7] We had misunderstood what was going on in the period just before the Cold War ended: the Soviet empire was on the verge of collapse. The unipolar moment was appearing before our eyes, but our Cold War blinders did not allow us properly to appreciate it.

We write this chapter less than two months after the failed coup of August 18–21, 1991, in the Soviet Union. It is now impossible to miss the unipolar implications of recent events. The bungled, misguided attempt at a coup d'état became the final catalytic coup de grace of Soviet communism. Just as Frederick the Great could once characterize the Holy Roman Empire as neither holy, nor Roman, nor an empire, one must now acknowledge that the Union of Soviet Socialist Republics is neither a union, nor socialist, nor Soviet, nor even a collection of ostensible republics, many of which appear to be breaking up along ethnic lines. Many Russians, traditional virtuosos of black humor, have taken to calling their former country the "UFFR" (Union of Fewer and Fewer Republics), and also the "USS Were."

Implications of these events for the Third World are, however, far from humorous. Consider the fate of Cuba in the immediate wake of the

Soviet implosion and entry into the new "Northern Third World." Desperate both to remove barriers to US aid to Moscow and to outflank Russian radicals seeking to end all foreign involvement, Mikhail Gorbachev has now done the formerly unthinkable: he has publicly proclaimed the intention to abandon Cuba. In September 1991, he appeared in Moscow with Secretary of State James Baker to announce that all Soviet troops would be withdrawn from Cuba and that aid to Cuba would cease.[8]

The severity of this announcement and the finality with which it signaled the Soviet withdrawal from the Third World might usefully be compared with, say, a hypothetical US announcement that Israel was being analogously abandoned due to a deal the US had made with Arab states, without the consultation of Israeli officials. The Cuban reaction was one of unmitigated bitterness. "We are marching," was the Cuban Foreign Ministry response to Gorbachev's announcement, "toward a world order in which the little countries of the Third World, like Cuba, whose social systems do not please the United States will have no choice but to submit or run the risk of disappearing,"[9] As often happens, Cuba's response to events, while stronger than some in the Southern Third World, nonetheless contains elements with which many in these countries can agree. And none can hereafter escape the conclusion that if the Soviets cannot, or will not, keep their commitments to their most important ally in the Third World, then the great post–World War II counterweight to US hegemony is no more, and they are all hereafter on their own.

What is the significance of having discovered that the Cold War ended because the Soviet Union collapsed, and that it had been collapsing for quite some time? The world for our near-term projections is likely to be one in which only the United States remains a military force worldwide.[10] And it is this new, unipolar world that was already emerging some years ago in the Third World.

The events marking the resolution of conflicts in these regions need to be understood at least as much in the context of US power, "hard" and raw as well as soft, to quote Nye,[11] without the counterbalance of Soviet power, as in the context of new thinking and cooperation. New thinking on the part of Mikhail S. Gorbachev, Eduard A. Shevardnadze and their colleagues, and its contagious effect on even hard-boiled Cold Warriors like Ronald Reagan and Margaret Thatcher, has been substantial. But the more significant point for the immediate future is that the former Soviet Union is effectively disappearing from the Southern Third World scene, as it becomes a collection of Northern Third World countries, each of which has become a competitor with regions such as the Caribbean Basin and Southern Africa for increasingly scarce resources of the G7 industrialized nations.

What Difference Did the Cold War Make?

For the countries of the Caribbean Basin and Southern Africa, superpower antagonism was of primal significance. The rescinding of superpower tensions brought into stark relief the position Moscow and Washington had among the players in the Cold War conflicts explored in our case studies.

The Caribbean Basin

The somewhat paradoxical picture emerging from the United States and the USSR may be summarized this way: While the Cold War had everything to do with interstate conflict in the Caribbean Basin, the Soviet Union had very little directly to do with it. Moscow recognized its interests there as peripheral (except for Cuba) and that the US would always be the regional behemoth. The Soviets have, with the exception of the Cuban missile deployment, displayed considerable caution in the region. To the radical Marxists around Maurice Bishop in Grenada, for example, they contributed only small arms, uniforms, and other supplies.

Nevertheless, the appearance of *any* Soviet assistance in the region was regarded, by the Reagan administration of the early 1980s as completely unacceptable. It was "evidence" that the Soviets were once again on the move, looking for other Cubas. In Nicaragua, the Soviets at first stayed aloof altogether, as the Carter administration tried to assist the Sandinistas, specifically to avoid "another Cuba."[12] Later their aid increased, though never to an extent remotely resembling US assistance to the contras in the Reagan period. As Sergo Mikoyan, a longtime observer of superpower politics in Cuba, put it: "It was not primarily Soviet aid in the region that contributed to conflict; it was rather the mere existence of the Soviet Union, a country hospitable to revolution, that both provided psychological sustenance to insurgencies, and irritation to US policy makers concerned to keep the Caribbean Basin a pristine American lake."†

It hardly needs mentioning that US contributions to conflict in the region have been large and various. In Nicaragua and El Salvador, massive military aid has come from Washington to rebels and government, respectively. In Grenada and Panama, the United States intervened with its own military forces. Both interventions had clear Cold War overtones. Both involved US calculations about Soviet influence, though mainly through what were regarded in Washington as Cuban proxies, who were said to be disguised in Grenada as construction workers, and who were supposedly working hand-in-glove with Panamanian strongman Manuel Noriega.

In this context, with the United States "sniffing everywhere for Marxists," and the International Department of the Communist Party of the Soviet Union "sniffing for opportunities," on its own or in the wake of the adventurous and enterprising Cubans, political systems in the region became polarized and corrupt. The Cold War, as refracted through the lenses of various US security agencies, has wreaked havoc on the Caribbean Basin every bit as tangibly as the hurricanes, which are an unpleasant reality in the region. In fact, the Cold War has been the dominant fact of political life in the area since the Cuban revolution of 1959.

Angola/Namibia

Whereas the Cold War *caused* much of the conflict in the Caribbean Basin, the principal conflicts in Angola and Namibia predated US and Soviet involvement or even interest in the region. In fact, superpower concern was the *effect* of conflicts already under way, prompted by the intervening variable of global competition during the Cold War. The spark that lit the fire in Southern Africa was the sudden collapse of Portugal as a colonial power and the resulting "power vacuum." Into this vacuum rushed advocates of all sorts of ethnic and class-related strife that had, for a brief moment in the mid–1970s, the look and feel of what Southern Africa watcher Robert Jaster called "a conflict typical of age-old bush wars in the region."† Whether ethnic identity or class issues were more salient in producing the fierce conflict is a point that is contested by experts.

The superpowers were several steps removed from the conflict that followed in the wake of the Portuguese collapse. The South Africans were of course professed and virulent anticommunists. The Angolans were avowedly Marxist. When the South Africans moved into Angola, the Cubans were fraternal socialists to a fault and answered a call from Luanda. They came by the tens of thousands to help. Mobutu's Zaire and the South Africans made sure that Henry Kissinger took due note of the presence of Cubans in their neck of the woods. The United States, reflecting the prevailing wisdom about Moscow-Havana relations, concluded that the Cubans had gone to Angola at the behest of the Soviets. However, the Soviets did not even receive advance warning about the Cuban airlift to Angola. "Gromyko and Kissinger both read about it in the newspaper,"† said Sergo Mikoyan, who was in a position to know the details.[13] The logic of global containment intervened. In operational terms, what had looked initially like a bush war became a tragically bloody, high-tech war, the site of the largest tank battles in Africa since World War II. With hundreds of thousands of casualties, reconciliation had become problematic.

South Africa

Through an incremental and step-by-fateful-step process of decisionmaking leading to the Angolan/Namibian war, South Africans slithered into a quagmire of their own creation. Analogies to US involvement in Vietnam are apt. In quick succession, the South Africans were surprised by the collapse of the Portuguese, and mistakenly confident of the opportunity to expand their influence into Angola. They were shocked by the Cuban sea- and airlift to Luanda, but decided to push on, convinced that they would retain command of the air over Angola and thus the course of the war. They were troubled by what they detected as increasing Soviet involvement, but they could not foresee that Soviet surface-to-air missiles would be difficult to knock out and thus that they would fail to achieve air superiority. Finally, South Africans were angered at what they eventually took to be their betrayal and abandonment by Washington, which they apparently believed would offer unconditional support because the enemies of South Africa—the Angolans and Cubans—were Marxists. This disastrous string of miscalculations meant that the South Africans could not fight what Annette Seegers, a South African military analyst, called the "Afrikaner way of war: letting blacks die in the place of whites."† Instead, they began to suffer casualties at an alarming rate, which the population would not support and could not sustain.

Viewed in hindsight, the South Africans' fate may be seen as a distant early warning of the coming end of the Cold War. The old generation, firmly in charge when the SADF moved into Angola in the mid–1970s, was soon challenged by what Seegers called "a new bourgeois generation of white politicians,"† for whom anticommunism and white supremacy would become more of an embarrassment than a dominant ideology. The picture that emerged was of an aging leadership increasingly out of touch even with its own white supporters, deluded into thinking that anticommunism would be enough to carry the day in Washington, regardless of the consequences. The radical wing of the Afrikaner leadership had thus sown the seeds of its own destruction. Out of the ruins of the Angolan/Namibian war came the realization that Cold War politics would thereafter provide insufficient international cover for the repugnant, racist society over which they ruled.

Cuba

Since the abortive episode at the Bay of Pigs in April 1961, Cuba has not been attacked by significant US-backed forces. Nevertheless, a discussion of Cuban involvement in the conflicts of the Caribbean Basin and Southern Africa should reflect continuing Cuban efforts to deter a US invasion of their island. In his contribution to this volume, Jorge Domínguez calls this "managing the debris of the Cuban missile crisis," following which the Cubans, with very significant Soviet assistance, worked feverishly to build up the defenses of the island. Their goal was to demonstrate that a US invasion, no matter how massive, would be too costly in blood to be worthwhile.

To Havana's obsession with deterring such an invasion, one must add the overwhelming personality of Cuban leader Fidel Castro—who came to power when Dwight Eisenhower was president and is still younger than George Bush. Castro's propensity to take risks, his apparent revolutionary fanaticism, his frequent expressions of fraternalism with Third World insurgents, and his regime's ability to organize Cuba into a formidable military power provide the background for understanding the Cubans and regional conflict. For decades Washington has viewed Castro's Cuba as a pariah, a troublemaker of the first magnitude. Moscow, however, viewed Cuba as a very useful ally in the global competition with the United States.

In the Caribbean Basin, the Cubans have in the past two decades supported revolutionary insurgents or governments in El Salvador, Nicaragua, Guatemala, Grenada, Colombia, and elsewhere. They have done so not only militarily, but also by sending doctors, teachers, and an array of advisers who have often been much appreciated by their hosts. But it has been in Africa that Cuba has most openly displayed its "pipsqueak power." Everything about aid for Angola was in character for Castro and the Cubans: assisting black Africans against racists; opposing US allies like South Africa and Zaire; and proving to the Soviets, whom they eventually pulled into the conflict, that Cuba is worth the billions in aid it has received yearly for so long.

But the Cubans, like the South Africans, seriously miscalculated. Although Cuban officials seldom admit it publicly, several have stated privately that in 1975 they believed that the Angola operation would last only about six months, long enough to turn the tide, after which they would return home as triumphant warriors. But six months became sixteen years, thousands of Cuban deaths, and a war that exacted a terrible toll on Cuban society. Moreover, the Cold War ended before the Angolan war. Ironically and bitterly, the Cubans must note that as Luanda becomes increasingly pragmatic in its international relations and consequently turns to the West for assistance, Cubans may no longer be welcome in the country that they believe they liberated.[14]

What Difference Did "New Thinking" Make?

Soviet new thinking in the conduct of foreign policy seems to have arisen primarily from the conviction of Gorbachev, Shevardnadze, and their colleagues that US-Soviet competition is too dangerous in the nuclear age to be conducted as it has been during the Cold War. New thinking is characterized by a concern for positive sum solutions in which all sides gain, rather than for zero-sum competition in which one side gains at another's expense. Its main tenet for issues in the regions under study in this volume is the repeal of superpower spheres of influence.

Caribbean Basin

In the midst of the upheaval of late 1989, in his address before the United Nations, Shevardnadze placed the goal of superpower diminution in Third World affairs in the context of the rapidly evolving international situation:

> We see nothing threatening in the fact that in accordance with the will of the Polish people a coalition government has been formed. . . . Tolerance is the norm of civilized behavior.
> But if it is obligatory for us in our attitude toward the government of Poland, why are others so intolerant toward, for example, Cuba? And if a non-Communist Prime Minister is possible in a socialist country, why should the appearance of a Communist as head of a Western government be perceived as heresy? The days of the traditional demarcation lines are numbered.[15]

Shevardnadze's sentiments are noble, but they are profoundly naïve. If he actually expected something like full reciprocity, a kind of Sinatra Doctrine for the Western Hemisphere, in which each state might go its own way, he was mistaken. The United States, in its dealings with Cuba and the other governments of the Caribbean Basin, has shown no interest in *ending* the Cold War without also *winning* it.

The resolution of recent conflicts in the Caribbean Basin are thus most usefully explained by Soviet withdrawal and accommodation to the Monroe Doctrine rather than by its repeal. In Washington's direct interventions in Grenada and Panama, the issue has not been conflict resolution, but simple emplacement of regimes whose views accord with those of Washington. In Nicaragua, a good deal has been made of the impact on the peace process of negotiations between Assistant Secretary of State Bernard Aronson and Soviet Foreign Ministry official Yuri Pavlov. Some believe the Soviets pressed the Sandinistas to call elections in February 1990, and to abide by the results. The Sandinistas eventually lost to a coalition led by Violeta Chamorro, whose campaign was backed and financed by the United States. In fact, the evidence suggests that the

United States was far more interested in winning in Nicaragua than in sustaining the fragile democracy there. Aid to the Chamorro government is nowhere near the level of aid given to the contras. Rather than genuinely playing by positive-sum rules, Washington seems to have taken advantage of Moscow's new thinking as a cover to whip the Sandinistas.

One significant development derived from Soviet new thinking is the emergence of the United Nations as a player in regional affairs.[16] Previously, Washington had systematically prevented UN involvement in the Caribbean Basin, a curious permutation of the Monroe Doctrine. However, beginning in 1989 the US reversed its policy toward the world organization, which has subsequently taken a significant role in conflict management in a number of capacities: sending unarmed military observers for Central America, soldiers to disarm the contras, civilian observers and police to oversee domestic elections in both Nicaragua and Haiti, and most recently, unarmed military observers to monitor human rights violations in El Salvador. Although the UN's press coverage during the gulf crisis was more dramatic, the turnaround of the world organization's fortunes in the Caribbean Basin was no less spectacular.

Angola/Namibia

There are two arguments, somewhat at variance with received wisdom, concerning the role of the superpowers in resolving the conflict in Southern Africa. Robert Jaster has said, "The Soviets' role in the peace process consisted mainly of hand-holding. They really weren't very important."† At no point, according to specialists from the United States, the USSR, Cuba, and South Africa, did Moscow exert pressure on the Cubans. According to Jorge Domínguez, "the Cubans and Angolans noticed the changing world around them, and decided it was time to negotiate."† The Cubans agreed to a phased withdrawal of their armed forces at the same time emphasizing the fundamental necessity of Namibian independence.

It is sometimes argued that, for the United States, constructive engagement, coined and implemented by Reagan's assistant secretary of state, Chester Crocker, was fundamental to the peaceful outcome. According to this view, the Reagan administration's policy of engaging the South Africans eventually paid off, as they too came to the conference table. Few independent observers believe this. Jaster characterized constructive engagement as a "broken clock that eventually told the right time," and an obstructionist policy, because of the "wedding gift" the Reagan administration gave to the South Africans—linkage of an agreement to a Cuban pullout.† Without this linkage, peace would have come to the region far sooner than it did. As it turned out, a hurting stalemate finally caused so much suffering on all sides that the participants, in effect, stumbled to the conference table. Yet in this region, the eventual settlement was relatively fair and equitable, far more so than the one-sided "victories" required by Washington in the Caribbean Basin.

Again, new thinking made possible the UN's success story in helping to end the carnage in Angola and to terminate South African control over Namibia. The military observers in Angola were a helpful addition to the December 1988 agreements. In Namibia the world organization was essential in overseeing the long-awaited independence process and plebiscite. UNTAG had been on hold since 1978, and the UN "invasion"—some 5,000 troops and police and almost as many civilians, not to mention associated representatives from nongovernmental organizations—in 1989–1990 was possible because of the sea-change in Moscow's policy and a reciprocal response from Washington.

South Africa

Though few could have discerned it at the time, South Africa was already in the throes of a societal revolution during the Angolan war, dramatically symbolized by the release of Nelson Mandela, the legalization of the ANC, and the dismantling of the legal basis for apartheid. A new generation, barely visible politically, was making itself felt in the South African peace movement, particularly after the battle of Cuito Cuanavale in January-February 1988. The battle itself was only the occasion when the government recognized that it had reached a stalemate and could not win the war. The real battle was being fought within South Africa, and it was generational. Comparisons to the US experience on the home front during the Vietnam War are appropriate.

In the negotiations the South Africans proved willing to give up a lot to achieve peace. They forsook the UNITA rebels, led by Jonas Savimbi, whom SADF particularly liked, and they were forced to live as neighbors with Namibian leader Sam Nujoma, formerly spoken of in official South African circles as "conceived in communist sin in Moscow." Was this new thinking by the South Africans? Perhaps. But it was made necessary by a revolution within their country. This situation resembles the Soviet Union's in that ideologically driven foreign adventures are no longer supported by an increasingly restive and divided domestic constituency.

Cuba

The official view in Washington, almost from the moment Fidel Castro came to power, is that the Cubans export revolution in the Western

Hemisphere, and in so doing act on behalf of the Soviets, in violation of the Monroe Doctrine. The Cuban view is that because the US props up vile, right-wing regimes whose leaders toe the line for Washington and business interests, it is the Cubans' duty to respond when insurgents or beleaguered governments ask for help. There is more than a grain of truth in the accusations of both.

The relevant point here is that the call by Shevardnadze, in his September 1989 address to the UN, has fallen on deaf ears in the Caribbean Basin. There is little evidence of new thinking in the resolution of conflicts in the region. The United States killed or captured dozens of Cubans during the US invasion of Grenada in 1983, harassed Cuban officials in Panama after the invasion in 1989, and resolutely refuses to negotiate. Both Washington and Havana seem to feel that the United States won and Cuba lost in Nicaragua. In none of these zero-sum transactions is there any evidence that the Soviets brought pressure to bear on the Cubans.

Whereas the Cubans may have fallen on hard times in the Caribbean Basin since the early 1980s, their official view is that they and their allies won in Southern Africa. Jorge Risquet, Cuban Politburo member and chief Cuban negotiator of the Angola/Namibia accords, put it this way in a recent interview:

> Cuito Cuanavale was decisive. The negotiations came later. The battle of Stalingrad took place three years before the fall of Berlin, but it was at Stalingrad that the outcome of World War II was decided. . . . The South Africans realized that putting up a frontal battle in southern Angola and northern Namibia would amount to the swan song of apartheid. So they decided to concede Namibia.[17]

In mid–1991, the last of approximately 300,000 Cuban troops who had served in Angola returned home to a hero's welcome, ending this chapter of Cuban involvement in the region. The view espoused by Risquet is disputed, especially by those who emphasize that the Cubans could hardly have continued to sustain the war much longer in light of imminent reductions in Soviet aid. But this only reinforces the point that the end of the Angola-Namibia war had little to do with new thinking and everything to do with the regional collapse of South Africa and the nascent global collapse of the Soviet Union.

Uncertainties Between Two Epochs

While the Cold War is identified universally as losing its relevance in Third World affairs, the new epoch has not yet formed. Between the old and the new, there is much conjecturing about future relations among the superpowers and their former allies.

Caribbean Basin

Many Caribbean Basin nationals are profoundly disturbed by an emerging post–Cold War pattern. The invasion of Panama showed that Washington will act unilaterally, embodying what Sergo Mikoyan called "F–16 diplomacy," an updated version of the gunboat diplomacy of yesteryear. The unwillingness or inability to boost democracy in Nicaragua shows that the United States once again cares only that its people are in power and has no more interest than formerly in fostering genuine economic development in the region. Most ominously, the Gulf War proves that the United States can move with impunity, seemingly where it wishes. The Soviets, who could once be counted on to resist US adventurism, will hereafter knuckle under and rapidly disappear as an important actor on the world stage.

These developments are occurring when alienation in the region is increasing dramatically because of the inability of governments to meet the basic needs of their people, making them vulnerable to coups, insurgencies, and other sorts of chaos. These conditions will tempt Washington to intervene and thus perpetuate the militaristic paternalism that has characterized US–Caribbean Basin relations for 200 years.

However, the taste for representative democracy, once almost the exclusive regional province of the insular Caribbean states, is now being more widely acquired, with the significant exception of Castro's Cuba. There is interest in switching to market-oriented systems—for example, in the return of Jamaica's Prime Minister Michael Manley, formerly a "fidelista socialista," now a born-again advocate of the market.

Yet, the transition from a Cold War environment to a post–Cold War regime is unlikely to be easy. Democracy has not brought prosperity to the islands: many governments in the region are thoroughly corrupt; all are poor, and most are getting poorer; increasing mass emigration and brain drain are all but inevitable; and coups and drug smuggling are ever increasing. In addition, the collapse of the Soviet Union and the end of the Cold War will likely render the only remaining great power capable of having an effect in their countries—the United States—likely to take an interest only after a coup, revolution, or societal collapse, and then only a military interest. The United States is likely to remain just long enough to restore order before moving on to the next disturbance. Thus, deep pessimism remains.

Angola/Namibia

The prognosis is less somber for the transition to post–Cold War politics in Southern Africa. Free and fair elections are fraught with ethnic rivalries and class issues of major proportions. Yet, with the withdrawal of South Africa as the major destabilizing force in its Frontline States, the area stands a decent chance of evolving into a group of democratic, market-oriented states. Angola is rich, as is Namibia, with natural resources. SWAPO, the rebel group that fought for Namibian independence, has demonstrated an ability to forge a consensus, to hold fair elections, and to agree on what many have called a model constitution. The Angolan government of José Eduardo dos Santos, formerly enamored of Castro, shows signs of opening to Western investment and ideas. In all, guarded optimism is the watchword on the transition in Southern Africa. However, a positive outcome in this critical transition period is largely contingent on Washington's actually retaining some semblance of a policy toward the region.

There are also some ominous signs. The current assistant secretary of state for African affairs can no longer even get onto the national security adviser's calendar, a far cry from Chester Crocker's high profile during the Reagan administration. Abdul Mohammed, from the Inter-Africa Group, saw the superpowers' abandonment of all of sub-Saharan Africa symbolized in the joint escape from Somalia of the US and Soviet ambassadors in the same helicopter during the uprising that overthrew Mohammed Siad Barre, leaving the country in the throes of anarchy and war. These sentiments were recently expressed passionately by Mervyn Dymally, the chairman of the US House Foreign Affairs Subcommittee on Africa:

> Southern Africa . . . is being marginalized in President Bush's new world order. . . . If we ignore the poorer nations in favor of the rich, if we turn our backs on Third World friends such as Namibia, the new world order may only be a euphemism for the old world order that saw rich nations get richer and poor poorer. That type of inequity and disparity will only promote political instability and social chaos.[18]

The central question of the transition for the region has changed: Will the United States as the remaining superpower find the moral and financial resources sufficient to meet the needs of this tragically war-torn area?

South Africa

The security arrangements of the entire region depend on a relatively peaceful transition in South Africa itself. This pariah state has heretofore been seen as a problem without a solution. For a brief time, following the release of Nelson Mandela and the legalization of the ANC, there was genuine optimism. But in the wake of terrible factional township violence, and in the absence of any clear path to majority rule in South Africa, its fate must remain quite uncertain.

Some believe that the South African regime possesses the ability to make nuclear weapons. This is a chilling thought for much the same reason that we must now ponder the internal security of the Soviet nuclear arsenal during some unforeseen domestic chaos. What would happen after a coup by right-wing elements in the Afrikaner minority? In no place on earth, therefore, with the exception of the former Soviet Union itself, is the transition to a post–Cold War regime likely to be more complex than in the Republic of South Africa.

Cuba

Cuba is now in the midst of what Fidel Castro began in March 1990 to call the "special period in time of peace."[19] With the former Soviet Union rapidly losing its ability and will to supply Cuba with such staples as oil and grain, Cubans are desperately striving toward self-sufficiency. Recently, officials have begun to speak of "option zero," in anticipation of the moment when they awaken to discover that the Soviet Union, perhaps having erupted in civil war, will no longer supply any of Cuba's needs. What then? In preparation for this day of judgment, Havana is expanding the tourist industry, which flourished in prerevolutionary times but has languished ever since, and seeking trading partners elsewhere, especially in Latin America. In so doing, the leadership has asked its people to make ever greater sacrifices and has exhorted them to do so under the slogan of "socialism or death." Although there is yet no sign of serious opposition to the regime on the island, there is talk elsewhere among the community of Cuba-watchers about civil war, suicidal attacks on the US mainland, and the danger of a Caribbean catastrophe over Cuba in this transition period.[20]

Cuba presents the clearest case of how important it is to the US to win the Cold War. Traditionally, Washington has maintained that two obstacles stand in the way of normal relations with Cuba: export of revolution and Soviet influence, especially the military presence, on the island. All Cuban troops had left Africa by July 1991, and Cuban support for insurgencies in the Caribbean Basin presently consists probably of modest support for the FMLN in El Salvador. The Soviets have now said publicly that they have begun to normalize their own relations with the Cubans, implying just the kind of cutbacks the US has long sought. But the Soviets also add that there can be no completely satisfactory solution to the Cuba puzzle while Washington retains its threatening posture

toward Cuba.[21] The US has responded by raising the ante and now requires
the equivalent of unconditional surrender by the Castro government—
renouncing socialism, holding elections, switching to a market system—
before normal relations can ensue. Wayne Smith has remarked that by
"moving the goalposts" the Cubans are left with nothing to negotiate.†
The Cold War may be over elsewhere, but in the Caribbean it lives on
like a land mine from a previous war.

The Fate of the Soviet Union

Lurking not far offstage during many policy discussions, not least of all
in the G7 in London in July 1991, is a deep concern for the fate of the
Soviet Union. Possibilities fall into three broad categories:

- *Adjustment*: The Soviets cum Russians will find a way to
  negotiate their transition and will emerge again as a great power,
  seeking to retain ties of mutual interest and friendship with their
  traditional allies.
- *Implosion*: The Soviet Union, which has already ceased to exist
  formally, will collapse into chaos, ethnic conflict, perhaps even
  civil war, and it will thus simply cease to be relevant to the
  countries of the Caribbean Basin and Southern Africa.
- *Reversion*: As a result of a successful right-wing coup d'état, or a
  resurgence of socialist fundamentalism, the Soviets will seek
  actively to reestablish their power and influence in the
  regions.

Neither the contributors to this volume nor its editors are sufficiently
courageous to guess which of these possibilities is the most likely. Yet
all agree that even the third scenario, reversion to Cold War attitudes,
perhaps as a result of a coup that is better organized than that of August
1991 is unlikely to produce the result that Soviet Cold Warriors might
seek. The former Soviet Union is too poor and its people far too
preoccupied with internal problems to begin building, as in the days of
Khrushchev, bridgeheads in the Third World, a category to which the
Soviet Union increasingly belongs, except for its nuclear arsenal.

These considerations have prompted a good deal of discussion of an
idea associated most famously with the Melian Dialogue of Thucydides:
"The large and powerful take what they want, while the small and weak
relinquish what they must." What leverage will small, poor, weak
countries have in the wake of the Soviet collapse? Most observers lament
this development even if not enamored of socialism or of the often dismal

past performance by the Soviets in sticking up for the little guy in international affairs.

Third World countries now have no alternative to seeking the attention of Western powers, particularly Washington, yet they can foresee no reliable way to interest the Americans in the absence of a Soviet embrace of their cause. Without the counterbalance of Soviet power, without the luxury of assuming that US responses to Third World entreaties must include calculations of Soviet reactions to similar requests directed to them, representatives from the Caribbean Basin and Southern Africa see little hope of what Anthony Bryan, director of the Institute for International Relations of the University of the West Indies, has called "encouraging civilized behavior on the part of the US."†

The new Soviet position concerning these regions emphasizes their abandonment of past confrontational attitudes in favor of more pragmatic cooperation. This is the regional essence of new thinking, as exemplified in the remark of Leonid Fituni, director of the Soviet Institute for African Studies: "It took the Soviet Union almost thirty years," he said recently, "to recognize that much that was happening in Africa could not be fitted into the grand ideological design."[22] This represents, among other factors, the triumph of the Soviet Foreign Ministry over the International Department of the Central Committee of the Communist Party of the Soviet Union and especially of the influence of Eduard Shevardnadze in the new approach. While there is indeed resentment, as evidenced by Shevardnadze's resignation under fire from communist hard-liners in December 1990, most Soviet officials and academics are relieved and proud of their escape from past rigidities.

Yet, what may appear to be positive-sum new thinking to officials in the Soviet Foreign Ministry often looks like capitulation in Third World capitals. The much-heralded propensity to compromise can be interpreted as a two-edged sword. It advances Soviet interests relative to the United States, which in the new post–Cold War climate is helpful; but at the same time, Moscow may compromise the interests of small countries of the Third World. Representatives of the Caribbean Basin and Southern Africa emphasize that new thinking may only be a transitional strategy. Now that almost all Cold War–driven Third World fires have been cooperatively doused and after the formerly competitive superpowers have left the scene, the former Soviet Union has practically disappeared from the regions.

This, then, is the great regional trade-off at the Cold War's end: the imminent end of superpower exacerbation of regional conflicts, with perhaps greater capacity for reconciliation at their conclusion, as well as the suspicion in Third World capitals that their influence in Moscow and Washington will soon end. In fact, the post–Cold War world is likely to resemble, in places like the Caribbean Basin and Southern Africa, nothing so much as the pre–Cold War world that was dominated by the old colonial powers.

While this may be putting the matter a bit too starkly, such feelings are strongly in evidence at a variety of international gatherings. As Bryan put it pithily: "While the US emphasizes the importance of democracy and the market in the world at large, in our part of the world there is neither. We are not permitted to vote, and there is only one supplier of goods in the marketplace, and that is the US and its group of like-minded, rich and powerful friends."† It is in this sense that the fate of the Soviet Union seems so central to many in the Third World. Hereafter, no large country will be under any sort of pressure to take their needs, their possibilities, or even their wars, into account.

US Policy Choices for a Post–Cold War Security Agenda for the Regions

In thinking about post–Cold War security arrangements, we restrict ourselves to policy options for the United States, schematically addressing the interests and responsibilities of the remaining superpower, the pole of influence at this unipolar moment. We assume that in the very short term the former Soviet Union will remain a player in the Caribbean Basin and Southern Africa, and therefore the Soviet Union and the United States must for a time continue to find ways between them to manage the debris of the Cold War. The sorts of collaboration we will suggest here, therefore, are meant to be consistent with Soviet new thinking, called mutual security in the central theater,[23] which we take to mean primarily seeking solutions that are in the best interests of all concerned. In these respects, we recommend that the principles that have promoted settlements of Cold War disputes so far be applied to remaining real or potential hot spots.

We also assume that in the long run, consistent with emerging policy consensus and the arguments in this volume, the constituents of the former Soviet Union as such, even Russia, will hardly matter in either the construction or operation of the security arrangements of these regions. What is of interest in the long term, therefore, is transcending neocolonialism and avoiding a reversion to pre–Cold War paternalism, resentment, inequity, and instability. Here we enter uncharted territory as we seek to articulate the outline of a security agenda based on a definition of security that has yet to appear to any significant degree in US relations with the countries of either region in question.

In effect, we suggest that the principles of new thinking, or mutual security, be applied to the relationships between a superpower and its small, relatively powerless neighbors. We admit that our argument is open to the charge of wishful thinking—that it violates the dictates of the Melian Dialogue. If it is wishful thinking, we believe it is only because American leaders lack the political will and ability to sell it to their constituents. It requires not altruism but the ability to think in the longer term—the five to ten year time horizon—a luxury now affordable with the Cold War's end.

Caribbean Basin

In the short term, Washington should engage Moscow and Havana directly in a range of issues related to US-Cuban difficulties over the years, including outright US hostility toward Cuba, Soviet military presence and influence on the island, and Cuban support for revolutionary movements and governments.[24] The Cubans have demonstrated that, when given the chance, they do negotiate in good faith, as they did in the discussions that resulted in the resolution of the Angola-Namibia war. The Soviets are keen to talk; Washington should join them. As Rafael Hernández, of Havana's Center for the Study of America, put it, this would amount to "burying the ghost of the Cuban missile crisis of 1962, and it's about time!"† The United States should also join the Soviets and Cubans in negotiating an end to the terribly destructive war in El Salvador, in which all three countries have been involved over the years. The time is ripe for a solution that would save lives, money, and prestige on all sides.

It is in the long term interest of the United States and the small countries of the region to reduce the incidence of illegal drug trafficking, massive and illegal emigration to the United States, and threats to the Panama Canal. These regional issues are of concern to the United States and will supersede efforts to limit the vestiges of Soviet and Cuban influence in the Basin. Attending to these difficult problems might include jointly staffed teams in the region dealing, respectively, with the drug trade, disaster relief, weather tracking (especially hurricanes), antiterrorism, establishment of reliable police forces in the insular Caribbean, and a regional arms control regime in Central America.

The role of regional (OAS) and universal (UN) organizations should expand. The present is the most propitious time since the end of World War II to expand multilateralism. US reaction to the Haitian coup of early October 1991—working through the OAS and the United Nations—is a hopeful sign. The Reagan administration's UN bashing was automatic, systematic, and almost mindless. This ideological stance was particularly applicable to the Caribbean Basin, where the world organization had never been allowed to operate. This policy has given way under the Bush administration to an active embrace of the UN as a result of the Gulf War. In fact, stated US policy objectives—the end of the Sandinista rule and the spread of democracy in Nicaragua—were hindered by bilateral aid to the contras and the mining of Nicaragua's ports, but they were brought about through multilateralism. A variety of US interests could be better served by making use of international institutions rather than by shunning them, and it is imperative that the Bush administration investigate greater use of them in the 1990s.[25]

If the Caribbean Basin is relatively stable, relatively able to meet its own needs and deal with its own problems, US security will be enhanced. In the sense that neighbors have common interests, common responsibilities, and common needs, if all are secure, each is secure. Security in the sense of defense against a foreign military threat is no longer necessary, for no such threat exists.

Southern Africa

In Southern Africa, the United States should in the short term discuss with the former Soviets and the Cubans how all three governments can smooth the way to a peaceful future in the region. Each has a long history of direct and indirect involvement in the region, and each has important contacts within and outside regional governments. In particular, the ethnic rivalries that threaten to shatter the tenuous peace processes in Angola and Mozambique should usefully be assisted by outside mediators, especially the UN, but not excluding direct involvement by US, Cuban, and Soviet mediators as well as those from contiguous countries. In addition, the United States should participate with regional actors, especially the SADCC, in assisting South Africa toward a successful transition to majority rule. At the same time, it must be recognized that apartheid has run its tentacles into every nook and cranny of South African society and psychology, and it will not go as quickly or as quietly into oblivion as one might wish.

It is time for Washington to throw its considerable weight behind an array of long-term UN initiatives in peace and security, including support for peacekeeping forces, humanitarian aid, monitoring of elections, and investigation of allegations of human rights abuses.[26] These are issues that former UN Under-Secretary General Sir Brian Urquhart has alluded to in his remarks about "the rush to join the industrialized North," which leaves behind "a residual, undeveloped, unindustrialized South . . . the ultimate formula for an unstable world."[27] Washington's direct involvement in the security affairs of Southern Africa is recent, unlike its historical and geographical preoccupation with the Caribbean, and motivated almost exclusively by geopolitical concerns about the expansion of Soviet influence, which are unlikely to survive the end of the Cold War. This is, however, an opportunity for the United States to earn the mantle of moral leadership it so often claims is rightfully its own, and to demonstrate that the phrase *new world order* is meaningful.

In fact, too much of the literature about Third World security has been written almost exclusively from the point of view of superpower competition.[28] This perspective ignores what is certainly the most important source of Third World instability, namely extreme poverty coupled with fundamental domestic roots of conflict, resulting in the fragility of many governments. The weaknesses and nonviability of many Third World states is probably the single reason for the contamination and even expansion of regional conflicts.[29]

In this context, the Beltway's decisionmakers must keep in mind that great powers historically are compelled to protect their interests as they see them whenever instability appears. If war again breaks out in Southern Africa, if by then the United States has important oil interests in the area, or black constituents are pressing Congress, or a nuclear weapon is brandished, then a replay of the Gulf intervention is not out of the question. As Stanley Hoffman recently put it, for the United States in the new world order surely "an ounce of prevention is worth a ton of punishment."[30]

Postscript: Revisiting the Carter Approach

As we survey the chapters in this volume, we are struck by the following hypothesis: The world at large, and the Caribbean Basin and Southern Africa in particular, may at last be ready for Jimmy Carter. The reader should not fear: we are not advance men for another Carter run at the presidency. Nor are we blind to the tremendous disappointments in US foreign policy toward these regions that is part of his legacy.

Yet, for a very brief moment Carter brought to the White House an attitude that can only be thought of as post–Cold War. He indicated in various ways during his campaign, in the transition period, and early in his presidency that he sought a full partnership with the Soviet Union on bilateral issues; new means to manage complex interdependence; greater tolerance for ideological pluralism, but coupled with vigilant human rights monitoring; normalization of US relations with Cuba under terms not requiring surrender of the island's sovereignty; negotiated settlements for the conflicts in Central America and Southern Africa; and finally a greater reliance on multilateral institutions. In general, his approach was that of seeking positive-sum solutions.

In a trenchant essay called "Why Carter Failed," historian Gaddis

Smith offers this explanation of the great lost opportunities of those years:

> Finally and tragically, Carter failed because he asked the American people to think as citizens of the world with an obligation toward future generations. He offered a morally responsible and far-sighted vision. But the clamor of political critics, the behavior of the Soviet Union, the discordant voices of his advisers, and the impossibility of seeing clearly what needed to be done—all combined to make Carter's vision appear naïve.[31]

Everywhere, the world of the Cold War was too much with him—in Moscow, Addis Ababa, Havana, Managua, San Salvador, Luanda, Pretoria, and last, but far from least, in Washington. The Cold War intervened in conflicts associated with each of these capitals and forced zero-sum attitudes to harden. Hundreds of thousands of people died, treasure was wasted, and Carter was swept out of office. Détente became a memory, and the Cold War started anew with a vengeance after the Soviet invasion of Afghanistan.

But, as we know now, the 1980s saw the swan song of the Cold War and of the Soviet Union as a first-class world power. In certain ways, the Carter approach to foreign policy seems to have required one to act as if these events had already occurred, as was the case in Carter's persistent recommendation of representative democracy, the market, and universal moral principles of human rights as everywhere applicable, even to the Soviet Union itself. Now they seem to be generally so regarded. To say so is not, as it was for Carter, to run the risk of being excoriated as naïve, or to make an unwarranted intrusion into the affairs of another country. It is simply to restate the prevailing conventional wisdom. This may not be the "end of history,"[32] as some have oddly claimed, but it is certainly the end of serious opposition to the ideas for which Jimmy Carter briefly and prematurely stood as president.

Although we cannot in this space argue the case adequately, we have the impression that as US policymakers and analysts try to imagine the shape of post–Cold War security regimes in the two regions of present inquiry, they would be well-served to look back at the Carter years. The formula might be to ask what the Carter approach would have been to a given set of regional issues; to measure its success and failures; to subtract the Cold War from the outcome; and to see if the Carter years don't provide some help in proceeding into a murky future in which US leadership is likely to be unchallenged—but also a future in which the nature of that leadership awaits definition.

As Carter discovered, the grass must suffer when the elephants make war, even Cold War. And in making Cold War, the elephants did not

172 ■ JAMES G. BLIGHT & THOMAS G. WEISS

prosper. In the post–Cold War era, a single unifying consensus is becoming evident: Only one elephant remains. Surely there is a way for the survivor to get along with a Soviet mammoth and in so doing to tread lightly upon the Third World's grass. Just as surely, we believe, this is the sort of world to which the Carter approach can eloquently speak.

Notes

† In this chapter, a dagger indicates passages quoted from the April 1991 Brown University conference.

1. See Thomas G. Weiss and Meryl A. Kessler, eds., *Third World Security in the Post–Cold War Era* (Boulder, Colo.: Lynne Rienner, 1991), and G.R. Berridge, *Return to the UN: UN Diplomacy in Regional Conflicts* (London: Macmillan, 1991).

2. See the views of Stephen Lewis, Clovis Maksoud, and Robert S. Johansen in "The United Nations After the Gulf War," *World Policy Journal* 8, no. 3 (Summer 1991): 537–574, and a special issue of *The Fletcher Forum of World Affairs* 15, no. 2 (Summer 1991), entitled "What's New About the New World Order?"

3. Fidel Castro, speech at Camaguey, Cuba, 26 July 1989, on the anniversary of the attack on Moncada. In W. Raymond Duncan and Carolyn McGiffert Ekedahl, *Moscow and the Third World Under Gorbachev* (Boulder, Colo.: Westview Press, 1990), 229.

4. "The Mind of Saddam Hussein," *Frontline* special report, PBS, narrated by Hodding Carter, 26 February 1991. On the issue of coming desperation in traditional Soviet client states, see James G. Blight and Aaron Belkin, "Déjà Vu, '62?: Avoiding New World Desperation and Disorder," in *Foreign Policy* (Winter 1991–1992), forthcoming.

5. See Robert S. McNamara, "The Post–Cold War World and Its Implications for Military Expenditures in Developing Countries," in *Toward Collective Security: Two Views*, Occasional Paper No. 5 (Providence, R.I.: Thomas J. Watson Jr. Institute for International Studies, Brown University, 1991), 21–42.

6. The Soviets do not believe talk of a possible catastrophe over Cuba is mere hyperbole. For a summary and analysis of the concerns of Soviet policymakers on Cuban issues see James G. Blight, janet M. Lang, and Bruce J. Allyn, "Fidel Cornered: The Soviet Fear of Another Cuban Crisis," *Russia and the World* (Fall 1990): 21–25, 39–40.

7. Charles Krauthammer, "The Unipolar Moment," *Foreign Affairs* 70, no. 1: 23–33.

8. See David Hoffman, "Soviet Brigade to Leave Cuba, Gorbachev Says," *Washington Post*, 12 Sept. 1991, A34, 1; and Gerald Seib, "Soviets Plan Troop Pullout from Cuba," *Wall Street Journal*, 12 Sept. 1991, A13. On September 30, Foreign Minister Boris Pankin explained that the Soviet announcement was part of a series of "confidence building measures" that he hoped would be followed by each side. He compared the unilateral Soviet announcement of the troop pullout from Cuba with President George Bush's announcement on September 27 that the United States would begin unilateral dismantling of its tactical nuclear weapons in Europe. Pankin further suggested

that an appropriate US response to the Soviet troop withdrawal would be a reduction in the US military presence at the Guantánamo Bay naval base in Cuba and a cessation of US naval maneuvers around Cuba (remarks on PBS, "McNeil-Lehrer News Hour," 27 Sept. 1991.

9. "Cuba Will Never Accept Being Delivered or Sold to the United States," Cuban Foreign Ministry Statement, regarding the withdrawal of Soviet troops from Cuba, Havana, 14 Sept. 1991.

10. Sobered by the failure of recent predictions, we nevertheless hazard this one with some confidence. Albert O. Hirschman warns: "It does not seem to have occurred to these people that if the events, which are the point of departure for their speculations, were so hard to predict, considerable caution is surely in order when it comes to appraising their impact. . . particularly with respect to the less developed countries," "Good News Is Not Bad News," *New York Review of Books* 27 (11 Oct. 1990), 20.

11. Joseph S. Nye, Jr., *Bound to Lead: The Changing Nature of American Power* (New York: Basic Books, 1990).

12. This story is marvelously rendered in Robert A. Pastor, *Condemned to Repetition: The United States and Nicaragua* (Princeton, N.J.: Princeton University Press, 1987).

13. See also Henry Kissinger, *The White House Years and Years of Upheaval* (Boston: Little, Brown & Co., 1979).

14. See Kenneth B. Noble, "As Angola Turns to West, Cubans Are Resentful," *New York Times*, 9 Apr. 1991, A8.

15. Eduard A. Shevardnadze, Speech to the UN General Assembly. Excerpts in Pravda 28: 4. Robert A. Pastor argues forcefully for the repeal of spheres of influence on both sides in "The United States and Central America After the Cold War: Seal, Peel or Repeal the Sphere of Influence," in Albert Fishlow, ed., *Superpower Conflict and Cooperation in the Third World* (Berkeley, Calif.: Institute of International Studies, 1991).

16. For a detailed discussion, see Thomas G. Weiss and Meryl A. Kessler, "Moscow's UN Policy," *Foreign Policy* 79 (Summer 1990): 94–112.

17. Jorge Risquet, interview with David Deutschmann, in David Deutschmann, ed., *Changing the History of Africa: Angola and Namibia* (Melbourne, Australia: Ocean Press, 1989), 32.

18. Mervyn M. Dymally, "Unshackle Namibia," *Boston Globe*, 6 July 1991, 11.

19. Fidel Castro first used this phrase to describe Cuba's post–Cold War situation in his speech to the Fifth Congress of the Federation of Cuban Women, 7 March 1990.

20. See, for example, Georgie Anne Geyer, *Guerilla Prince: The Untold Story of Fidel Castro* (Boston: Little Brown, 1991); and Susan Kaufmann Purcell, "U.S. Policy Towards Latin America After the Cold War," *Adelphi Paper No. 256* (London: International Institute for Strategic Studies, 1991); and Carlos Montaner, "Gorbachev, Bush and the Cuban Obstacle," *Wall Street Journal*, 1 March 1991, A9.

21. Official and unofficial Soviet views have for some time emphasized that, while the Soviets seek long-term "normalization" of their relations with Cuba, there is no possibility of cutting back so-called aid because of US pressure. See, for example, the remarks of Valery Nikolayenko, Deputy Foreign Minister for Latin America, in Wayne S. Smith, ed., *The Russians Aren't Coming: Soviet Policy in Latin America After the Cold War* (Boulder, Colo.: Lynne Rienner, 1992); and the remarks of Soviet Foreign Ministry

spokesman Vitaly Churkin, in TASS, 10 June 1991 (reported in the daily report of Radio Free Europe, 17 June 1991, 12). In unofficial circles, the Soviet position on Cuba has been articulated most forcefully by Sergo Mikoyan. See his "We're Not Your Man in Havana," *New York Times*, 2 July 1991, A17; and "Soviet Foreign Policy and Latin America," *Washington Quarterly* 13, no. 3 (Summer 1990): 179–191.

22. Leonid Fituni, cited in Neil Henry, "A New Age for Africans?" *International Herald Tribune*, 1–2 June 1991, 2.

23. For a comprehensive treatment of mutual security in the context of US-Soviet relations, see Richard Smoke and Andrei Kortunov, eds., *Mutual Security: A New Approach to Soviet-American Relations* (New York: St. Martin's Press, 1991). For an application of the principles of mutual security to Third World–Great Power relations, see Aaron Belkin and James G. Blight, "Triangular Mutual Security: Why the Missile Crisis Matters in a World Beyond the Cold War." *Political Psychology* (Winter 1991–1992), forthcoming.

24. These issues are explored in James G. Blight, Aaron Belkin, and David Lewis, "New Rules of the Game: U.S.-Cuban Relations After the Cold War." In Smith, ed., *The Russians Aren't Coming*.

25. For a further discussion of these issues, see Thomas G. Weiss, "Superpowers, The United Nations and the Post-Cold War Era: More than a Blue Fig Leaf?" in ibid.

26. See Augustus Richard Norton and Thomas G. Weiss, *U N Peacekeepers: Soldiers with a Difference* (New York: Foreign Policy Association Headline Series 292, 1990), and the special issue of *Survival* 32 No. 3 (May/June 1990).

27. Sir Brian Urquhart, "After the Cold War: Learning From the Gulf," *Toward Collective Security: Two Views*, 16. See also the argument made by a group of Third World intellectuals under the chairmanship of Julius Nyrere, *The Challenge to the South* (New York: Oxford University Press, 1990.)

28. See, for example, Michael Nacht, "Toward an American Conception of Regional Security," *Daedalus* 110 (Winter 1981): 1–22; and Neil S. MacFarlane, "The Soviet Conception of Regional Security," *World Politics* 37 (April 1985): 295–316. For an effort to explore the theoretical implications of using northern security lenses to examine Third World instability, see Edward E. Azar and Chung-In Moon, eds., *National Security in the Third World* (College Park, Md.: Center for International Development and Conflict Management, 1988).

29. This argument is made convincingly by Mohammed Ayoob, "The Security Problematic of the Third World," *World Politics* 32 (January 1991) 257–283; see also Yezid Sayigh, "Confronting the 1990s: Security in the Developing Countries," *Adelphi Paper No. 251* (London: Institute for International Strategic Studies, 1990); and Joel Migdal, *Strong Societies and Weak States* (Princeton: Princeton University Press, 1988).

30. Stanley Hoffmann, "Avoiding New World Disorder," *New York Times*, 25 Feb. 1991, A19.

31. Gaddis Smith, *Morality, Reason and Power: American Diplomacy in the Carter Years* (New York: Hill and Wang, 1986), 247.

32. See Francis Fukuyama, "The End of History," *National Interest* 16 (Summer 1989): 1–18.

About the Authors

JAMES G. BLIGHT is senior research fellow with Brown University's Center for Foreign Policy Development, where he directs the Cuban missile crisis project and a study of the US-Cuban-Soviet relationship and its implications for security in the Caribbean Basin. He is the author of *On the Brink* and *The Shattered Crystal Ball.*

JORGE I. DOMINGUEZ is professor of government and chairman of the Committee on Latin American Studies at Harvard's Center for International Affairs. He is the author of *Cuba* and *To Make the World Safe for Revolution: Cuban Foreign Policy.* He collaborated with Cuban scholars at Havana's Center for American Studies on the book *U.S.-Cuban Relations in the 1990s.*

GILLIAN GUNN is senior associate with the Carnegie Endowment for International Peace in Washington, D.C. Her recent publications on Cuba and Angola have appeared in the *Christian Science Monitor, Foreign Policy, Current History,* the *Miami Herald,* and the *Chicago Tribune.*

FEN OSLER HAMPSON is associate professor at the Norman Patterson School of International Affairs, Carleton University, Ottawa, and editor of a special issue of *The International Journal* dealing with regional conflicts. He is the author of *Unguided Missiles* and coauthor of *The Allies and Arms Control.*

LLOYD SEARWAR is visiting fellow with the Institute of International Relations, University of the West Indies, Trinidad and Tobago. He has been a senior member of the Guyana Foreign Service, with the rank of ambassador, specializing in UN and multilateral and special missions' diplomacy. He recently contributed a chapter on Caribbean small states in *Peace, Development and Security in the Caribbean.*

WAYNE S. SMITH is professor of Latin American studies at the Paul H. Nitze School of Advanced International Studies, Johns Hopkins University. He is a former foreign service officer and is the author of *The Closest of Enemies: A Personal and Diplomatic Account of the Castro Years*.

NEWELL M. STULTZ is professor of political science at Brown University. Among his publications are *Transkei's Half Loaf: Race Separation in South Africa* and *The Apartheid Issue in the Security Council*. He has recently completed a study of the evolution and development of the UN's opposition to apartheid, and the internationalization of South Africa's internal conflict over apartheid.

THOMAS G. WEISS is associate director of Brown University's Thomas J. Watson Jr. Institute for International Studies. His most recent books include *Third World Security in the Post–Cold War Era* (coeditor); *Soldiers, Peacekeepers and Disasters* (coeditor); *Humanitarian Emergencies and Military Help in Africa* (editor); *U.N. Peacekeepers: Soldiers with a Difference* (coauthor); and *The U.N. in Conflict Management: American, Soviet and Third World Views* (editor).

Index

About the Book

Detailed case studies of regional conflicts in the Caribbean Basin (including Central America) and Southern Africa furnish insights into the origins and the eventual resolution of Third World strife and instability. Each region provides raw material for in-depth evaluations of Soviet and US roles in fueling conflicts and, more recently, in helping to wind down long-standing wars. There is also an examination of the respective contributions of the regional hegemons, Cuba and South Africa, and the influence of both regional and international organizations. Similarities between the two regions emerge, in particular the extent to which internal factors (poverty, ethnic troubles, the legacy of colonialism) are at the root of conflicts and remain a continuing threat to future stability, in spite of warming East-West relations and the disappearance of the Soviet Union from the Third World. Prescriptions for US policy figure prominently in the conclusions.

Brown University's THOMAS J. WATSON JR. INSTITUTE FOR INTERNATIONAL STUDIES was established in 1986 to ensure the continuous development of the University's international dimension, for the benefit of students, faculty, and, ultimately, society. The institute supports faculty teaching and research and sponsors lectures, conferences, and visiting fellows. Its thirteen affiliated centers and programs engage in a broad range of activities, from improving the teaching of international relations and area studies to contributing to policy-oriented research and public outreach.